300 home-improvement TIPS

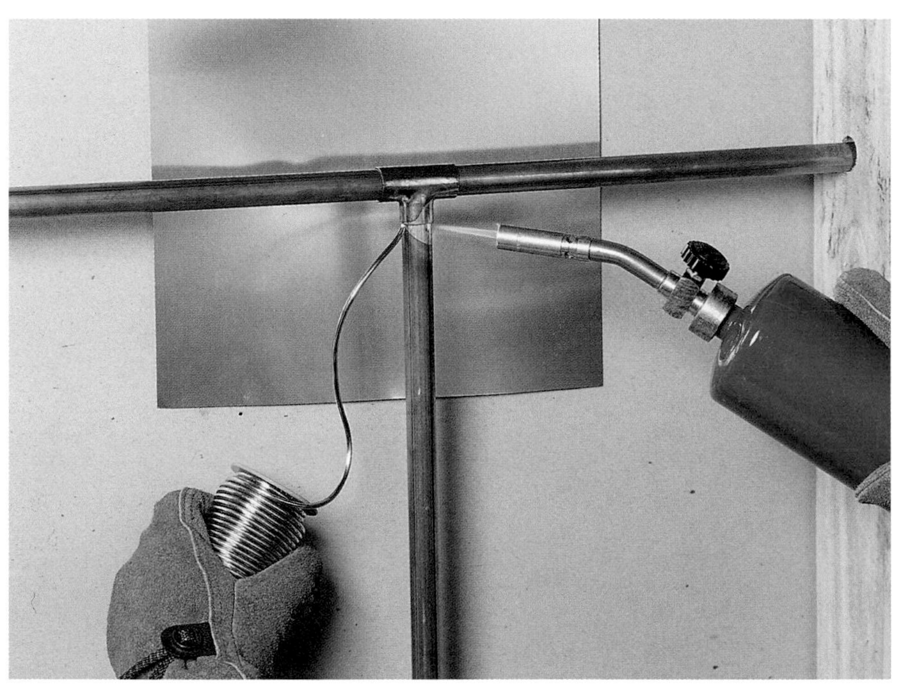

CREATIVE HOMEOWNER®

300 TIPS home-improvement

for working smarter safer greener

CREATIVE HOMEOWNER®, Upper Saddle River, New Jersey

A Division of Federal Marketing Corp.
Upper Saddle River, NJ

300 HOME-IMPROVEMENT TIPS

PRODUCED BY Home & Garden Editorial Services
PROJECT MANAGER Joe Provey
CONTRIBUTOR Steve Willson
COPY EDITOR Owen Lockwood
COVER DESIGN Glee Barre

CREATIVE HOMEOWNER

VICE PRESIDENT AND PUBLISHER Timothy O. Bakke
MANAGING EDITOR Fran J. Donegan
ART DIRECTOR David Geer
PRODUCTION COORDINATOR Sara M. Markowitz

Manufactured in the United States of America

Current Printing (last digit)
10 9 8 7 6 5 4 3 2 1

300 Home-Improvement Tips, First Edition
Library of Congress Control Number: 2009941177
ISBN-10: 1-58011-490-3
ISBN-13: 978-1-58011-490-5

CREATIVE HOMEOWNER®
A Division of Federal Marketing Corp.
24 Park Way
Upper Saddle River, NJ 07458
www.creativehomeowner.com

GREEN EDITION

Planet Friendly Publishing

✓ Made in the United States
✓ Printed on Recycled Paper
Text: 10% Cover: 10%
Learn more: www.greenedition.org

At Creative Homeowner we're committed to producing books in an earth-friendly manner and to helping our customers make greener choices.

Manufacturing books in the United States ensures compliance with strict environmental laws and eliminates the need for international freight shipping, a major contributor to global air pollution.

And printing on recycled paper helps minimize our consumption of trees, water, and fossil fuels. *300 Home-Improvement Tips* was printed on paper made with 10% post-consumer waste. According to the Environmental Defense Fund Paper Calculator, by using this innovative paper instead of conventional papers we achieved the following environmental benefits:

Trees Saved: 19

Water Saved: 8,500 gallons

Solid Waste Eliminated: 516 pounds

Greenhouse Gas Emissions Eliminated: 1,765 pounds

For more information on our environmental practices, please visit us online at www.creativehomeowner.com/green

Safety

Although the methods in this book have been reviewed for safety, it is not possible to overstate the importance of using the safest methods you can. What follows are reminders—some do's and don'ts of work safety—to use along with your common sense.

- Always use caution, care, and good judgment when following the procedures described in this book.
- Always be sure that the electrical setup is safe, that no circuit is overloaded, and that all power tools and outlets are properly grounded. Do not use power tools in wet locations.
- Always read container labels on paints, solvents, and other products; provide ventilation; and observe all other warnings.
- Always read the manufacturer's instructions for using a tool, especially the warnings.
- Use hold-downs and push sticks whenever possible when working on a table saw. Avoid working short pieces if you can.
- Always remove the key from any drill chuck (portable or press) before starting the drill.
- Always pay deliberate attention to how a tool works so that you can avoid being injured.
- Always know the limitations of your tools. Do not try to force them to do what they were not designed to do.
- Always make sure that any adjustment is locked before proceeding. For example, always check the rip fence on a table saw or the bevel adjustment on a portable saw before starting to work.
- Always clamp small pieces to a bench or other work surface when using a power tool.
- Always wear the appropriate rubber gloves or work gloves when handling chemicals, moving or stacking lumber, working with concrete, or doing heavy construction.
- Always wear a disposable face mask when you create dust by sawing or sanding. Use a special filtering respirator when working with toxic substances and solvents.
- Always wear eye protection, especially when using power tools or striking metal on metal or concrete; a chip can fly off, for example, when chiseling concrete.
- Never work while wearing loose clothing, open cuffs, or jewelry; tie back long hair.
- Always be aware that there is seldom enough time for your body's reflexes to save you from injury from a power tool in a dangerous situation; everything happens too fast. Be alert!
- Always keep your hands away from the business ends of blades, cutters, and bits.
- Always hold a circular saw firmly, usually with both hands.
- Always use a drill with an auxiliary handle to control the torque when using large-size bits.
- Always check your local building codes when planning new construction. The codes are intended to protect public safety and should be observed to the letter.
- Never work with power tools when you are tired or when under the influence of alcohol or drugs.
- Never cut tiny pieces of wood or pipe using a power saw. When you need a small piece, saw it from a securely clamped longer piece.
- Never change a saw blade or a drill or router bit unless the power cord is unplugged. Do not depend on the switch being off. You might accidentally hit it.
- Never work in insufficient lighting.
- Never work with dull tools. Have them sharpened, or learn how to sharpen them yourself.
- Never use a power tool on a workpiece—large or small—that is not firmly supported.
- Never saw a workpiece that spans a large distance between horses without close support on each side of the cut; the piece can bend, closing on and jamming the blade, causing saw kickback.
- When sawing, never support a workpiece from underneath with your leg or other part of your body.
- Never carry sharp or pointed tools, such as utility knives, awls, or chisels, in your pocket. If you want to carry any of these tools, use a special-purpose tool belt that has leather pockets and holders.

Contents

CHAPTER SIX

74 Windows and Doors

CHAPTER SEVEN

86 Floors, Walls, and Ceilings

CHAPTER EIGHT

96 Paint and Other Finishes

CHAPTER NINE

114 Trim, Roofing, and Siding

CHAPTER TEN

126 Masonry

CHAPTER ELEVEN

140 Landscaping

Introduction

On Being Knowledgeable

There are two ways to be a do-it-yourselfer. You can learn as you go, making your share of mistakes along the way. Or you can pick up tips from professionals who have been there before—and save yourself a lot of time, money, and aggravation. This book presumes you're in the latter camp—or are ready to join it—and that you're willing to study up a bit before plowing headlong into your next home-improvement project. We're not saying we can prevent you from ever making a mistake again—just that we've written this book with the hope you'll make far fewer of them. As a bonus, we've salted these pages with tips that allow you to make your improvements without hurting yourself, your wallet, or the planet.

The Whole House Within these pages you'll find tips for just about every type of remodeling and building activity you can think of, from framing to landscaping. Find out how to be more accurate in your measurements when installing trim. See how to build a jig for making straight cuts in plywood. Learn about a new type of piping that makes plumbing jobs easier and faster. Discover simpler ways to handle all kinds of electrical tasks, from stripping cable to adding new outlets. Unearth the right way to build a freestanding stone wall or a retaining wall.

You'll find valuable tricks for doing things you think you already know how to do, too. Read about the proper working order for painting a panel door, a double-hung window, or an entire room. Learn how to hang wall-coverings with perfect seams and without waste. Find better ways to create edges around your garden beds and along paths.

Making home improvements yourself can be tremendously satisfying. It can also be frustrating and even hazardous. It's our wish that *300 Home-Improvement Tips* will help make the former a reality.

Discover new, easy-to-use polyethylene tubing.

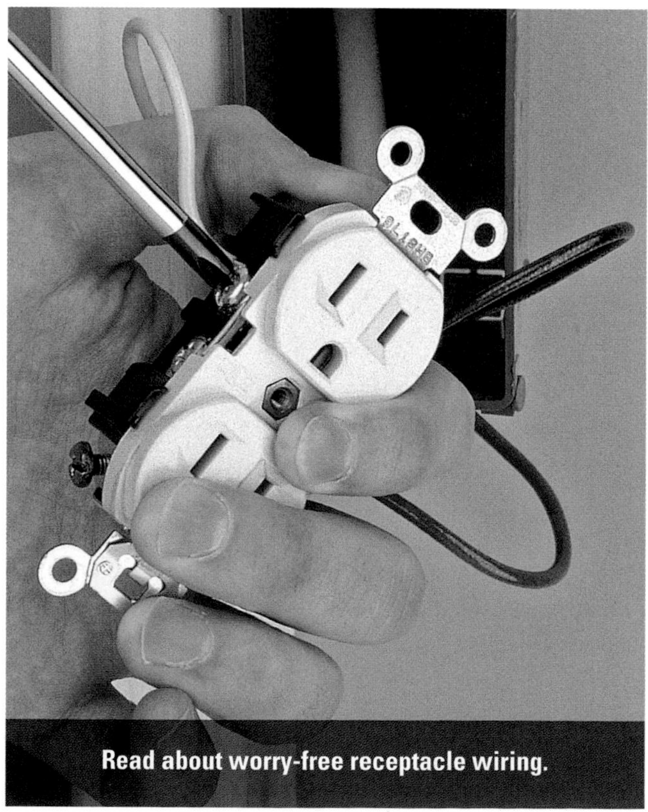

Read about worry-free receptacle wiring.

Hang drywall like a professional.

1 Framing

- HOW TO DRIVE NAILS • HOW TO MAKE BETTER CUTS
- PUTTING UP WALLS • PROPER VENTILATION

1 Wall Structure

The anatomy of most house walls is very similar. You start with a bottom plate and a top plate and then fill in between them with vertical studs. Once the wall is built, an additional top plate, called a cap plate, is usually added to increase the overall stiffness of the wall and to help tie adjacent walls together. Headers are another major component. They are designed to transfer weight from the top of the wall down through adjacent (trimmer) studs to the floor below. Studs come in three types. The first are full-length studs that extend from plate to plate. These are often called king studs when they are next to window and door openings. The second type is a trimmer stud (often called a jack stud), which is nailed to a king stud to form the sides of any wall opening and to support the header above. Cripple studs are the third type. They fit between headers and top plates and sills and bottom plates.

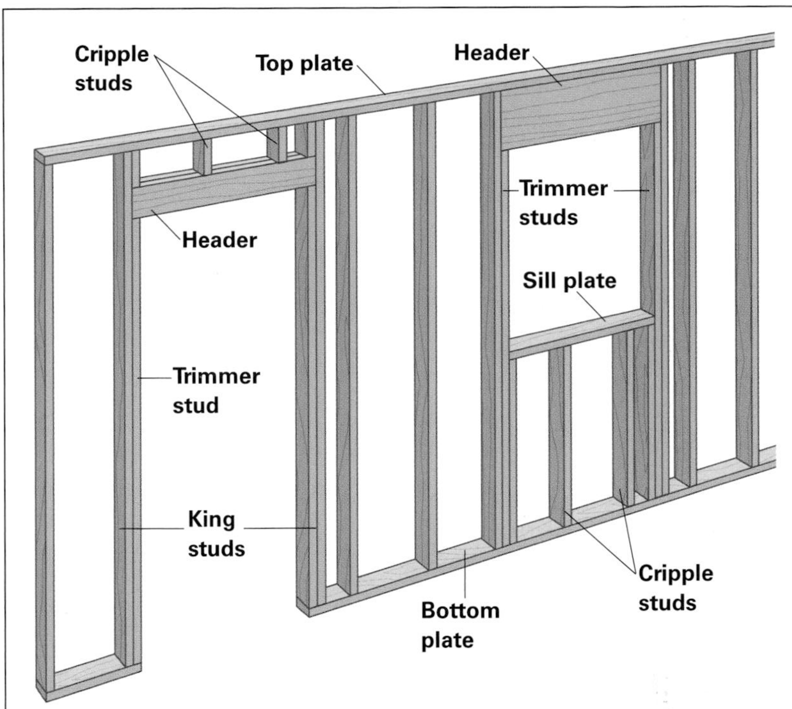

Though wall terminology may change slightly from region to region, the wall shown here is typical of the walls in most houses.

2 How to Drive Toenails Properly

The best way to nail together two boards that meet at a 90-degree angle is to drive the nails through the face of one board into the end of the other. This approach is fast and strong, and it requires little technique. But many times you won't have access to the face of one board. In these cases, you must toenail the perpendicular parts together. This means driving the nails at an angle through one part and into the other. Although this looks easy, it takes some practice to do well. Do it wrong, and the base of the veritcal board can split and become loose. The right way: start driving the nail at a 45-degree angle about 1 inch above the joint. When the nail is about ⅛ inch into the wood, increase the angle to about 60 to 70 degrees and finish driving the nail. When nailing studs to plates, drive two nails on one side of each stud and a single nail on the other side.

A Toenail Trick To prevent a stud from shifting as you drive a nail, hold it in place using a spacer block cut to fit your stud spacing. Make sure the nail doesn't hit the block, and remove it when you're finished nailing.

Too shallow · Too steep · Correct

When toenailing perpendicular boards together, you must drive the nail at the correct angle.

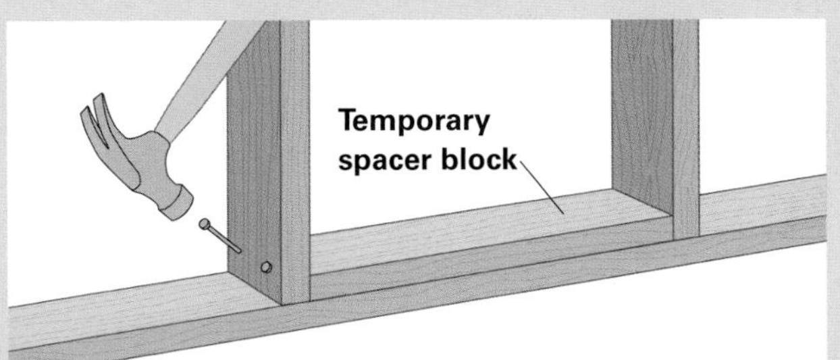

To keep studs in place when toenailing, use a temporary spacer block cut to fit your stud spacing.

Greener Ways

3 Sill Gasket for Energy Savings

Using vapor barriers under drywall, house wrap under siding, and caulk in every crack you can find are all good energy-saving practices. But one that sometimes gets overlooked is adding sill sealer between the top of the foundation and the bottom of the sill. This material is usually sold in rolls and is made of flexible foam. To install it, just roll it out on top of the foundation, cover it with the sill boards, and then tighten these boards in place with the sill bolt nuts. The sealer will be compressed between the sill and the foundation wall and will form an air-tight joint.

4 Easier Square Cuts

Power miter saws and radial-arm saws are both great at making square crosscuts on boards, but buying one of these expensive saws, or carrying them around, is not much fun. Fortunately, you can make square cuts to rival these machines with nothing more than a circular saw and a rafter angle square (Speed Square). Just hold the square on the board so that when the foot (base) of the saw bears against it, the saw blade will be on the waste side of the cut line. Then hold the square firmly, turn on the saw, and push it across the board, making sure it always stays against the square. If you don't let the square move, you'll have a perfectly square cut.

A Speed Square is an excellent cutting guide when making crosscuts with a circular saw.

5 A Reciprocating Saw

If you need to cut down a wall, cut a hole in the floor, or cut through pipes, wires, ducts, plaster, drywall, flooring, siding, roofing, or countless other building materials, this tool is for you. It has a reciprocating (in and out) sawing action that drives its sturdy narrow blade, which comes in lengths from 4 to 12 inches. Other saws, both hand-powered and electric-powered models, can do some of the things that a reciprocating saw can do. But none of them can do the work easier or faster. The tool is available in corded and cordless models. The former are more powerful; the latter are more convenient and best suited for smaller jobs.

A reciprocating saw is great for cutting all kinds of materials, including roofing and sheathing (shown).

6 Fasteners for PT Wood

Place two dissimilar metals together, and they will react to one another and start to corrode. The same kind of reaction will occur when you drive a nail or screw into a piece of lumber that has been treated with copper—and today's pressure-treated (PT) lumber processors have replaced arsenic with copper compounds such as alkaline copper quaternary and copper azole. Consequently, when using PT lumber, don't use standard nails, fasteners, or hangers anymore. Use stainless-steel or hot-dipped galvanized products. Do not use electric-galvanized fasteners; the zinc coating may be too thin to last long. To be safe, look for a package that says it's ACQ- or CA-approved. Most home-improvement centers and lumberyards now have a full line of these new fasteners at reasonable prices.

7 When to Blunt a Nail

Anyone who has nailed a board too close to its end knows that a split is often the result. Sometimes, however, the nail location isn't negotiable. In these cases, try this pro trick. Blunt the nail point with a hammer before driving it home. This reduces the chance of splitting because the blunted point crushes the wood fibers as it makes its way through the wood, instead of splitting the fibers apart.

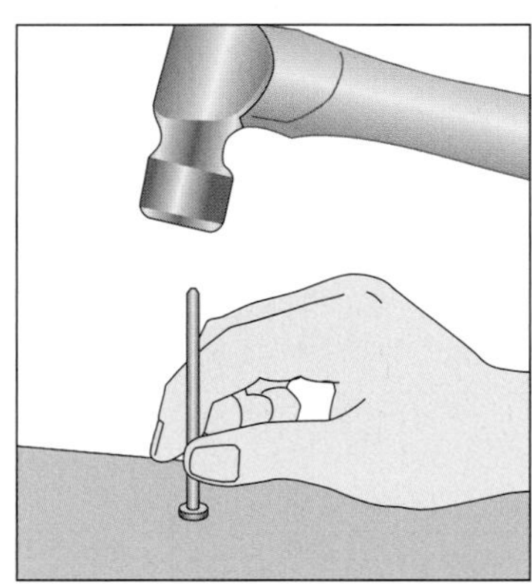

A few hammer taps on the pointed end of a nail will usually prevent the nail from splitting a board when you must drive a nail close to the board's end and you can't predrill.

8 Nailing Basics

Much of your framing-construction time will be spent nailing lumber. We've already touched on one nailing approach, toenailing. (See page 11.) You're likely to encounter a few other situations that will require different nailing methods. Here are a few:

When nailing through the end of a board, stagger the nails so they don't penetrate the same grain line. Otherwise, you risk splitting the board. You'll also want to avoid splitting when nailing from the face of one board into the end grain of another. To do so, angle your nails so they penetrate across the end grains.

The Clincher Clinching is another nailing technique. Clinching is driving a nail all the way through two boards and then bending over the pointed end to hold the nail in place. This technique comes in handy in rough work where you need a good hold.

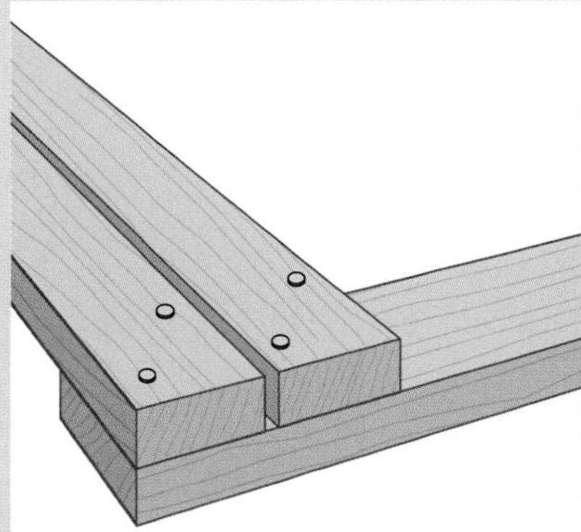

When driving more than one nail through the end of a board, stagger the nails to avoid splitting the wood.

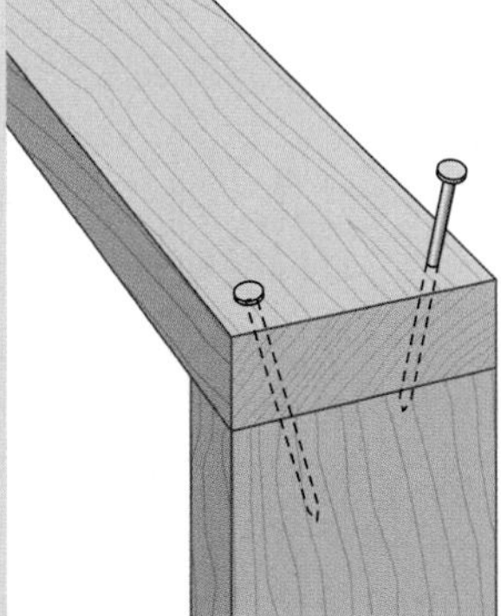

When nailing one board into the end-grain of another, angle the nails so they'll hold better.

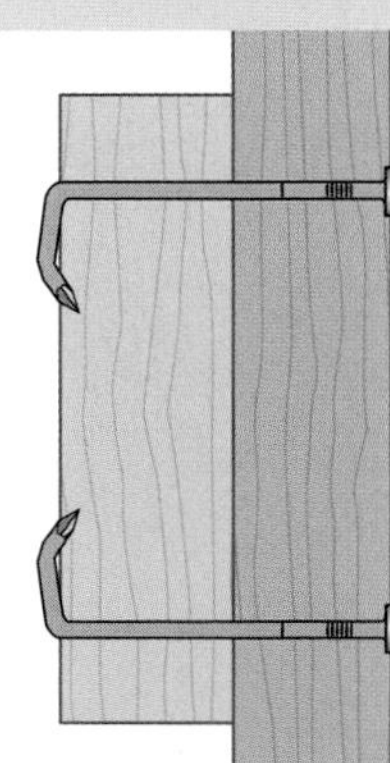

Clinching is a nailing technique common in scaffold construction and concrete formwork.

9 For Stronger Joints

You can attach joists to the side of beams, headers, and ledgers with toenails as mentioned on page 11. But a much stronger approach is to use joist hangers. These U-shaped galvanized-steel fasteners are designed for nailing into the sides of the joists and onto the surface of the mating parts. Commonly available sizes fit 2×4s, 2×6s, 2×8s, and 2×10s. The fastest way to install these hangers is to first lay out the joist locations. Then nail the hangers in place, and drop the ends of the joists into the pocket formed by the hanger. Make sure that the joist is tight to whatever framing member you're attaching it to. When it is, nail the hanger sides into the sides of the joist. Many carpenters use roofing nails or other short nails for this job. But hanger nails that are sized perfectly for the holes and the thickness of the joists are the smartest choice.

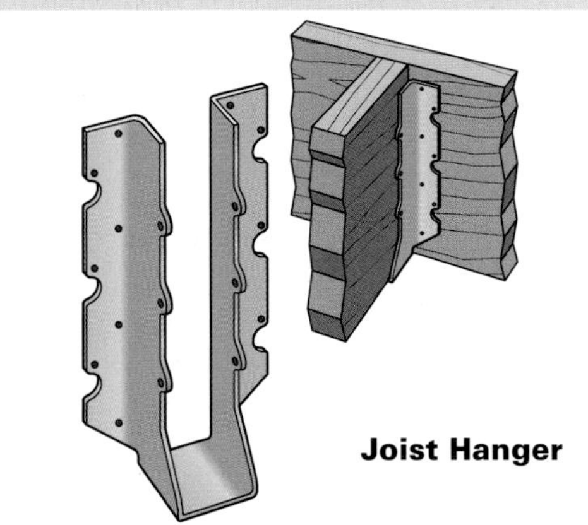

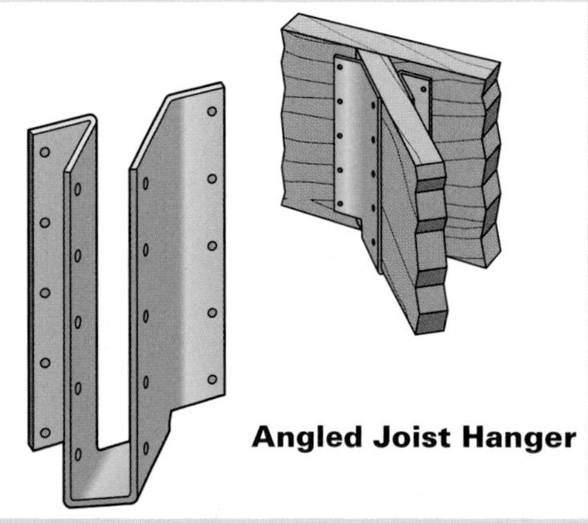

Galvanized-steel joist hangers are designed to attach joists to the side of beams, headers, and ledgers.

10 Lag-Screw Recess

Typically, you use lag screws to attach ledgers to a house. Lag screws are strong and easy to install, but they are not perfect fasteners because they are almost always in the way. No matter how carefully you plan, before you're done, their protruding heads will make part of the job harder than it has to be. Sometimes they'll fall between the end of the joist and the ledger. Other times they'll appear where a part of a joist hanger has to go. You can work around these problems easily enough, but you can eliminate the trouble altogether by recessing the heads below the surface of the ledger. Use a spade bit with a diameter slightly wider than the screw head and washer to bore a recess about ¼ to ⅜ inch deep. Then bore a clearance hole for the screw body through the rest of the ledger. Once the ledger is installed, you'll have a smooth surface on which to work.

Bore the recessed hole about ⅜ in. deep with a spade bit that's a little wider than the lag screw's washer.

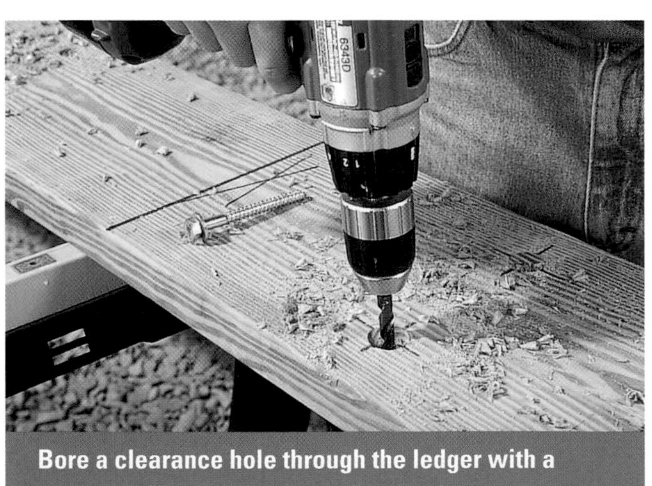

Bore a clearance hole through the ledger with a twist drill bit slightly bigger than the lag screw.

11 Wall Plates

When you are framing walls, mistakes can happen. You can put window openings in the wrong place or make them the wrong size. You can cut the studs to the wrong length, or build the wall out of square, which means you'll have to tear it apart and rebuild it. One good way to reduce mistakes is to lay out the top and bottom wall plates at the same time. You can still put a window opening in the wrong place, but it's pretty hard to build a wall that isn't square when the two plates are identical.

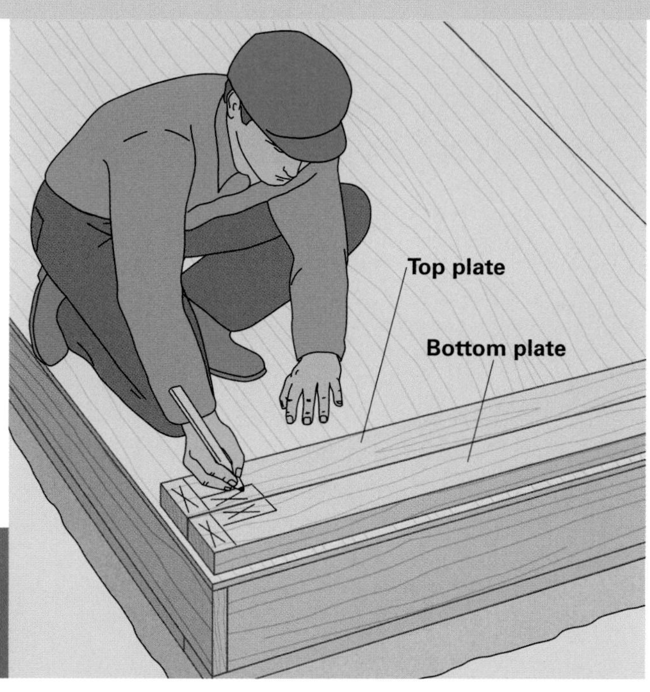

Place identical wall plates next to each other so that both ends are flush. Mark the stud locations on both plates at the same time to ensure alignment.

12 Raising and Bracing Walls

One of the great things about standard platform framing is that the walls all fit between the floor decks. (In balloon framing, the studs extend from the foundation to the roof.) This means that once the first-floor deck is done, you have a huge work surface, the entire floor, on which to build the walls. Construct the outside walls first, working in pairs: the front and back walls, and then the two side walls. Lift each wall into place, and brace it before you build the next wall. When all the outside walls are raised, plumb the corners, and nail the corner studs together. Then build the interior partitions. If a brace is in the way, you can remove it temporarily to build and raise a wall. Then you can replace the brace.

Braces Don't forget: all the walls have to be braced in a plumb position in both directions (in and out, and side to side) until the sheathing is installed. Once the sheathing is in place, you can remove the braces.

Temporary stops

1 Nail stops to the side of the floor deck. Then lift the wall, pushing it against the stops. Align the plate with the outside of the deck, and nail the plate to the deck.

2 Once the plate is nailed to the deck, one person holds the wall while another nails braces to the wall studs and to cleats that have been fastened to the deck.

13 Smarter Header Construction

When building headers, there is a natural tendency to create a solid-wood header. However, this is a waste of wood because in most situations you don't need a solid-wood header, especially for nonload-bearing walls that do not support heavy loads.

For cold-wall applications, solid-wood headers actually reduce the R-value of the wall from what could be achieved if the header were properly insulated. So consider using so-called "insulated boxed headers."

An insulated boxed header is typically made of engineered wood that sandwiches an expanded-polystyrene-foam core. An insulated boxed header for a 2×6 wall can achieve R-15 compared with around R-6 for a solid-wood version. Though they can be engineered for various wall thicknesses, the most common product is a 5½-inch-thick header designed for 2×6 walls.

Engineered headers also solve another problem: drywall installed over headers often cracks, but an engineered header can help reduce that problem by providing consistency and stability at that wall juncture.

Working Safer

14 Gear That Protects You

A basic assortment of personal safety equipment is a necessity for anyone who does work around the house. Most of this stuff isn't glamorous, but the "tools" can make any number of jobs easier and safer.

Must-Haves A hard hat is indispensable when doing demolition work, especially if someone is working above your head. Knee pads, on the other hand, may not prevent serious injury, but they can make long work sessions on floors and roofs more comfortable. To protect your eyes you need safety glasses or goggles. To protect your ears you need ear plugs or head muffs. And to protect your lungs you should have paper masks for dust and a respirator with replaceable cartridges for chemical fumes. Leather gloves protect your hands from splinters while rubber gloves protect them from harmful chemicals. And lastly, you should never overlook a first-aid kit with plenty of bandages, eye wash, and disinfectant.

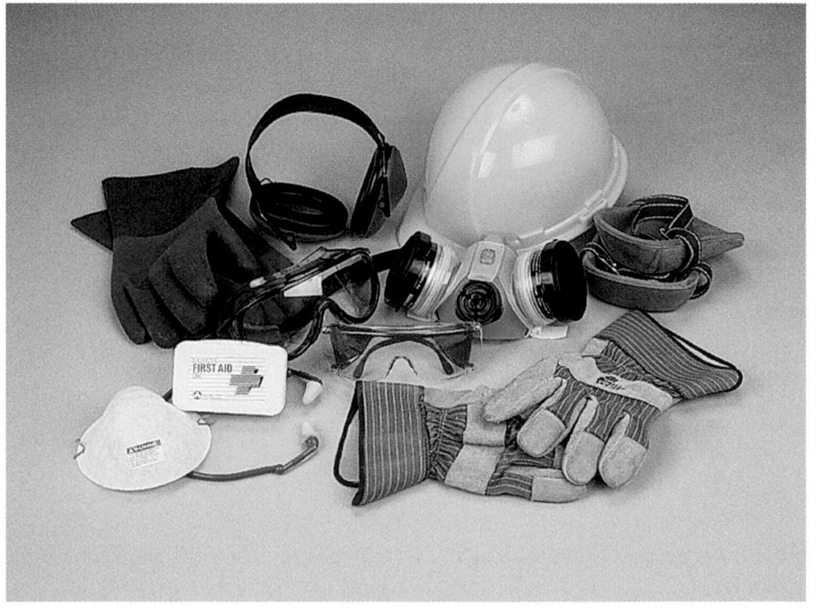

15 Easy Nail Removal

Hammers aren't just for driving nails; they're for pulling them, too. But hammer heads frequently damage the surface of the board when the nail is pulled, especially if the nail is hard to get out. By sliding a scrap block under the head and prying against it, you can protect the surface of the lumber and gain some extra leverage in the bargain.

Using a scrap block when pulling nails works for hammers with bent claws (left) and for hammers with straight claws.

Saving Money

16 Standard Sizes

Walls should be built in standard dimensional lengths to reduce waste and construction time, and to save money. Build your walls in 4-foot increments, or at the very least in 2-foot increments. For example, if you were to frame a 9-foot-long wall, you would have to cut down 10-foot boards to make the top and bottom plates, and those 1-foot stubs are hard to reuse elsewhere. A 10-foot wall is a little better, but when you go to apply drywall you will have to trim down the 4-foot panels, thereby "wasting" 2 feet. You may be able to use the 2-foot pieces elsewhere, but the best thing to do is to have a wall that is 4, 8, 12, or 16 feet long, so you are using exterior panels and drywall in their full dimensions.

17 Framing Outside Wall Corners

The first way to frame an outside corner is the traditional approach, and it's the strongest. The second is less strong, and the third is the weakest of all.

Go Strong Given these options, why wouldn't a carpenter always choose the strongest? Probably because the first corner would be harder than the other two to insulate. It would require adding fiberglass batts to the wall cavities and then packing the corner with smaller sections of insulation. If you are working on your own home, speed isn't much of an issue. Choose the strongest design, and make sure to fill the corner with insulation before you sheathe the wall.

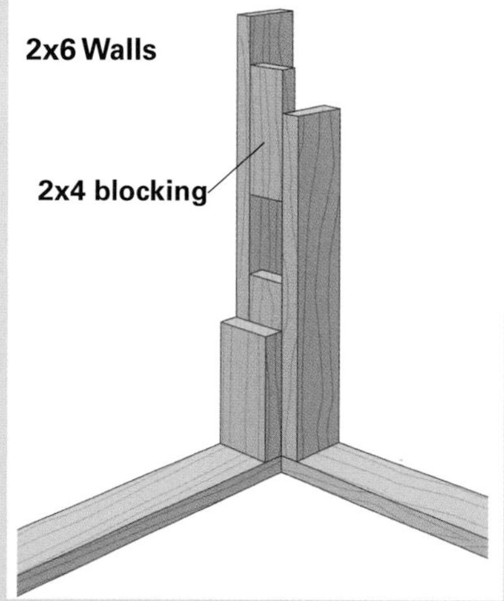

Outside corners made of three studs and blocking—the strongest option.

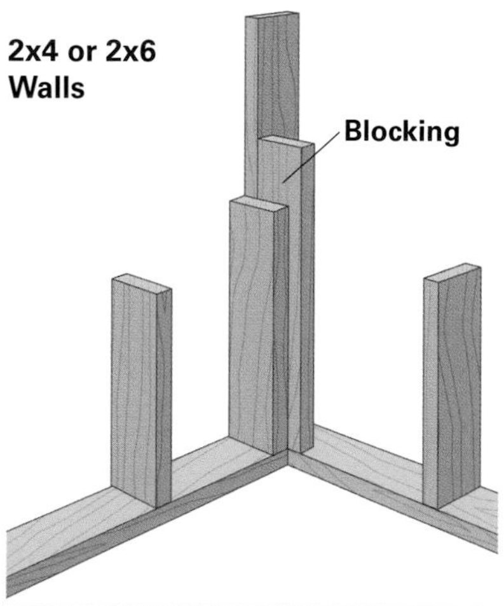

Outside corners made of three studs—the second-strongest option.

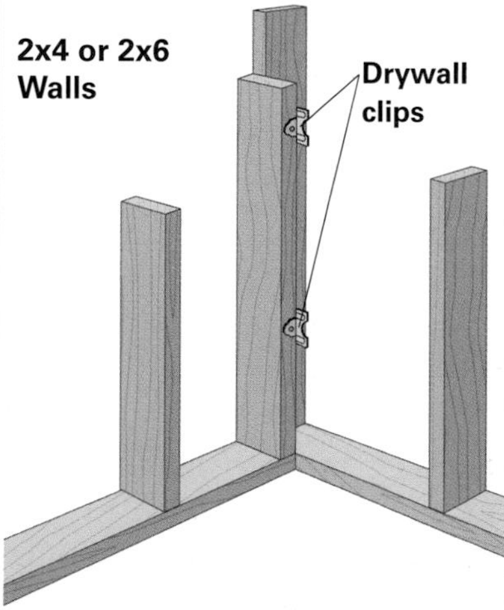

Outside corners made of drywall clips—the third-strongest option.

18 Best Underlayment

Underlayment must be stable, water-resistant, and free of defects. Vinyl flooring, for example, will reveal even small underlayment defects like raised grain, splits, or knotholes. And if the underlayment is not water-resistant, it may absorb spilled water or other liquids and swell. Tile adhesive and ceramic-tile grout will quickly fail with water-swollen underlayment.

There are a variety of underlayment materials, including hardboard, particleboard, OSB, and plywood. Of these, every type except plywood has exhibited failure in one or more applications. You can use APA-approved plywood underlayment beneath carpet, ceramic tile, vinyl, and wood flooring. Be sure the APA stamp says "underlayment" or "plugged cross bands," and that the exposure rating is either "Exposure 1" or "Exterior" to ensure moisture resistance. Also, the underlayment should have a "fully sanded" face (not "plugged and touch-sanded").

19 Undercutting Sill Plates

You'll eventually need to remove the sill plate where rough openings for doors will occur. Cutting through the installed sill is difficult. To make the job easier, cut a saw kerf halfway through the lumber on the underside of sills to mark the inside edges of rough openings before putting the sill plates in place. Later you'll be able to cut the sill plates out of the way using a reciprocating saw or circular saw set to the proper depth.

Cut a ¾-in.-deep kerf in the sill plate beneath rough openings for doors to make removal easier later.

20 Plywood-Cutting Guide

It's easy to allow the saw blade to wander when cutting plywood, so use a guide such as a shoot board to ensure clean, straight cuts. The shoot board is simply a straight-edged board that's fastened to a tempered hardboard base. For your straightedge, use a length of plywood or solid wood that has straight edges and is at least 2 inches wide. Fasten the straightedge to a length of ¼-inch-thick tempered hardboard using glue and wood screws, allowing about 8 inches of hardboard on both sides. Screw through the hardboard into the straightedge, countersinking the screws. Now trim off one side of the base by placing the jig on scrap plywood, squaring the blade to the base of the saw, adjusting the depth of cut to ¼ inch, and running the edge of the circular saw's base against the straightedge. This will create a straight base edge that shows the saw's exact cutting line.

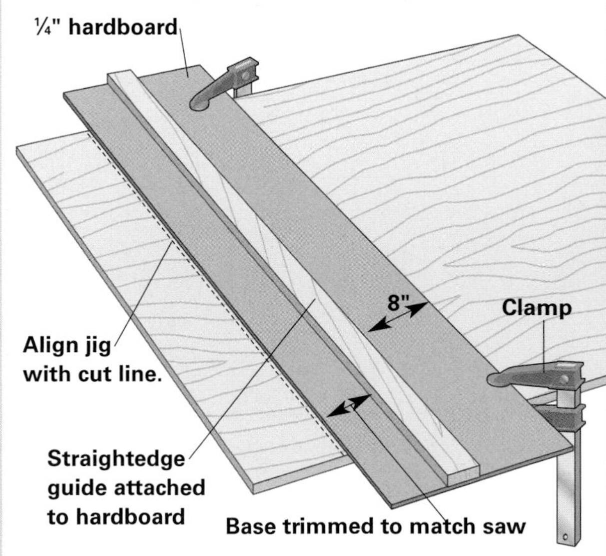

Using the Jig Clamp the jig onto the workpiece, and align the edge of the jig base along the cutting line. Be sure to place the clamps so that the saw's motor won't run into them while you're making the cut. When you must replace the saw blade, retrim the base edge of the jig to ensure that the cut line will, once again, coincide precisely with the edge of the jig.

21 Using Sawhorses

When cutting on sawhorses, never cut between the horses. Always rest the work on both horses; cut to the outside; and let the scrap fall away. If the piece you're cutting off is big enough to bind your cut, get a helper to support it until you finish the cut. Lastly, no matter what kind of cut you're making, always cut away from your body.

Safety First Cutting plywood takes great care. It's tempting to zip through plywood cuts without having someone hold the scrap piece you're cutting away. But because plywood is so flexible, it can easily bind your saw, risking kickback. When cutting plywood, follow these simple safety precautions:

- Cut on a good stable surface.
- Make a highly visible cut line.
- Always be aware of where the saw cord is as you work.
- Have a helper support the weight of the piece you're cutting away when necessary.

To make cutting plywood or lumber easier and safer, bridge two sawhorses with scrap 2x4s, and set the blade depth to workpiece thickness. The workpiece will not droop, nor will the saw bind. Have a helper hold the waste end of very large workpieces.

Working Safer

22 Holes and Notches

Few things in the building business are more visually appealing than a freshly framed house. The bones of the building are all on view, and the color of the structure makes it stand out from the background. When done well, a framed house is almost too crisp. But if you want to see this vision, you better look fast. By the next morning, the hordes will descend—plumbers, electricians, HVAC contractors, and others will start to cut it apart, making way for pipes, wires, vents, and other mechanical devices. While this creative destruction can seem haphazard, usually it's not. The size and position of the various holes and notches are governed by codes. Here are some of the basic guidelines:

- Never cut a hole closer than 2 inches to the board's edge.
- Never make a hole bigger than one-third the depth of the joist.
- Never cut holes or notches in the middle third of the board as measured from one end of its span to the other.
- Never cut notches deeper than one-sixth the depth of the board, except at the ends, where they can be one-fourth the depth.
- Never make notches longer than one-third the depth of the board.

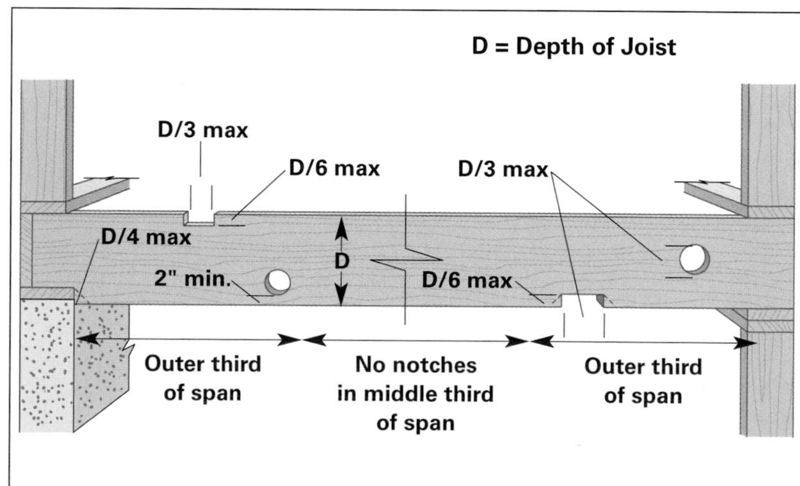

23 Venting Attics

A good attic ventilation system will reduce home energy and maintenence costs for the life of the house. Such systems keep air flowing, eliminating hot air in the summer and excess moisture in the winter.

How It Works Vents placed in the soffits allow in fresh air, which rises through the attic as it warms up and is expelled through ridge vents, gable vents, or other high roof vents. Local codes will specify the ratio of vent square footage to total floor space.

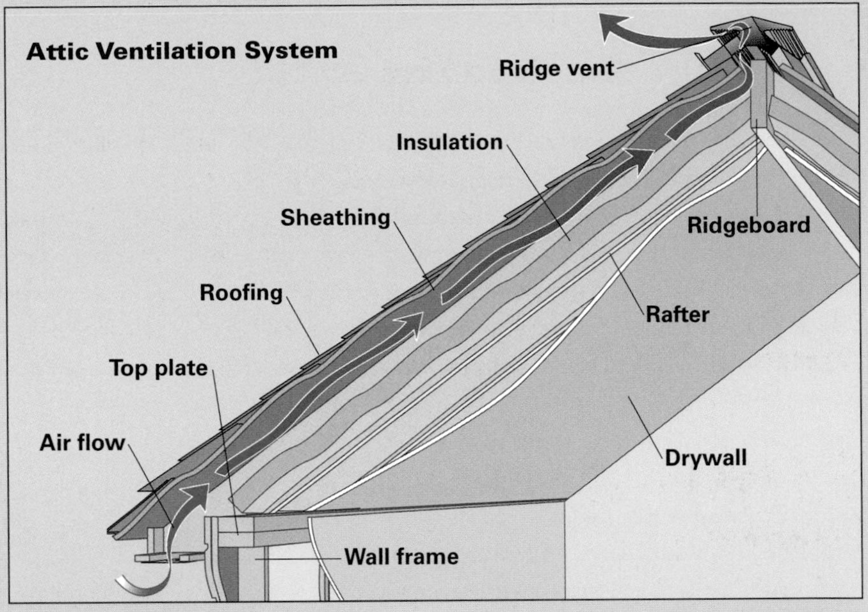

Perforated soffit vents, made of aluminum or vinyl, draw in cool air.

A ridge vent may be hidden under ridge cap shingles.

Motorized exhaust fans are typically mounted on an exterior attic wall.

24 Better Soundproofing

You can attempt soundproofing 2×4 partition walls, the nonload-bearing walls that divide the interior of a structure. You can't expect to make any walls in the house truly soundproof, but you can effectively cut down the transmission of sound through some walls, including those separating bedrooms and bathrooms.

A simple approach to controlling sound involves filling the interior partition wall with batts of R-11 unfaced fiberglass insulation or rigid foam rated at around R-11. If you want to make the wall even more soundproof, double the drywall on each side of the wall.

Probably the best soundproofing technique involves using 2×6s for the top and bottom plates and framing the wall with staggered 2×4 studs. Set the studs at 12 inches on center, so that every other stud is at 24 inches on center on the same plane. It's best to weave unfaced fiberglass insulation between the studs and use double layers of drywall on each side of the wall.

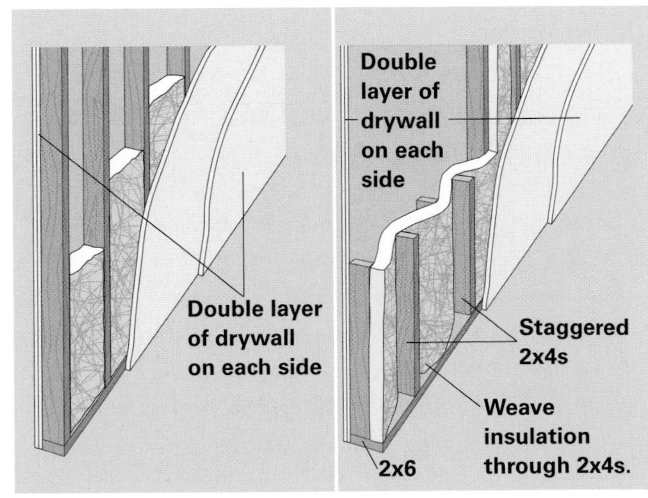

Working Safer

25 When You Need Fire Blocking

Most building codes require fire blocking—two-by stud material that runs horizontally between studs. Blocking is typically called for every 10 feet, measured vertically from the floor plate. Fire blocking interrupts the upward flow of flames and heat should there be a fire. If there were no blocking and a fire started in the basement walls, it could easily and quickly reach the roof and consume the house in flames by following the unobstructed path of the stud bays. If you're framing typical 8-foot walls, the first- and second-floor top plates will serve as the fire blocking. But if your walls are 10 feet high or more without blocking of some sort, you must install fire blocking.

26 Easier Sheathing

When sheathing walls, it's easiest to sheathe right over the rough openings that you created within your stud framing for doors and windows. When you're finished sheathing, you can mark the openings and cut them out.

From the inside, drive nails or drill holes to mark the corners of the opening. Snap chalk lines to connect the corners outside.

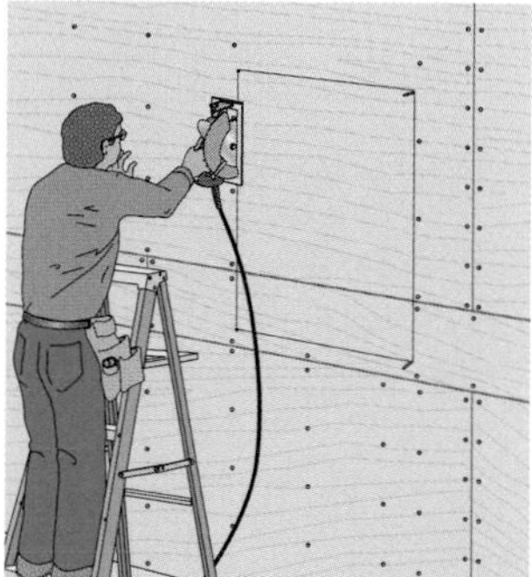

Cut out the rough opening along the chalk lines using a circular saw with the depth of cut set slightly deeper than the sheathing.

27 Wire and Pipe Setback

Drywall screws can easily puncture or penetrate copper pipe or wire, so you must set plumbing and wiring back from the side of the stud that will be receiving screws. Mark for holes so that when the tubing or wire is in place it will be no closer than 1½ inches from the stud edge.

Drill for wires with a ⅝-inch spade bit and for tubing with a ⅝- to 1-inch spade bit, depending on the size of the tubing. Maintain a consistent elevation from one stud bay to the next. Drill for larger plumbing members, such as drains, only in non-structural partition walls.

Where it is impossible to set the wire or tubing back from the wall, install a metal shield (1⁄16 inch in thickness) on the edge of the stud's inside face to prevent screws from entering. You'll find the protective metal plates in most home centers.

28 Properly Bearing Rafters

In the midst of a roof-framing job? Well, to make sure the roof looks great long after its been framed, don't overlook the following detail.

Roof sag can be one result of a rafter that improperly bears on a top plate. If the toe of the rafter (with no overhang) rests on the top plate, for example, the rafter may split, causing the sag. But if the heel rests on the top plate, the rafter is far more stable.

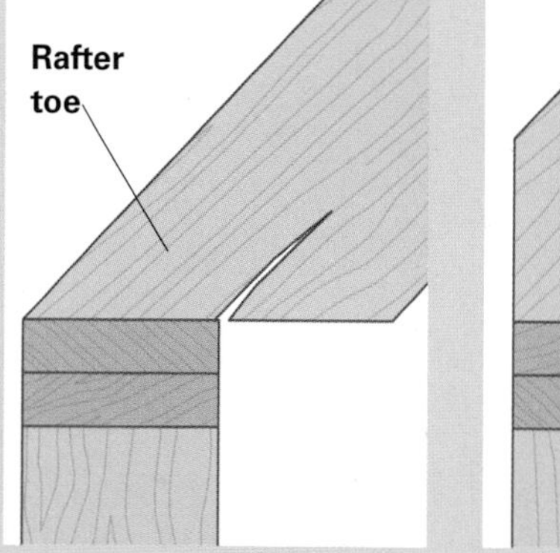

2 Finish Carpentry

- TAKING ACCURATE MEASUREMENTS • IMPROVING TOOL PERFORMANCE
- BETTER-FITTING JOINTS • FINISHING TOUCHES

29 Better Measuring

On most rough carpentry jobs, close is good enough. An eighth of an inch here or there will almost never cause a problem. The same can't be said of finish carpentry. Gaps as small as ⅛ inch between casing boards, along baseboards, or around door and drawer fronts can make a room look like it was cobbled together. They can also cause drawers and doors to stick, stairs to squeak, and countertops to leak. Accuracy is the benchmark of good finish carpentry, and no part of this work is more important than careful measuring. When absolute precision is required, don't measure from the end of your tape, where the built-in hook can be bent or loose. Instead, start at the 1-inch mark and carefully align it with the end of the board. Then make your measurement on the other end. Just be sure to subtract this inch when you do.

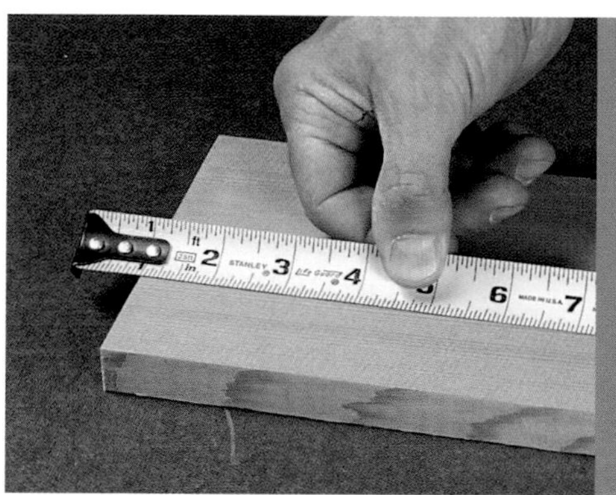

Measure from the tape's 1-in. mark, rather than from the hook, to improve accuracy.

31 "Inside" Measuring Jig

Taking an accurate inside measurement—such as an exact window or door opening—is one of the challenges of trimwork. To obtain exact measurements, take two sticks, each somewhat longer than one-half the overall dimension. Hold the sticks together and slide them apart until the ends touch the walls of the opening. Use clamps to lock the dimension, you can then use the guide to transfer the measurement to your trim piece.

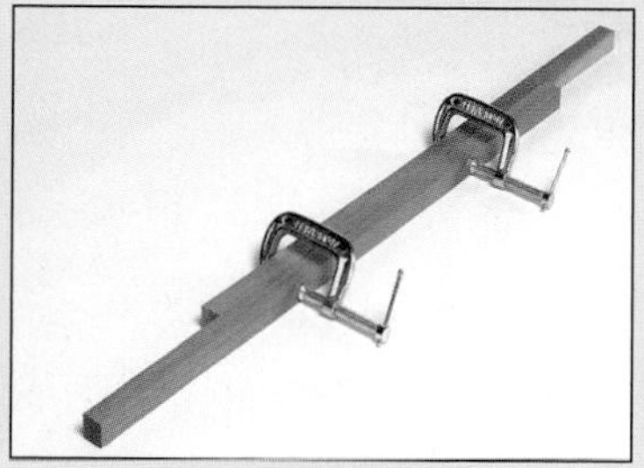

30 Getting Good Marks

In some cases, it pays to make *light* reference lines because you will have to sand away the mark later. (Who wants to do more sanding than is absolutely necessary?) But in most situations, a clear, precise line is essential. And the best way to get one is by using a V-shaped mark, as shown here. The point of the V should be located at the exact measurement, but the two lines extending from this point can be drawn casually.

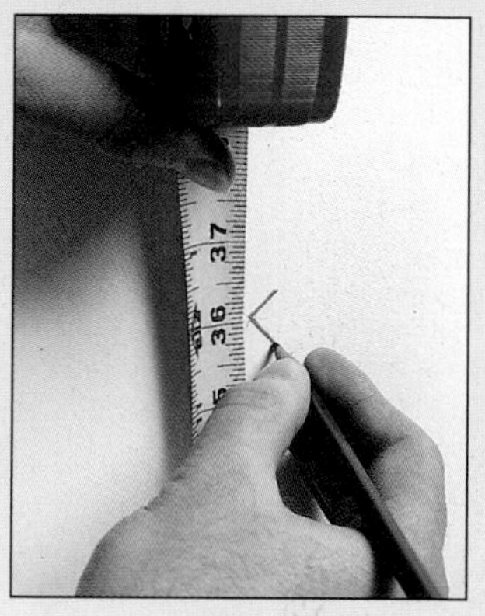

32 Perfect Parallel Lines

Everybody knows that a combination square is used primarily to mark square cut lines on boards and pieces of molding. But this tool can do other things, too. It can be used to mark accurate 45-degree angles; to measure the depth of openings, notches, and recesses by adjusting its sliding blade; and to quickly make accurate parallel lines, as shown here. To do this, simply adjust the blade to the width you need, tighten it securely, and hold the tool against the edge of the board. Then press the tip of a pencil against the end of the blade, and pull both along the board together. It usually takes a few tries to keep the pencil from wandering. Once you get the feel of it, however, you can mark a parallel line in just a couple of seconds.

Use a combination square to mark parallel lines.

33 Working Faster with a Stud Finder

Most finish carpentry requires attaching something to a wall or a ceiling, and this usually means attaching it to the underlying framing members. You can locate these studs and joists without removing any drywall or plaster by driving a small nail repeatedly across the surface and marking where it hits something. This is a fairly reliable method, but it's far from precise, and it can take quite a bit of time if you need to locate a lot of components. The smarter and faster approach is to use a stud finder. Current models feature a kind of radar technology that uses sounds or lights to indicate what's behind the surface. As you move the tool across the wall or ceiling, make a light pencil mark when the center of a framing member is reached.

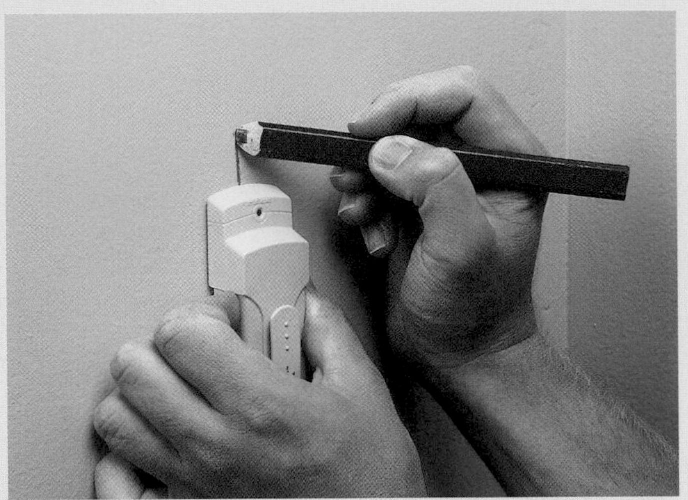

Stud finders can locate framing members within walls and ceilings without making holes in the drywall or plaster.

Working Safer

34 Keeping Up Your Guard

Trimwork is not very dangerous, but there are two areas where it pays to be cautious. The first is with power tools, particularly saws. You should check the manufacturer's operating instructions and follow the rules for safe operation. The second is with wood chips and sawdust. Guard against injury by wearing safety glasses or goggles (A) and, in some situations, by wearing a dust mask (B) or respirator (C). Gloves (D) are handy for sanding and finishing work. You will come to appreciate knee pads (E) when installing baseboard or wainscoting. Wear ear protectors (F) when power tools are loud.

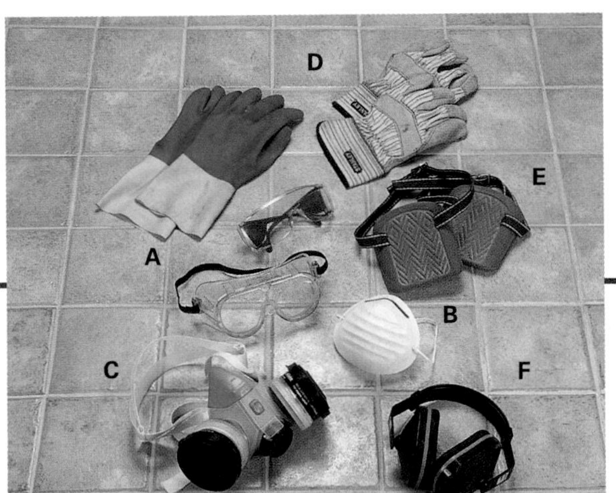

35 The Right Blade?

Just because a blade came with your circular saw doesn't mean it's the only type you should use. In fact, when it comes to finish carpentry, most stock blades do a poor job. This is because they are combination blades, designed to make both rip cuts and crosscuts. As such, they aren't great at making either. Usually these blades have 24 teeth. They sometimes feature a carbide tip on the end of each tooth for longer service and a reduced blade thickness, usually called a "thin kerf" design, to reduce resistance as the blade cuts through wood. Both features are good, but the 24-tooth design is not.

Counting Teeth To get smooth, straight cuts, a 40-tooth design is much better. If you need to cut plywood or other manufactured panels, a 140-tooth blade is essential.

These blades, from left to right, are a 24-tooth combination, a 40- tooth finishing, and a 140-tooth plywood.

36 Portable Worktables

Portable, folding worktables have been on the scene for a long time. Black & Decker's Workmate is so well known that its brand name is now used generically. The reason for their popularity must be based on how many little jobs they make easier. They are compact, so they can be moved from room to room and up and down stairs without damaging walls. And they are lightweight, which saves your back, knees, and arms. But the tabletop is the really ingenious part. It's made in two sections, one that stays put and the other that's attached to two threaded shafts. Depending on which way you turn the crank handles, this half of the top moves toward or away from the stationary half. Along the way, any number of things can be clamped and held in place, including boards that need to be planed smooth, doors that must be trimmed to fit, baseboard moldings that need to be coped, and jambs that need to be mortised for hinges.

A clamping worktable, such as this model, can make trim jobs go faster and easier.

37 Time-Saving Tools

Finish carpentry is a tool-intensive pursuit. It requires a full array of hand tools and portable power tools, and even some stationary tools, if the budget permits. And if you are doing a big job, the budget should permit, especially if you think your time is worth any money. Owning just three tabletop tools can save many hours of work and help you do a much better job in the process. The first is a sliding compound miter saw. This tool can accurately cut angles, miters, and wide crosscuts on both moldings and construction lumber. The second is a small table saw. It's needed for just one job, making rip cuts (cuts along the length of a board instead of across the width of a board), because this is the one cut that a sliding compound miter saw can't make. The last is a portable router table, which allows you to mount your router upside down. A router that is mounted is much easier to use than one that is handheld. It lets you form moldings, cut decorative profiles, and straighten the edges of boards before you glue them together. Don't forget: once you are done with the job at hand, these tools form the nucleus of a very capable home woodworking shop.

A sliding compound miter saw allows you to cut wide stock.

A table saw is the best tool for making rip cuts.

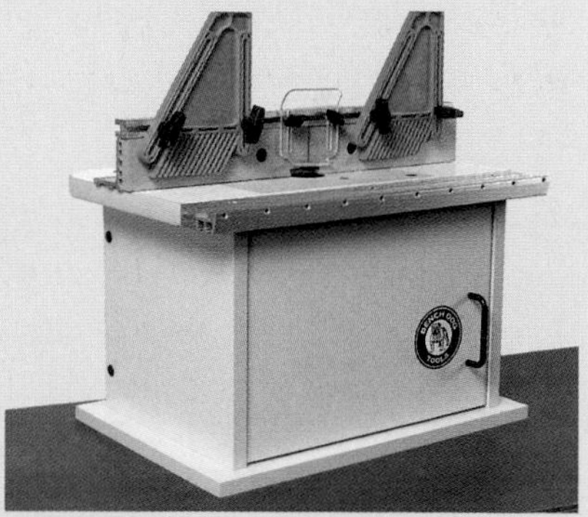
A router becomes more versatile when inverted in a router table.

38 Coped Joints for Tight Fits

The trim carpenter's job would be a lot easier if every inside and outside corner could be fitted with mitered joints. This way, a piece of trim could be cut quickly with a power miter saw and then immediately nailed in place without any muss or fuss. The best part about this dream is that once the board is up, everybody can stop for coffee. Unfortunately, this never happens, because walls are rarely perfectly square. Even if they were, when you nail the second mitered board into an inside corner, a gap in the miter always opens up. The only way to make tight interior corner joints is with a coped cut. This requires only a few simple tools: a coping saw and a couple of files. It does, however, take quite a bit of practice to get it right. The basic steps are shown here.

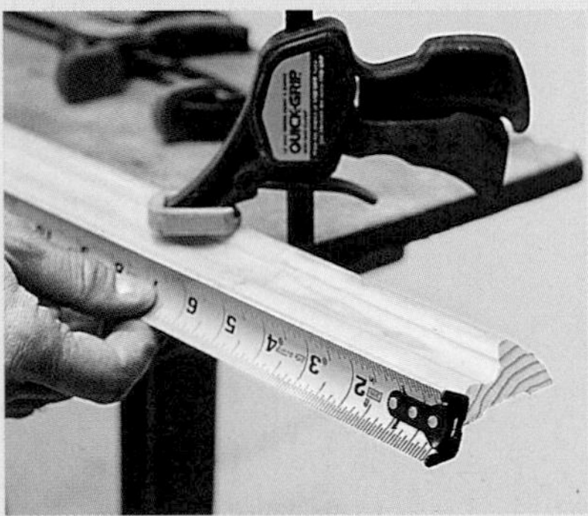

1 Make the miter cut, and measure the molding. Leave an extra inch or two to make adjustments.

2 Use a utility knife to trim off the feathered edge of the miter cut, which is easily broken.

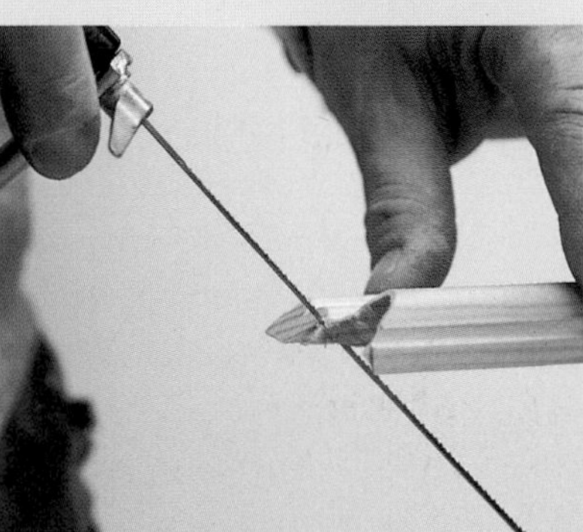

3 With the blade turned 90 deg. to the saw bow, back-cut the molding along the edge line of the miter.

4 After the initial cuts, make the file passes on curved sections with a tapered half-round rasp.

5 A flat rasp works well on square edges where the molding will fit into place against the adjoining section.

6 Test your work by placing the coped edge against the molding it will adjoin.

Saving Money

39 Stability for Power Miter Saws

Make your own power-miter-saw stand from scrap wood, and improve your cutting accuracy and safety. Frame the platform with 2x4s, and cover it with ¾-in. plywood. Attach outboard supports, level with the saw table. This will allow you to handle long, flat stock and moldings with ease.

Working Safer

40 Sharp Chisels = Safe Chisels

A basic set of butt chisels, ranging from ¼ to 1½ inches, is essential for trimwork. You'll find them handy for fine paring of joints and cutting mortises for door hardware. The old adage about a sharp tool being safer than a dull one is true. Keep your chisels sharp with a good-quality sharpening stone and honing guide—and always cut in a direction away from your body and hands.

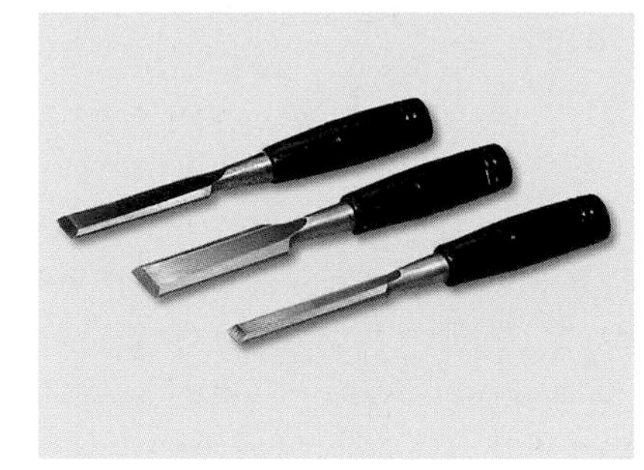

41 Cutting Baseboard

Whenever you cut a piece of baseboard, it is a good practice to add an extra ¹⁄₁₆ inch to the length to ensure a tight fit and allow you some room to adjust the joint. When fitting a piece of base between two surfaces, an extra ¹⁄₁₆ inch allows you to spring the molding into position, pushing the end joint closed. And when fitting an outside corner joint, the extra length gives you the opportunity to work toward a tight fit—something that does not always come automatically, especially in corners that are not perfectly square. Remember that some fitting and recutting is an expected part of trim installation.

Cut trim slightly long so that you can make adjustments and get a tight fit.

42 Short Cutoffs

It's tough, and hazardous, to cut short pieces of stock with a power miter saw because the fence on this type of saw is necessarily open around the cut and does not provide good support for short cutoffs.

Build a Jig A simple alternative is to build a crosscutting jig that you can use with a backsaw. Screw two pieces of scrap 1×4 stock to the edges of a piece of 1×6. Use a reliable square to mark across the top edges of the 1×4s, and carry the guide marks down the outside faces. Use a backsaw to carefully cut down along the marks.

43 The Finishing Touch

Sometimes a piece of molding will just end on a wall. This happens with aprons under window stools, moldings applied to the top of head casings, and chair rails that are installed over wainscoting. You can simply cut the end of these boards square, but a better approach is to cut a miter on the end of the board. Then cut a matching miter on a small scrap of the same type molding, and glue it in place. Hold it in position with a piece of masking tape until the glue dries.

For safety, cut the return in a jig as shown in tip no. 42.

Apply glue to both surfaces, and push the piece into place.

Greener Ways

44 Finger-Jointed Stock: Inexpensive Wood-Saver

A good way to reduce the impact of harvesting so much wood is to use more of what's been cut. This is the reasoning behind finger-jointed lumber and moldings. Small waste pieces of wood are machined so they have finger joints on both ends. They're glued together to form longer boards, and then they are cut into standard dimensions and shapes. Besides the environmental benefits of this lumber, you can save money and get a better product at the same time. Finger-jointed hardwoods, such as poplar, are standard trim stock. They are stable, resist damage very well, and look great when painted. Of course, this material is only suitable for trimwork that will be painted. A clear or stained finish would let the joints show.

45 Keeping Joints Closed

You may be working on square door or window jambs, and you may cut perfect miters on the matching casing boards. You may nail everything in place without splitting anything or leaving behind a hammer mark. But you can still discover a few weeks later that this joint has opened up and cracked the paint that was over it.

The Glue Trick You can cover this joint with paint every once in a while and let sleeping dogs lie. But the next time you do this job, remember a simple trick that can prevent most of these cracks: spread a little yellow or white glue on the ends of both boards before you push them together. Then once they're nailed in place, wipe up any excess glue with a damp sponge. This will keep the joint tight for the rest of its days.

For tight, long-lasting joints, apply glue to the mating pieces. Complete the job using finishing nails to hold the joint closed while the glue dries.

46 Crown Molding Support

When crown molding runs perpendicular to the ceiling joists above, nail it through the ceiling and into the joists at the top. Nail it into the wall plates at the bottom. When the molding must run parallel with the ceiling joists, there is often no framing member into which you can nail. You can solve this problem by installing backer blocks around the room to accept nails wherever necessary. Cut two-by stock to form blocks at the appropriate angle. Cut the blocks to allow a space of about ⅛ inch between the molding and blocks so you have some room to adjust the molding during installation.

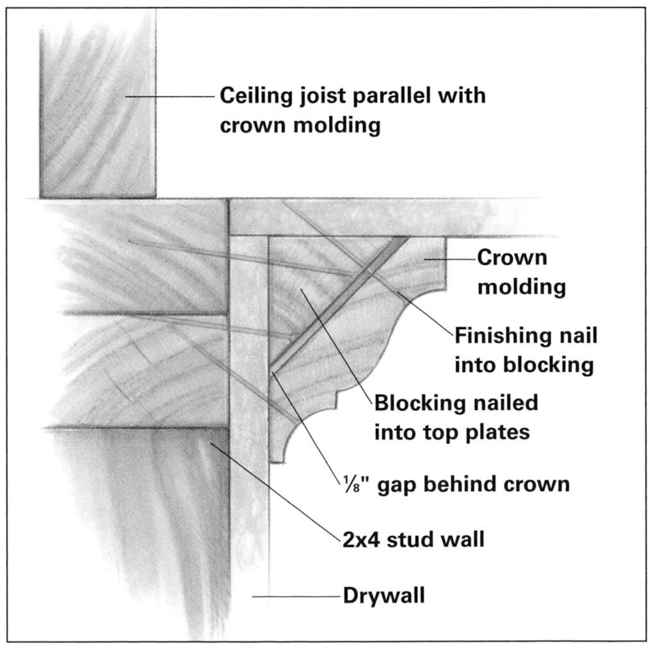

47 Open versus Closed Grain

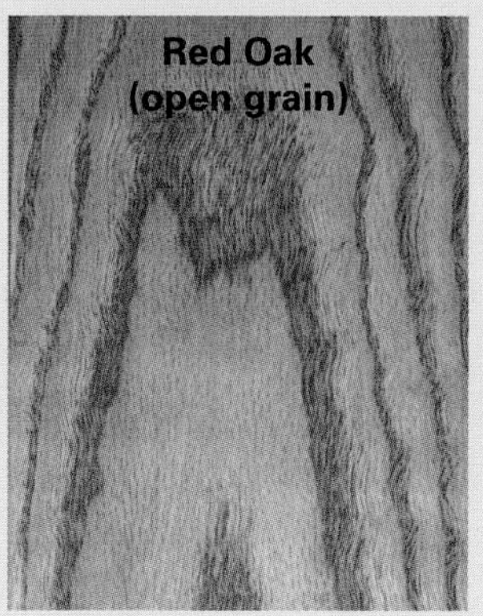

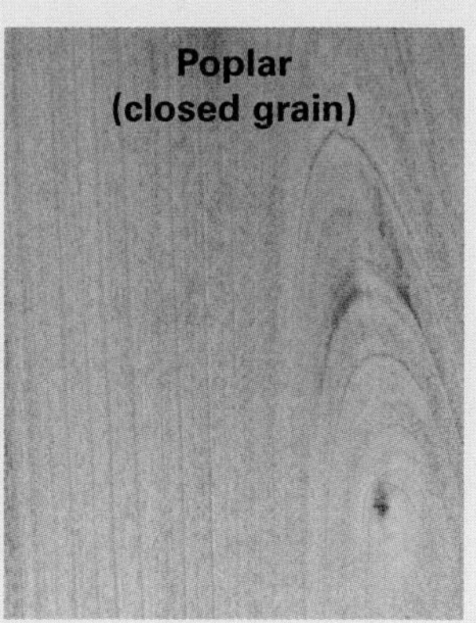

Hardwood lumber that's used for interior trim falls into two broad categories: open grain and closed grain. The first group is populated by common species such as ash, red and white oak, walnut, butternut, and mahogany. Closed-grain woods include birch, cherry, hard and soft maple, poplar, and sycamore. The biggest difference in appearance between the two is that open-grain woods tend to show more grain. The closed-grain species, on the other hand, have less contrast between the growth rings and therefore have a more uniform color. If the only difference between these two types of wood was their appearance, choosing between them would be simple. There's more to it. These woods also have different porosities. The open-grain types tend to absorb more finish and do it unevenly. Closed-grain woods aren't as absorbent and tend to accept finishes much more uniformly. To make the finish over an open-grain wood look better, you need to fill the grain with a paste filler. This intermediate step is not particularly difficult if you are working on a small area. But if you have a room or two with lots of open-grain trim, filling the grain before you apply the finish is going to cost some money and take a lot of time.

48 Easy-to-Install Ceiling Moldings

One of the good things about crown moldings and other ceiling trim is that they are up high and, as a result, more difficult to see. Because of this, the joinery between boards doesn't always have to be perfect, or the alignment on the ceiling can be a little off, and no one will notice. One of the bad things about these moldings is that they are hard to install, even if lower standards are permissible. Synthetic moldings, usually called resin moldings, make a virtue out of the good and correct the bad aspects of the conventional approach. They are very easy to install and don't require coped joints at inside corners. You just miter the ends and fill any gaps with caulk. Because these "boards" are always painted, the caulk can be easily covered so it's not visible from below. These moldings are available in many different designs. In fact, the larger, more ornate examples look more like traditional plaster moldings than wood trim.

Lightweight resin moldings are easy to install on ceilings.

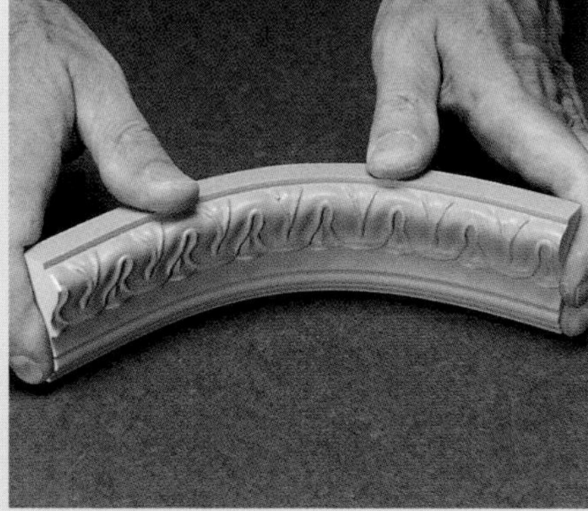

Some resin trim is very flexible and can be used on curved walls.

This room contains crown molding, casing, and panels made from resin.

49 Wall-Cabinet Support

Wall cabinets aren't very heavy, but they are bulky and hard to handle. If you attach a 1×2 support ledger to the wall just below the bottom of these cabinets, you'll make installing them much easier. Lift each cabinet; rest the back corner on the ledger; and have someone steady the box in place while you screw it to the wall. This will allow you to spend a little more time positioning each cabinet and making sure it's plumb and level before attaching it.

Install a 1x2 ledger to the wall just below wall cabinet height. Use a 4-ft. level to be sure it's level.

50 Scarfing for a Better Joint

Sometimes you need to splice boards together to make the best use of your materials. If you simply butt square ends, even the slightest bit of shrinkage in the boards will result in a visible crack between the parts. The better approach is to use a scarf joint, where the ends of both mating boards are cut at a 45-degree angle so that one overlaps the other. Typically, these joints are glued and nailed together. When the surface is sanded smooth, the seam is almost invisible. If shrinkage does occur, instead of a gap, more wood will be exposed.

Using a miter saw, cut matching 45-deg. cuts on each piece that will form the scarf joint.

51 Using Hollow-Wall Anchors

It's always best to fasten trim parts to the framing members inside a wall or ceiling, but this isn't always possible, depending on the location of the trim on the surface of the wall. In these situations, you have two options. You can open up the wall and install solid blocking between adjacent framing members. Then you have to close up the hole, repair the surface, and install your trim using conventional methods.

A Better Choice The other option is to use one of the various hollow-wall fasteners that are available these days. Clearly, the second option is the smarter choice. A typical installation is shown here.

1 Drill through the piece to be installed using a countersink bit. The bit will mark the drywall for drilling.

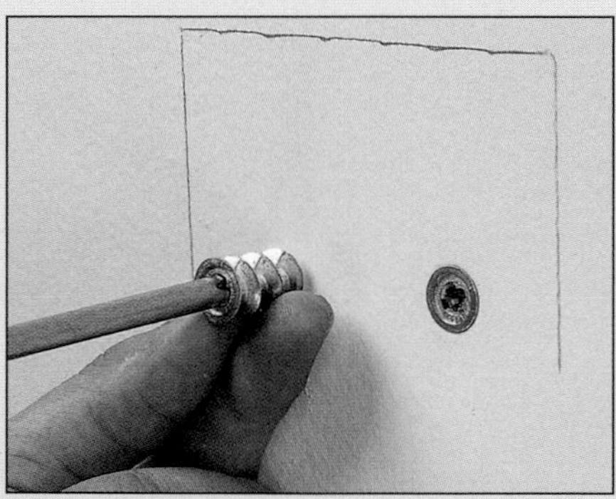

2 Remove the molding, and drill pilot holes. Screw anchors into the pilot holes.

3 Attach molding, and glue dowels into the holes. Trim excess, and finish the workpiece.

52 Scribing = Better Fit

When a floor is out of level a small amount, such as ¼ inch in 10 feet, it's hard to detect, especially if there's furniture in the way. But if it's worse than this and baseboard will be clearly visible, you should scribe the board to the floor and cut the bottom edge so that it fits properly. To do this, support the trim in a *level* position with small blocks and shims. Then adjust a scriber (or a simple compass) so that the space between the point and the pencil matches the thickness of the thickest block-shim combination. Tighten the screw on the scriber so that the distance between sides can't change, and use the tool to mark along the bottom edge of the board. Cut the baseboard to remove the waste below the line, and smooth the edge with a block plane. Test-fit the board, and when you're satisfied, nail it in place.

Place spacers beneath baseboard to level it, and then use a scriber to mark the bottom edge of the board for a tight fit between an uneven floor and baseboard.

53 Flattening Drywall Bulges

Sometimes a piece of trim can't be installed flat against a wall or ceiling, because sections of bulging drywall are in the way. Many tools can get rid of these bulges, but the easiest one to use is a simple surface-forming tool. This tool looks—and is used—just like a bench plane. But its replaceable blade cuts like a coarse rasp. It can scrape off drywall paper, and the gypsum underneath, in just a few passes. Different sizes are available, including one that resembles a block plane. This smaller tool is so easy to carry around that many trim carpenters keep one in their tool aprons at all times.

Before installing casing, use a surface-forming tool to flatten bulging sections of drywall until they are flush to the jamb.

54 Easier Casing Corners

Mitering is the standard method for corner-joining most kinds of trim, like casing on doors and windows, but that doesn't mean it's the only way to do this job. You can also use corner blocks, or rosettes, and save a lot of time and effort. Because these blocks are thicker than the casing boards, the casing doesn't have to fit flush against the blocks to look right. As long as the blocks are square and the ends of the casings boards are square, the joints will be tight, even if the casings are tipped a little in one direction or the other. Corner blocks can be made from wood stock or purchased as finished units in wood or plaster with various decorative faces, such as the one shown below. To install them, just butt the casing as you nail the blocks and casing to the wall. This approach is so fast that you may wonder why anyone started using miters in the first place.

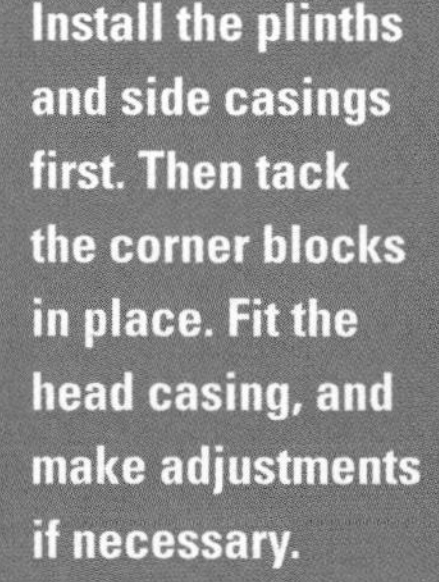

Install the plinths and side casings first. Then tack the corner blocks in place. Fit the head casing, and make adjustments if necessary.

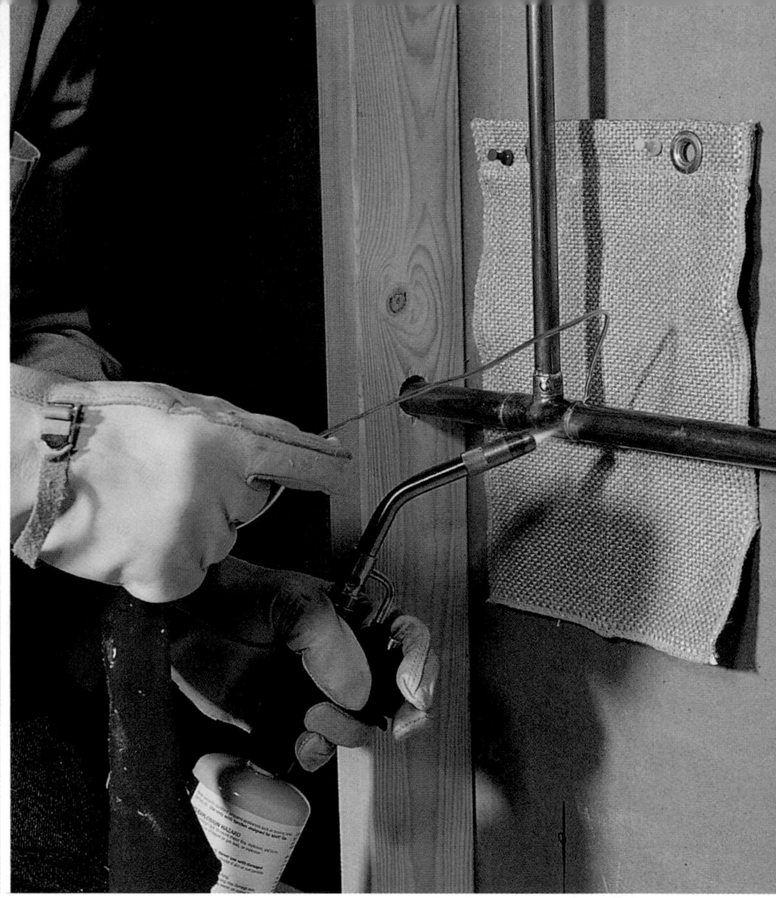

3 Plumbing

- EASY PIPE CUTTING • MAKING JOINTS
- HANDY TOOLS • SAVING ENERGY

55 Registration, Please!

Working with plastic drainpipe is easy and quick, as long as you assemble the parts in the right position on the first try. Once the pipe and fittings are glued together, there's no getting them apart, even to make the smallest of adjustments. To prevent mistakes, test-fit all the parts first, and indicate their proper positions with registration marks. Then separate the parts, and start to glue together the individual joints, making sure that the marks align.

1 Cut the pipe with a hacksaw. Be sure the cut is straight.

2 Remove plastic burrs from the pipe end using a deburring tool.

3 Apply primer—often required by code—to the end of the pipe.

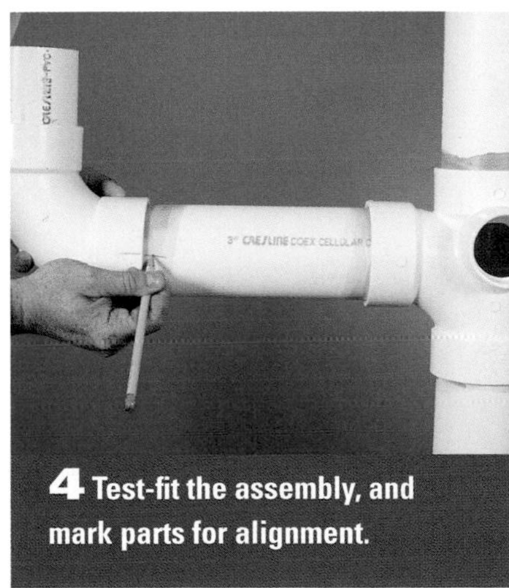

4 Test-fit the assembly, and mark parts for alignment.

5 Apply solvent cement to the mating surfaces.

6 Start fitting a bit out of alignment, and then turn parts to align.

Working Safer

56 Using Metal Flashing to Prevent Fires

Not all soldering jobs can be done out in the open where the torch flame can't cause any damage. In fact, when it comes to remodeling work, sweating copper is often done in tight spots. To avoid scorched wood, some plumbers use a piece of woven fireproof fabric placed behind the joint, but a folded piece of aluminum flashing works as well. Wedge a 6- or 8-inch-square piece behind the joint, and turn on the torch. Once the job is done, let the flashing cool for a minute before pulling it out. Wear leather gloves to prevent any burns.

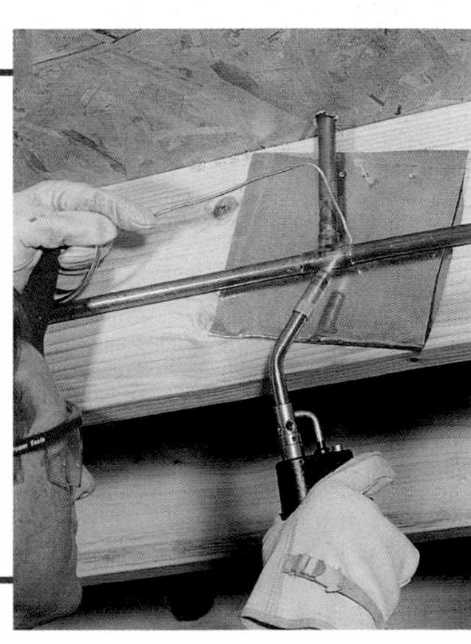

57 Bottoms First!

Always start soldering at the lowest part of a joint. The reason for this is simple: when you solder the bottom part first, the solder in that section has a chance to cool, and thicken slightly, before you start soldering the higher parts. When the solder is then applied to the upper areas, it can't drain through the bottom of the fitting, because the cooler solder is blocking its path. If no solder drains out of the joint, the chance of a leak is greatly reduced.

58 Cutter for Tight Spaces

You'll find a variety of copper tubing cutters on the market; most of them are 5 to 6 inches long. These work very well for just about every tubing-cutting job. But if you are working inside a wall between studs or between floor joists, you may not have room to swing one of these tools. Jobs like this are better done with a small tool called a thumb cutter. It has a knurled knob instead of a long handle. You twist the knob to tighten the cutting wheel, and then turn the tool around the tubing, as you would with one of the larger tools.

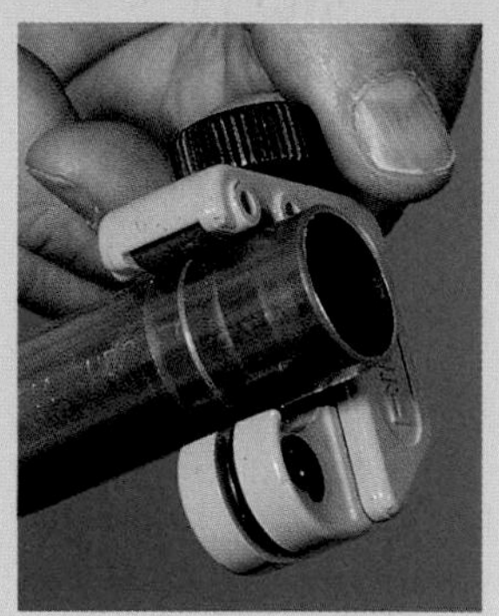

59 A Faster Way to Clean Tubing and Fittings

Always clean both mating surfaces of every solder joint before you sweat them together. Steel wool and sandpaper do a good job of this chore, and just about everyone has these items on hand. But if you have a lot of soldering to do, using an inexpensive combination tool can save a lot of time and do a better job. This tool has a plastic body with two openings that are ringed with short pieces of wire. One opening is sized for ¾-inch tubing; the other is for ½-inch tubing. Both ends of the tool have a short wire brush. One is for cleaning ¾-inch fittings; the other is for ½-inch fittings. To use this tool, insert the end of a tube in its proper opening and turn the tool completely around the tube a few times. To clean the inside of a fitting, push the correct-size brush into the fitting and twist right then left a few times. When you're done, wipe the parts with a dry rag.

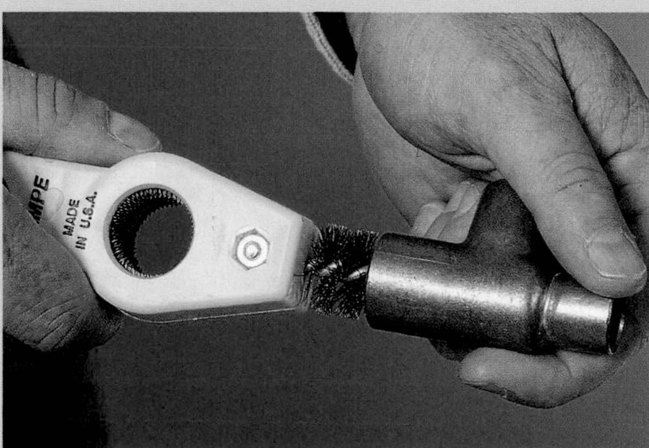

To clean a fitting, insert a combination tool (shown), a wire brush, or an abrasive pad into the end and twist.

To clean a tube, push the end into one of the holes on the combination tool and turn.

60 Speedier Plumbing Jobs with New Tubing

PVC and ABS plastic pipe have been around for a long time, and both are used primarily for waste and vent piping. But in the last few years PEX (cross-linked polyethylene) tubing has become very popular for water supply lines. It is code-approved for this purpose in most areas of the country. The tubing is very flexible (more like hose than rigid tubing), which makes new plumbing jobs go much faster. The ends are connected to standard fittings, such as kitchen faucets, with a barbed adapter and various types of crimped rings.

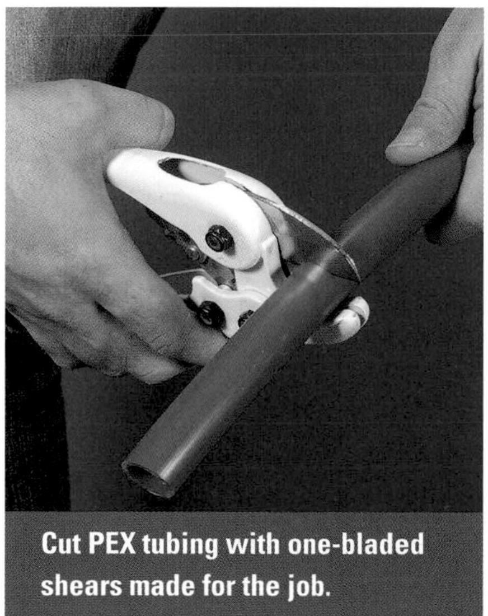

Cut PEX tubing with one-bladed shears made for the job.

The flexible tubing is fed through a bracket to hold it in place.

The tubing slides onto the valve. A crimped ring securely locks it.

Greener Ways

61 Water-Saving Toilets

In the average home, the toilet accounts for more than 25 percent of water use. You can use less of this valuable resource if you consider a low-flush, dual-flush, or composting toilet.

Low-flush toilets, which are mandated by plumbing codes, are required to use 1.6 gallons or less per flush, which is about half the water older models use. And today's low-flush models are better than the first ones that came along, so you don't have to flush multiple times to get the job done, which negated any water savings. A two-button or two-handle dual-flush toilet allows you to control the flushing—a small flush for liquid waste and a bigger flush for solid waste. A composting toilet, which converts human waste into organic compost through aerobic decomposition, uses little or no water.

62 Space Saver

If you have to accommodate the cramped space of a very small powder room, where a conventional toilet will be in the way, you can use a corner toilet. This design features a wedge-shaped tank to fit in a corner and free up some valuable floor space. The drain hole for one of these units is located the same distance (usually 12½ inches) from both walls.

A corner toilet is shaped to save floor space, but it is plumbed in place—and works—the same way as a standard toilet.

Working Safer

63 Avoiding a Stack-Cutting Hazard

If you need to cut out a section of a cast-iron stack on a lower floor, it's important that you make sure the stack above the cut can't come crashing down. Most stacks won't fall when cut, because upper-story vents or branch lines hold them in place. Still, it pays to check, especially when you consider the weight of a 20-to-30-foot cast-iron pipe. The most surefire precautionary measure is to install a stack clamp that grips the stack and is supported by nearby wall studs.

Install a stack clamp to secure the upper section of a cast-iron stack when cutting out a lower section.

64 No-Hub, No Hassle

For the do-it-yourselfer, plastic sanitary piping takes some of the fear out of major plumbing jobs. It's lightweight and easy to cut, and making joints is easy. Many existing drain, waste, and vent (DWV) systems, however, are made from cast iron. So if you hope to make changes or additions, you'll need to know how to make a transition from cast-iron to plastic.

The easiest approach is to splice in a no-hub, cast-iron fitting using banded couplings. Banded couplings consist of a neoprene rubber sleeve backed by a wide stainless-steel band or collar and at least two stainless-steel clamps. Because these couplings can join dissimilar materials, they are perfect remodeling fittings, making permanent, corrosion-free joints.

1 Hold the new, no-hub fitting against the pipe, and mark the segment to be removed. Add ½-in. clearance to the cutout for fitting room.

2 Roll the coupling's sleeve up, and slide the fitting in place. Then roll it back down, and tighten the clamps.

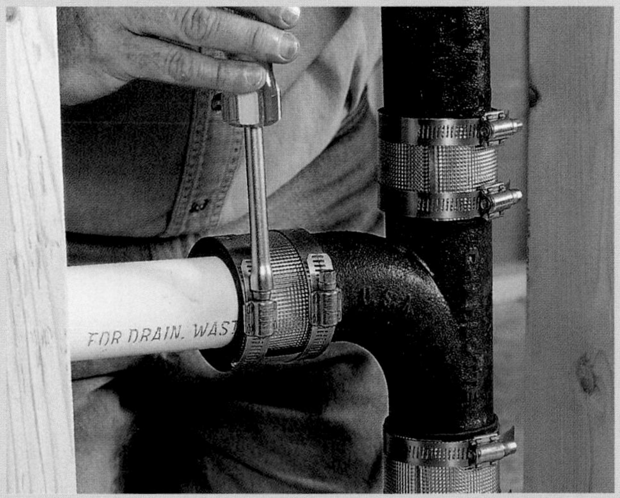

3 Attach the plastic piping to the no-hub, cast-iron fitting in the same manner.

65 Easy Ways to Cut Cast Iron

You have a choice of methods when cutting cast-iron pipe. A hacksaw will work, but it's a tedious job and will require several blades per cut. Another method is to repeatedly score the pipe with a ball-peen hammer and cold chisel. This method is slow and requires access to the entire circumference of the pipe, but it works surprisingly well. (See middle and right photos below.) When pros cut cast iron, they use a snap-cutter. As its name implies, this tool doesn't saw through but snaps—breaks—a pipe in two. A snap-cutter consists of a roller chain that has hardened steel wheels built into it, spaced an inch apart. The chain is connected to a ratchet head. As you lever the head, the chain tightens, and the cutter wheels bite into the pipe with equal pressure. When you apply enough pressure, the pipe snaps in two. Snap-cutters are common rental items.

A snap-cutter makes cutting cast-iron drainpipes quick and easy.

Another option is to draw a line around the pipe and score with a hammer.

If the cut is uneven, break off the high spots using an old wrench.

Saving Money

66 Air-Admittance Valves

Relatively new on the scene, air-admittance valves (AAVs) can sometimes be used to eliminate the need for multiple vent stack roof penetrations and to reduce the length of vent lines. They are especially useful in retrofit situations where venting may be difficult.

AAVs are pressure-activated, one-way mechanical valves. Normally closed, they open when wastewater discharges, allowing air to enter for proper drainage. When closed, AAVs prevent the escape of sewer gas and maintain the seals at traps.

AAVs can be located in any ventilated space. They are made of plastic and can be fitted to a drain, waste, and vent system with normal joint adhesives. Consult local codes to be sure AAVs are permitted in your area.

67 Speedy Demolition

To dismantle an old galvanized-steel or copper plumbing system, you can cut it apart with a hacksaw or reciprocating saw. You can also cut cast iron, but an easier method is to shatter the hubs with hammers. This may seem extreme, but it works well and gets the job done quickly.

You'll need to wear face and eye protection, of course, but the method is simple. Starting near the top of the stack, strike the first hub simultaneously on opposite sides with two hammers of equal weight. Three-pound sledgehammers work well. When you reach the lowest section of piping on the stack, stop. From the basement ceiling on down, use a snap-cutter to make clean cuts. At this point, either dig the lead and oakum from the lowest hub, or use a snap-cutter to cut the stack a foot or so above the floor. Using a neoprene gasket or banded coupling, you can then extend the new piping upward.

68 No More S-Traps!

If you are remodeling a kitchen or a bathroom in an old house, you may encounter S-traps connected to the bottom of sinks. These traps are hooked to pipes that go down through the floor instead of into the wall, and they are no longer code-approved, because they don't vent properly. Existing installations don't have to be changed, but if you are replacing a sink, it makes good sense to replace the trap, too. The performance of the drain will be much better.

Rework the piping as shown in this illustration. The pipe and fittings are all standard items, but the automatic vent (also called air-admittance valve, or AAV, Tip 66) is special. It has a one-way diaphragm inside that lets air into the system (like a traditional vent pipe) without letting sewer gases out. These units are sometimes called autovents or quick vents, and they are stock items at plumbing-supply stores and many home centers.

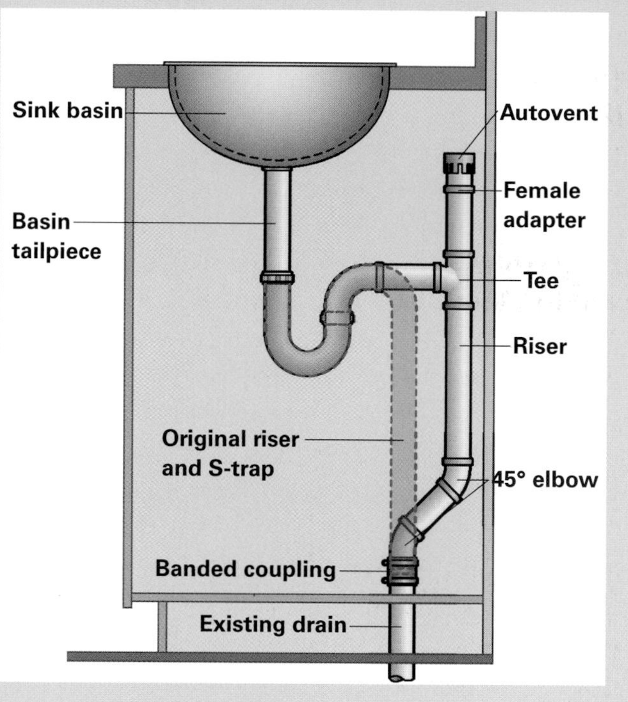

69 Great Gasket for Toilets—and Wax-Free!

Wax rings are the traditional way to seal the joint between the bottom of a toilet and the top of a toilet flange and drainpipe. You place one of these rings over the flange, lower the toilet onto the ring, and tighten the bolts that are hooked onto the flange. If your floor is flat and your toilet is not installed in very warm temperatures, the wax seal works well.

A New Way to Go But a newer approach works better, even if the floor is uneven or the day is very hot. It's a gasket that's mounted on a plastic horn that slides into the drain opening. The horn doesn't leak because it has a large O-ring on the outside that seals it to the pipe. And the toilet doesn't leak because the gasket seals the joint between the bottom of the bowl and the top of the gasket horn.

The gasket assembly fits inside 3-in.-dia. drainpipes and comes with a sleeve that fits 4-in. drainpipes, so you're ready for any situation.

70 To Caulk or Not to Caulk

Once you've installed a new toilet and tested it for proper operation, you may think you're done with the job. But you have one more thing to consider. Should you caulk around the base of the toilet or leave it as is? It's a little hard to believe that this could be an issue that any building codes would deal with, but they do. Some require it, especially for a bowl sitting on a concrete floor. The reasoning is that the caulk, once it's dried, will help keep the bowl from rocking from side to side. Other codes don't want the joint to be caulked, especially on wood floors because the caulk could trap water from a leak under the bowl and start rotting the wood flooring. Absent a governing code in your area, the best approach is something in between. Caulk the entire joint except for a 1-inch-long section at the back of the bowl. This will keep the toilet from rocking but let any water underneath escape. Use a silicone-based tub-and-tile caulk for this job.

When caulking around the base of a toilet, apply a uniform bead of caulk, and then smooth it in place with a wet finger.

Saving Money

71 Longer-Lasting Valves

When you install a new faucet as part of a larger remodeling job, you'd like to think it's a plug-and-play device. Install it and get on with all the other jobs that are waiting. If you take a few minutes to remove the valve stems and coat the new washers with some heatproof grease, however, you can prolong their lives and postpone repairs later on. Remove the faucet handles, and use an adjustable wrench to loosen the bonnet nuts that hold the stems in place. Spread a small amount of grease on each washer, and then reinstall the stems and the handles.

Coat the washer and stem threads on new faucets with heatproof grease to reduce the long-term wear on these parts.

72 Helpful Handle Puller

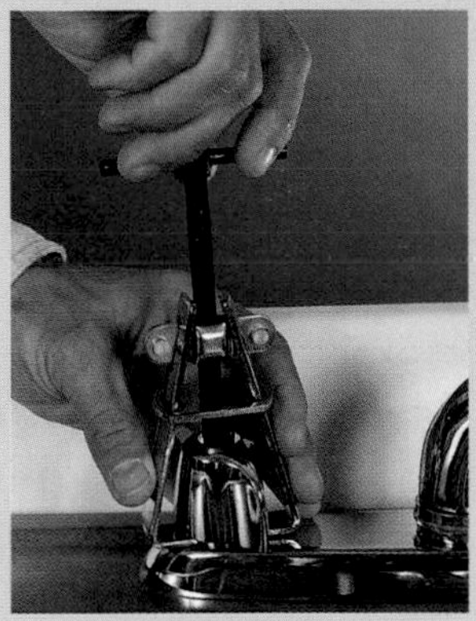

When working on a complete remodeling job, it's tempting to toss out everything and start from scratch. Your budget does not always make this possible. You'll often have to keep major items such as bathtubs, sinks, and toilets because replacing them is too expensive, in terms of money *and* time. A good cleaning will do wonders, and refurbishing faucet and toilet parts will make them work like new. Faucets are especially easy to renew. The hardest part of the job can be removing the faucet handles, which may be corroded on the inside and stuck to the valve stems, without damaging them. Fortunately, an inexpensive handle puller (usually less than $10) makes removing the handles a breeze. Simply remove the handle screw; slide the jaws of the puller around the bottom edge of the handle; and turn the puller head clockwise until the handle is free.

73 Tub Resurfacing

If you have an old bathtub that is showing some wear, you can usually have it resurfaced for less than $500. This can cost substantially less than buying a new tub and having it installed. The process consists of masking off the tub area and applying an etching solution. Then the installer sprays on several coats of a plastic-based product, not a porcelain coating. This new coating can last as long as 10 years if the installer does a good job and the homeowner keeps the surface clean with a nonabrasive product designed for this purpose.

Refinishing a tub requires several applications of a plastic coating.

Once the top coat dries, the surface is buffed to a smooth finish.

74 Preserving Chrome

Lots of fittings and fixtures are preserved instead of replaced to reduce the cost of a big remodeling job. This makes sense, but only if they look good when the job is done. One way to keep chrome faucets from looking worse for wear is to use a strap wrench when you have to remove visible parts such as this spout cap. To use a strap wrench, place the strap over the part and tighten it. Then turn the handle as you would a typical wrench. Some, like this one, are made with fabric; others are made of soft plastic.

75 Freeze-Proof Sillcocks

Freeze-proof sillcocks are designed so that the water connection to the valve is deep inside the house where it is warm, instead of on the outside of the house where it's cold. When the valve is turned off, the standing water never reaches an area that is cold enough to freeze it; thus, no frozen pipes and no broken pipes. These devices work very well, as long as you don't keep a hose attached to them in the winter. If you don't remove the hose, it will create an air lock that can hold water in the chamber, between the handle and the valve seat, which will freeze and break.

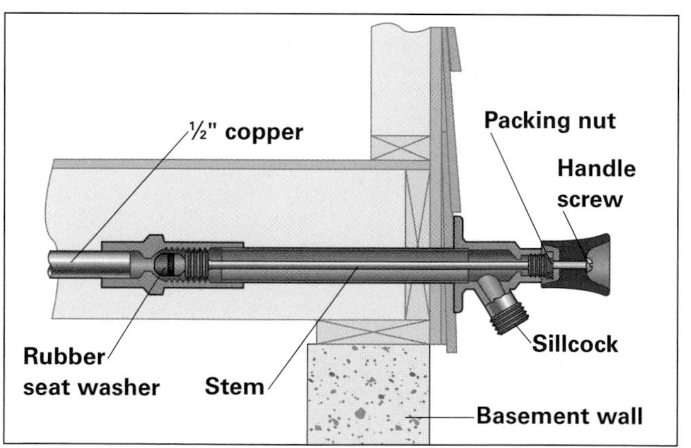

76 Getting the Kinks Out

Soft copper tubing is the preferred pipe for all sorts of jobs, from natural gas and propane lines to ice-maker supply tubes and water lines throughout the house, especially where they meander through tight spots.

Pros and Cons When you first pick up this tubing, it seems so workable because you can bend it easily with just your hands. This is the good news, but it's also the bad news. Because copper tubing is so flexible it also kinks easily, and once a section is kinked it has to be cut out and thrown away. Fortunately, inexpensive spring benders are available for all the standard tube sizes. To use one, simply slide the bender over the tube; center it at the middle of the bend; and then force the tube into the shape you want. The spring will bend but not distort, and it allows the tube to do the same thing.

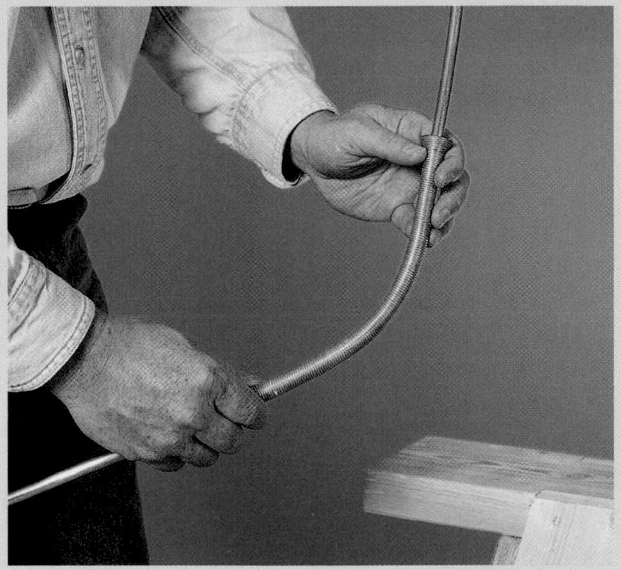

Use a spring-type tubing bender to avoid kinking soft copper tubing.

Greener Ways

77 Insulating Water Lines

Much of the energy consumed by a conventional water heater is devoted to storage costs: keeping the water in the tank hot until it's needed. But the tank isn't the only place where water is stored. It's also "stored" in the hot-water lines that travel throughout the house. Installing a well-insulated water heater is a good step, but so is wrapping the hot-water tubing in foam insulation. These foam sleeves are sized to fit different-diameter tubes and pipes, and each has a slit along one side, so it slides easily in place. The real energy savings result from treating the hot-water lines, but it makes sense to wrap the cold-water lines, too. This will reduce (if not eliminate altogether) the condensation that can drip off cold tubing in the summer.

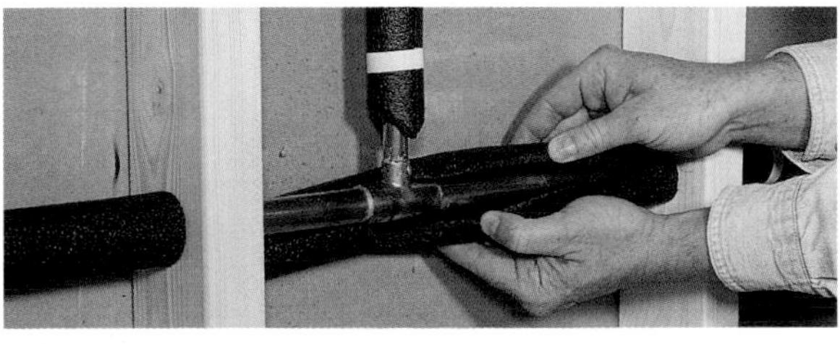

78 Right-Angle Drills

Right-angle drills do what their name implies. They take the rotary action of a typical drill and deliver it at a right angle to the work surface. Instead of the chuck being in line with the body of the tool, it's mounted at a 90-degree angle. This change in direction is accomplished by a group of gears located in the head of the tool. The design lets you easily drill pipe and tubing holes between wall studs and floor joists. You can use spade bits for smaller holes and heavy-duty hole saws for larger holes.

Rent or Buy? These tools can do a tremendous amount of work in a short time, but they are expensive—more than $200 without any bits. Because of this, they are standard rental items. If you have a lot of work to do, consider buying one. But if you are putting in a single bathroom, rent one for a few days to get all the pipes installed, and then take it back.

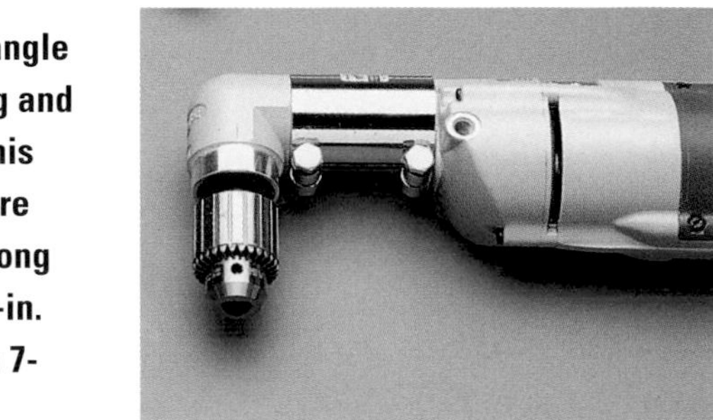

Most right-angle drills are big and powerful. This model is more than a foot long and has a ½-in. chuck and a 7-amp motor.

79 Solving for Basement Water Leakage

Water can get into your basement in a lot of ways. Your house may not have gutters, so the water from the roof drains down into the soil next to the foundation and comes in through cracks in the wall or under the floor. The same thing can happen with clogged gutters; the water just bypasses them on the way to the basement. You can also have poor soil grading around your foundation, which allows rainwater to drain back against the house instead of out into the yard. You could also be missing a perimeter drain system around the base of your foundation, which is designed to take away the water that gets to the bottom of the wall before it forces its way inside.

If you have water problems and you're doing remodeling work on the outside of your house, you should try to correct the problem. Solutions such as adding or cleaning gutters aren't too expensive, and regrading the soil around your house can sometimes be done without damaging expensive landscaping elements. But installing or replacing a perimeter foundation drain can cost a lot of money and spoil a lot of plants. Whatever method you choose for reducing the water in your basement, it's still a good idea to install a sump pump. This illustration shows the typical installation. A pit is dug through and under the basement floor for the liner that captures the water. Then a sump pump is installed in the liner to pump away the water that collects there. The water level usually activates the pump; when it rises above a certain point, the pump turns on.

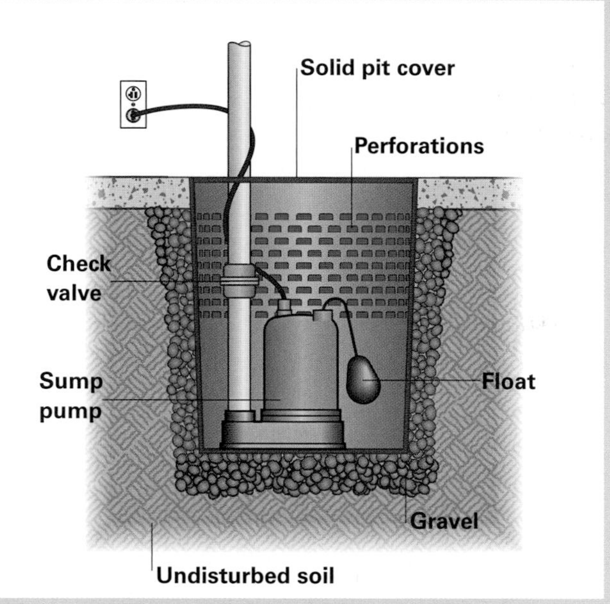

Sump pumps remove water from basements before damage occurs.

80 Power Venting

For some homeowners, a gas water heater is preferable to an electric unit. Many times gas is cheaper, and the heaters tend to have a quicker recovery time. But gas models must be vented to the outside, which is usually accomplished with a flue inside your chimney. Unfortunately, some houses don't have a flue, which means the only way you can have a gas heater is if you install one with a power vent. These direct-vent appliances have a sealed burner and a fan that expels the combustion gases through a PVC pipe. This pipe comes out at the top of the heater and is plumbed to the outside of the house through the floor's rim joist. Power-vent water heaters are more expensive than traditional gas units, but they tend to be more efficient. And for many people, it allows them to have the quicker recovery time of a gas unit even if they don't have a flue.

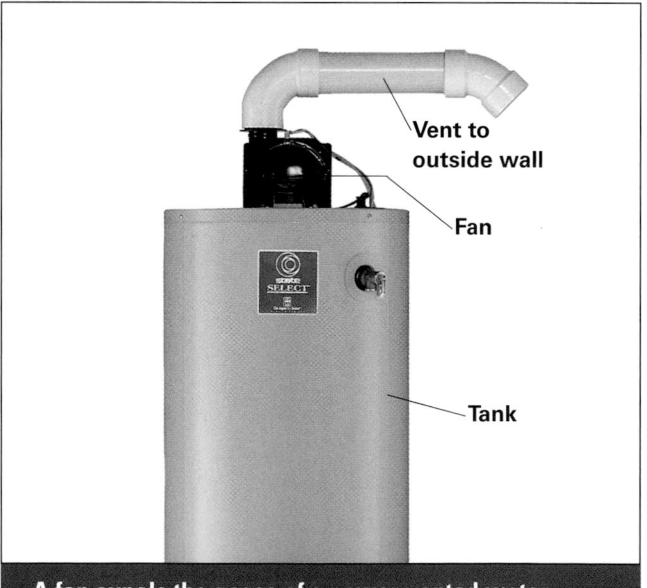

A fan expels the gases of a power-vented water heater, so the vent pipe doesn't need to be vertical.

81 Wiser Washer Hookup

Clothes washers—especially those in older houses—are often hooked up in a haphazard way. If you are remodeling your laundry room or simply replacing your washing machine, it's a good time to install a simple, plastic fixture called a laundry box. This is attached to the wall, usually between two studs, and it brings the hot and cold water lines and the drainpipe together in a single location. Make sure you install this box close enough to the washer so that the appliance's drain hose will reach the drainpipe opening and the shutoff valves are easy to reach and operate.

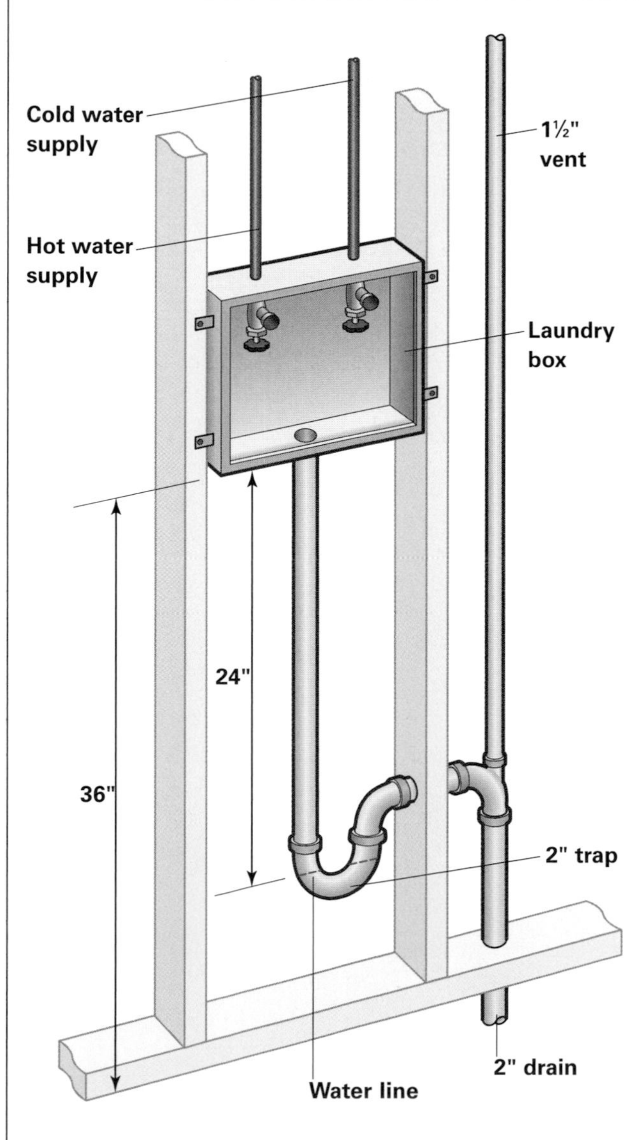

A laundry box provides easy access to the supply and drain lines.

82 Dishwasher Removal

It's easy to scratch or gouge flooring when pulling an old dishwasher from its cabinet space. To prevent damage, tape cardboard to the floor before you move the dishwasher. Turn off the dishwasher electrical circuit at the main breaker, and then turn off the water at the shutoff valve. Remove the unit's lower panel, and disconnect the water-supply and drain lines. Have a pan or bowl ready to catch spillage. Disconnect the wiring at the machine's electrical box by unscrewing the wire connectors.

83 How to Tunnel Under

Most yards have obstacles that can make installing all kinds of pipe below the surface more difficult. Pipes that carry electrical wires or water are often confronted with sidewalks, driveways, and even big trees that are difficult or impossible to go around. One solution is to tunnel these pipes under the obstacles, and one good way to do this is with sluice pipe. Excavate on both sides of the obstruction, and then attach a pointed spray nozzle to one end of a PVC pipe and a hose fitting to the other. Connect a hose to the hose fitting, and turn on the water. Push the pipe under the obstacle in short thrusts, pushing forward and backward. The water from the nozzle will wash away the soil as you work the pipe toward the excavation on the other side. Once the pipe is through, remove the hose from the back end; hook whatever pipe you want to use onto the sluice pipe; and pull both through the tunnel from the far side.

Use a sluice pipe to tunnel under sidewalks and other obstructions.

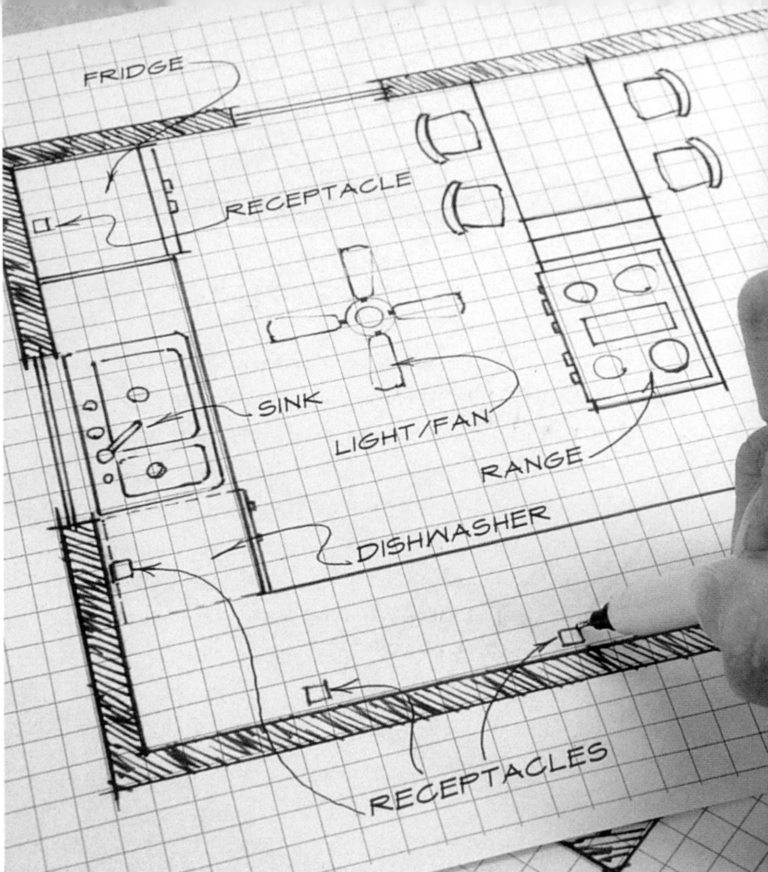

4 Electrical

- SAFER WIRING • BETTER BREAKERS
- CODE KNOW-HOW • LIGHTING OPTIONS

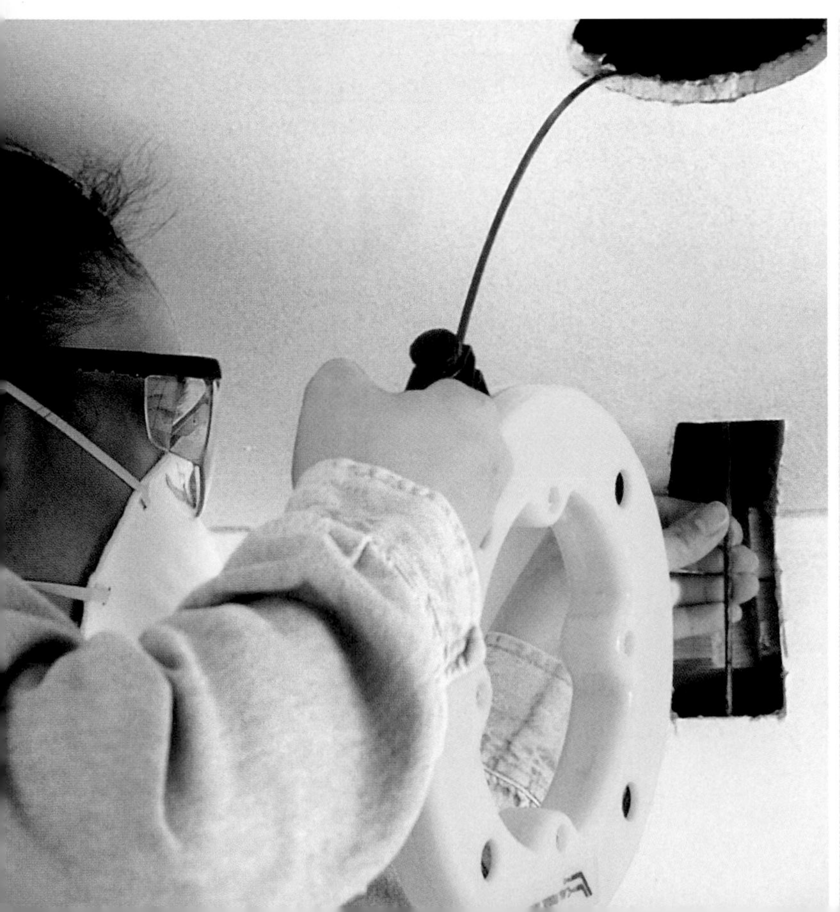

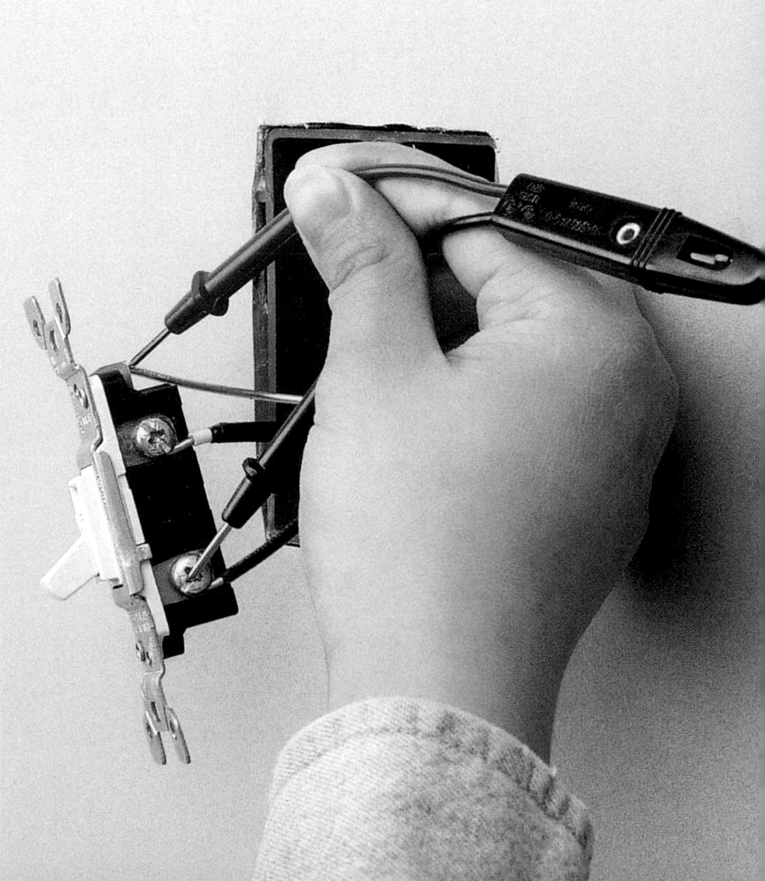

Saving Money

84 Finding Appliance Wattage—and Cost

Today, major appliances such as freezers, refrigerators, and water heaters are energy-rated for the amount of power (wattage) they use. This information appears on a large yellow "Energy Guide" label affixed to each device. Smaller appliances may not be so labeled, but their wattage rating should be listed on their packaging. The wattage rating can be used to calculate the actual operating cost of the appliance. The higher the wattage rating of the appliance, the more you will have to pay to operate it. For example, if a 4-foot-long baseboard heater uses 250 watts per foot, it will require 1,000 watts to run. At 10 cents per kilowatt-hour (1,000 watts used by an appliance in one hour), it will cost 10 cents per hour to run the heater. If the wattage is not listed on the appliance, look for the voltage and current. Multiply the two together to find the wattage.

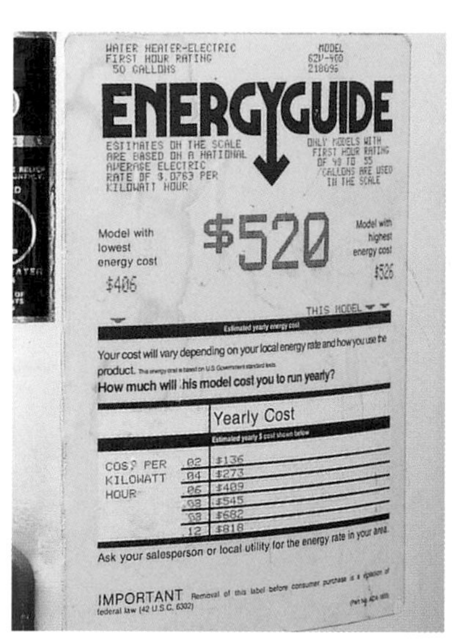

85 Wiring Receptacles

Oftentimes it's better to work smarter than to work faster. This is especially true when wiring electrical receptacles. Many of today's units have two ways to attach the wires. One is fast and convenient because it uses push-in terminals. Simply strip the end of a wire, and push this bare end into a hole. The other option is to strip the insulation from each wire, bend the end into a tight loop, and then wrap it around the appropriate screw terminal. The second method takes longer and is sometimes very frustrating, especially when big fingers are working with little loops and screws. Most electricians, however, never use the push-in connectors, because they're considered unreliable. The screws may take more time, but they are the better choice.

Color-Coordinated Connections Remember, the white wires go under the silver screws; the black wires go under the gold-colored screws; and a grounding wire (or pigtail) is attached to the green grounding screw and spliced to the other ground wire (or wires) from the cable (or cables) inside the box (and to the box) if applicable.

Push-in terminals
Terminal screws
Grounding screw

Securing circuit wires to terminal screws is smarter than simply pushing them into the push-in holes.

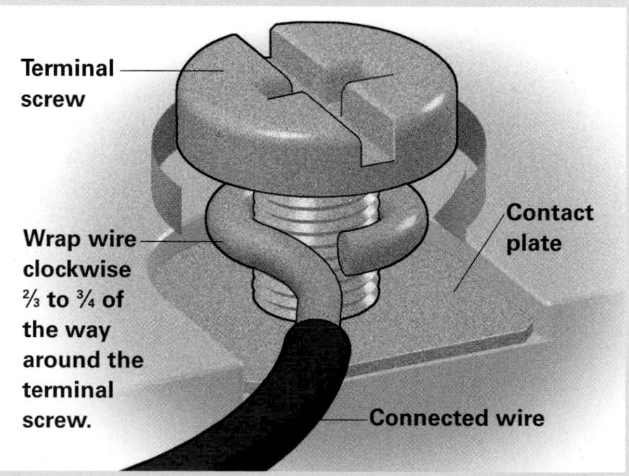

To connect a wire, wrap the stripped end clockwise around the terminal screw. Then tighten the screw.

86 What Cable Labels Mean

Standard residential wiring cables feature two or three conducting wires and a single grounding wire wrapped together in a plastic cover. These cables come in many different lengths, with different wires inside, and with different types of insulation protecting the wires.

Making Sense of the Markings The difference between a very big cable and a very small one is easy to see. But determining the difference between cables that look about the same isn't easy, unless you do the smart thing and look at the outside of the plastic cover. There you will find all the pertinent information printed repeatedly along the whole length of the cable. This information will usually look like what is shown below. It will note the gauge of the wires, the number of wires, whether there's a ground wire included, the type of cable construction (for interior or exterior use, for example), the voltage rating, and whether it's listed by Underwriters Laboratories (UL). If, for instance, you are working on a 20-amp, circuit you will know at a glance whether the wire is 14-gauge, which would be too small, or 12-gauge, which would be adequate.

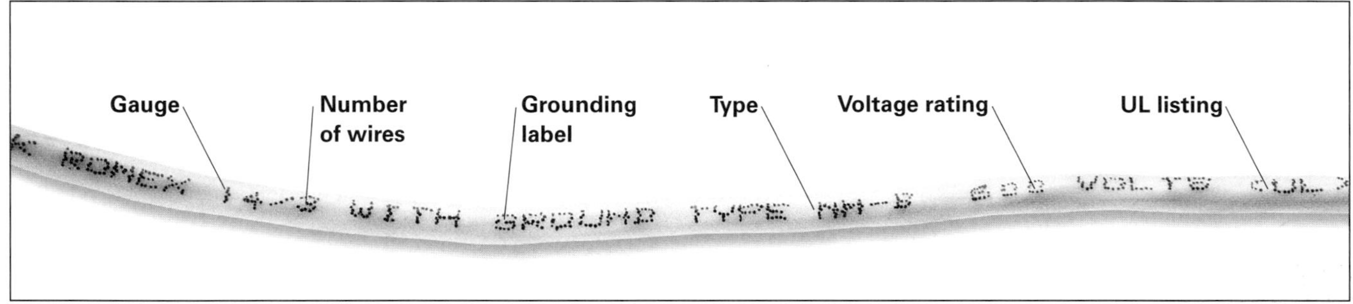

87 Two More Reasons Why Breakers Are Better

Circuit breakers are better protection devices than traditional fuses because they are easy to use and rarely need replacement. If they trip (turn off the current), they can be turned back on by simply pushing the toggle switch to the OFF position and then to the ON position. Fuses, on the other hand, can only be used once, and a ready supply of replacements must be on hand. If they aren't, the circuit can't work until you go to the hardware store to get a new fuse. Most breakers do the same job as traditional fuses: they protect the receptacle, light, and appliance circuits in the house. But they can also do smarter things that typical fuses can't. Two of the best breakers are shown here: quad breakers and GFCI (ground-fault circuit-interrupter) breakers. The first type comes in different configurations, but all are designed so that two 240V (or four 120V) circuits can be powered from a service panel slot that normally holds only one double-pole breaker. The second provides GFCI protection for an entire circuit, not just a few receptacles in the kitchen, bathroom, or basement. To wire a quad breaker, attach black circuit wires to the breaker terminal screws and the white and ground wires to the neutral/gounding bus bar in the service panel. To wire a GFCI breaker, attach the white and black circuit wires to the two terminals on the breaker. Then attach the coiled white wire from the breaker and the ground from the cable to the neutral/grounding bus.

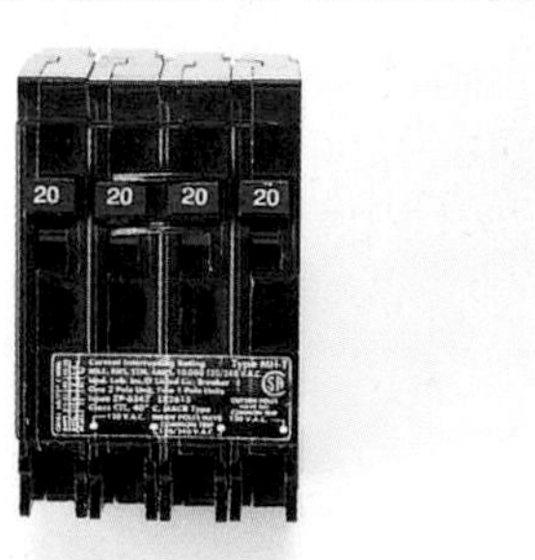

A quad breaker serves two 240V circuits in the same space as one double-pole breaker.

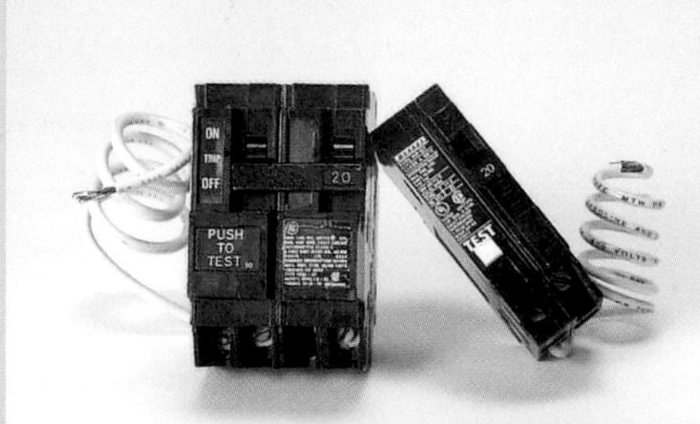

A GFCI breaker cuts power to a circuit when it's tripped by an imbalance in current flow.

Working Safer

88 Using the Right Wire Connector

It's hard to keep all the materials organized on any remodeling job, to say nothing of keeping your wits in line. Because of this, it's always tempting to use whatever is close at hand, whether it's the best choice or not. This usually doesn't make much difference, but making the safer selection is always best when dealing with electricity. Even though all wire connectors may look similar, they do have different colors, and these colors indicate size, or the minimum and maximum number of wires they can safely connect. Color schemes may vary from one manufacturer to the next, so stick to one maker, and use its color chart. Wire connectors must completely encase the bare ends of the wires joined by the connector. Green wire connectors should only be used for connecting grounding wires.

89 Extra Security with Crimping Ferrules

Wires can loosen from twist-on wire connectors. Crimping ferrules, shown at right, make a more permanent connection, especially when splicing bare grounding wires. After twisting the wires together, slide the crimping ferrule, or compression ring, over the wires, and crimp them together using a crimping tool. For insulated wire, the ferrule must be covered with a special wire cap.

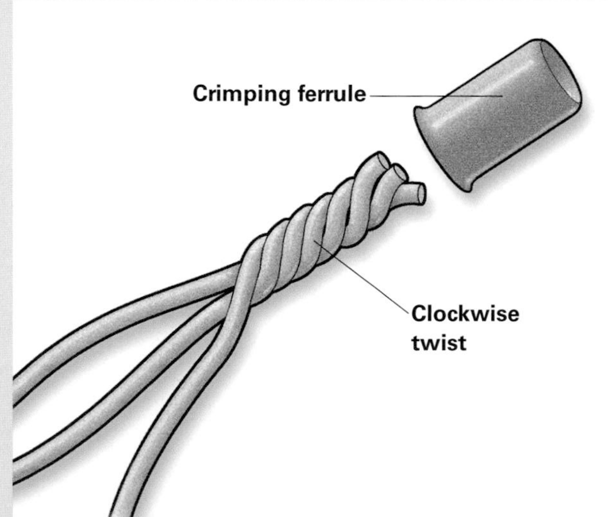

Twist the wires to be spliced together in a clockwise direction. Then cut them evenly at the ends.

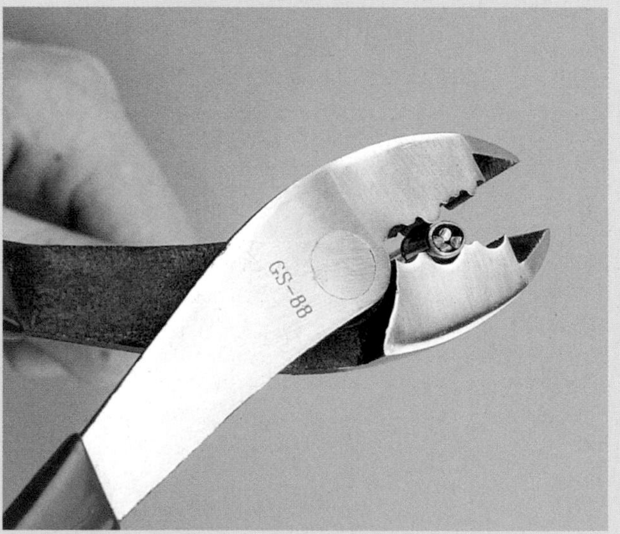

Use a wire crimper to compress the crimping ferrule around the twisted wires.

Working Safer

90 Nonconductivity!

Because electricity can be so dangerous, rethink your tools and gear before starting a job. Electrician's gloves, for example, are insulated. Some high-voltage gloves can protect you from up to 20,000 volts, while low-voltage gloves are sufficient for up to 1,000 volts.

Not all common tools can be used with impunity. Screwdrivers and hammers, as well as other metal tools, must have insulated handles to prevent current from flowing into the user's hand, causing a shock.

The ladder you use should be made of nonconductive wood or fiberglass. Conductive aluminum ladders can be an electrician's nightmare: should you accidentally cut into a hot wire, you must be insulated from ground—not connected to it! Always wear rubber-soled shoes and electrician's gloves to serve as additional insulators. Brace the ladder by hammering stakes into the ground.

91 Splicing Know-How

According to the National Electrical Code, all wire splices must be enclosed in a switch, receptacle, fixture, or junction box. Sounds straightforward enough, but be aware that you will have to confront several kinds of splices.

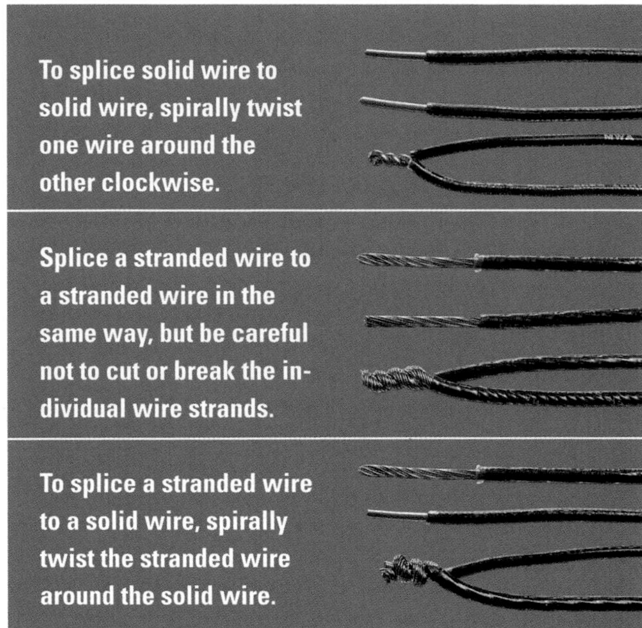

To splice solid wire to solid wire, spirally twist one wire around the other clockwise.

Splice a stranded wire to a stranded wire in the same way, but be careful not to cut or break the individual wire strands.

To splice a stranded wire to a solid wire, spirally twist the stranded wire around the solid wire.

92 Protecting Nonmetallic Cable in a Metal Box

Bringing nonmetallic (NM) cable into a metal box may seem puzzling at first. But it's not difficult. You must first remove one of the knockouts on the box. Some boxes have pry-out plugs built into them, which can easily be removed using a flat-blade screwdriver. Others also have circular knockout plugs, which must be punched out using a hammer and a screwdriver or knockout punch. Once the pry-out or knockout hole is open, a cable clamp can be inserted into the opening. The clamp secures the cable in place, ensuring that connections don't come loose and protecting the cable from chafing against the sharp metal edges of the box opening.

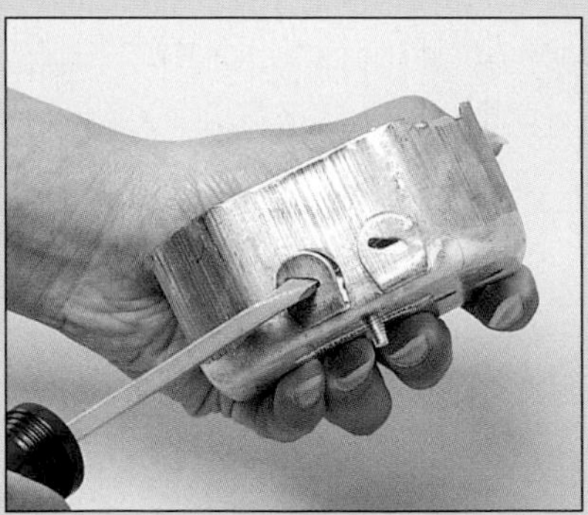

Some boxes have pry-out plugs. You remove them using a screwdriver.

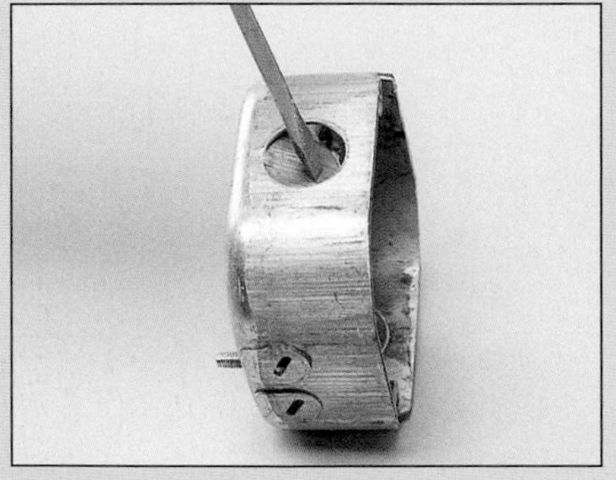

Other metal boxes also have knockout plugs, which must be punched out.

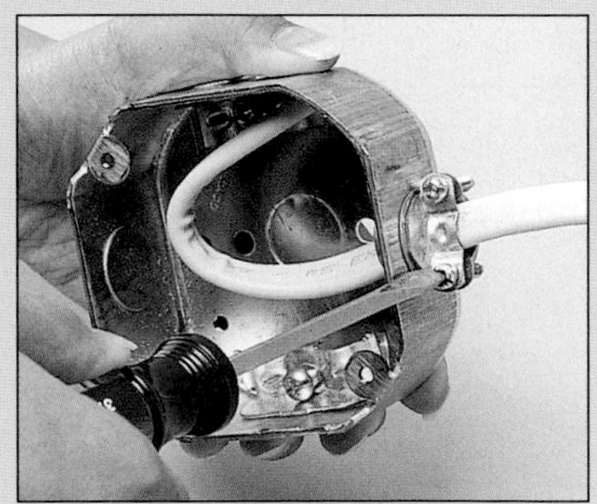

A cable clamp screws into the opening to secure the cable.

93 Stripping Cable

An inexpensive cable-ripping tool can save you time and conserve cable. It allows you to quickly remove the sheathing on NM cable. Insert the cable into the cable ripper, and squeeze the cutting point into the flat side of the cable 8 to 10 inches from the end. Pull lengthwise down the center of the cable. This method is forgiving, too. Because the center wire is the bare grounding wire, not much harm comes from accidentally cutting too far into the cable. If you do, it's unlikely that you will cut into the insulation on the conductor wires. Peel back the thermoplastic sheathing and the paper wrapping, and you're set to go.

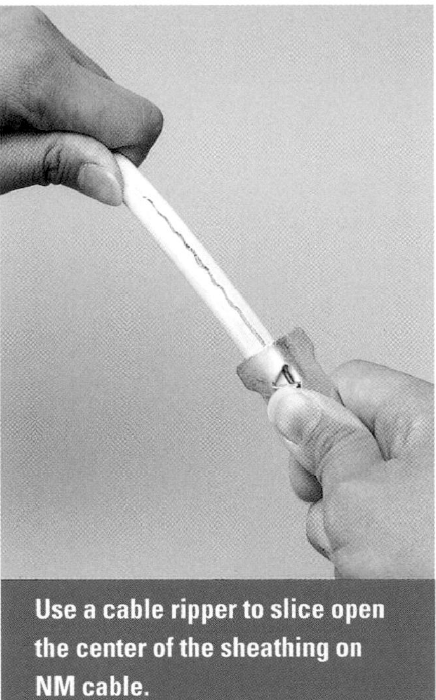

Use a cable ripper to slice open the center of the sheathing on NM cable.

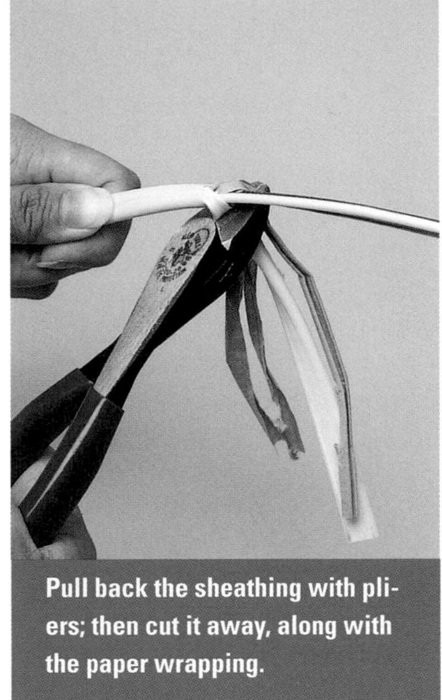

Pull back the sheathing with pliers; then cut it away, along with the paper wrapping.

94 Handy Wire Strippers

Before you can do any wiring, you must first strip insulation from the ends of the individual wires. Although you can use a utility knife for this, you may nick the wire with it. Instead, use an electrician's wire stripper or multipurpose tool. A wire stripper is operated either manually or automatically. A manual wire stripper requires that you cut the insulation before stripping the wire. You then pull the cut insulation from the end of the wire. Automatic wire strippers cut and strip the insulation in one motion.

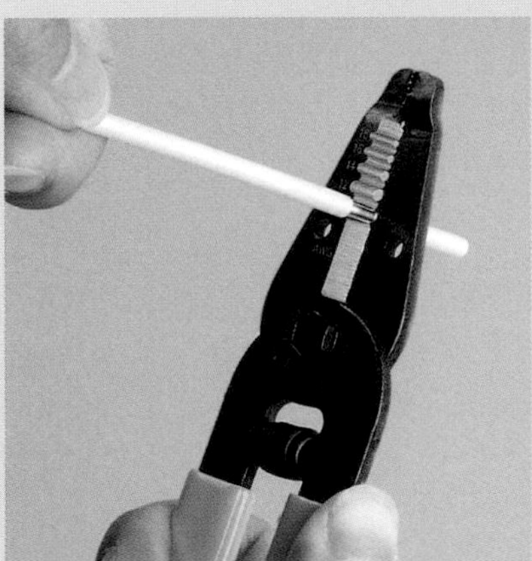

To use a manual wire stripper, insert the wire, close the stripper to cut the insulation, and pull the stripper toward the end of the wire.

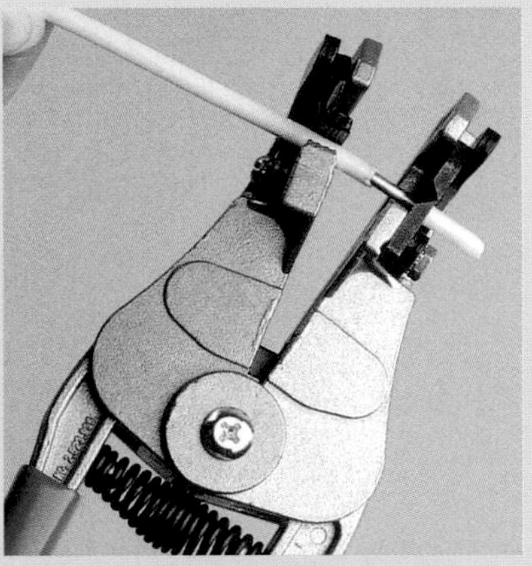

Though more expensive, an automatic wire stripper is easier to use than a manual one. One squeeze cuts and strips the wire insulation.

95 Armor Cutter

Although nonmetallic cable is almost always used these days, you may need to work around some existing armored cable when remodeling. Armored cable can be cut with a hacksaw, but if you're going to have to make a lot of cuts, invest in a specialized armored cable cutting tool. The tool just barely cuts through the armor, which is then twisted to break cleanly, exposing the wires inside. Install a small plastic sleeve on the sharp cut ends of the cable to protect the wires inside.

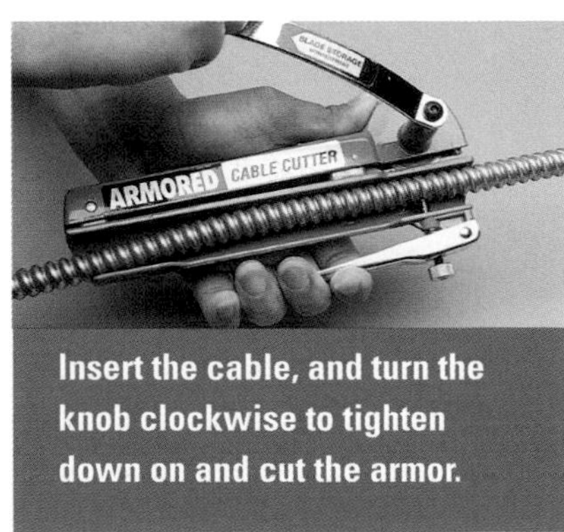

Insert the cable, and turn the knob clockwise to tighten down on and cut the armor.

96 The Smarter Choice

Plastic electrical boxes are almost the default choice these days for DIYers and professionals alike. They are cheap, easy to install, code-approved, and available in just about every configuration that you'll find for metal boxes. One of the small but smart strategies for using these boxes calls for installing the biggest one that the available space can accommodate, no matter how few wires are going inside. The cost difference between big and small is negligible, but the extra room makes everything easier.

Use the deepest box that can fit your space when installing receptacles, switches, and wires.

97 Planning with a Plan

For bigger remodeling jobs, especially in high-power areas such as kitchens, you should take the time to make a plan. One good way to do this is with a scaled drawing executed on standard graph paper. Sketch in all the pertinent fixtures and appliances, and then add the lights, switches, receptacles, and what type of outlets are needed for high-amp items such as electric ranges and clothes dryers.

Benefits Drawing this plan doesn't take much time, but it can save lots of time later on. It can also focus your attention and in the process reduce mistakes down the road. It's much easier to contend with the vagaries of the National Electrical Code when you are drawing on a piece of paper and can make changes easily. It's not nearly as easy to "erase" a circuit when all the cable and boxes are in place.

98 Quick Electrical Box Installation

Just about every remodeling adventure requires adding (or moving) electrical boxes, whether they hold receptacles, switches, or junctions, or they support ceiling fans and lights. This chore is sometimes easy, but most of the time it is much harder than it has to be. The smart (and quick) way to do this job is with a cut-in box. These devices, available in metallic and nonmetallic form, are made to mount directly on the drywall. All that's required is cutting a hole, pushing the box into the hole, and tightening three screws to pull the box wings tight against the back of the drywall. You still have to fish the cables you need into the box, which should be done before you install it. But you won't have to cut a big hole in the wall to attach the box, and then spend a lot of time repairing this hole. These boxes can be used for switches, receptacles, and ceiling fixtures.

Editor's Note: In photo 3 below, the view is from inside the wall.

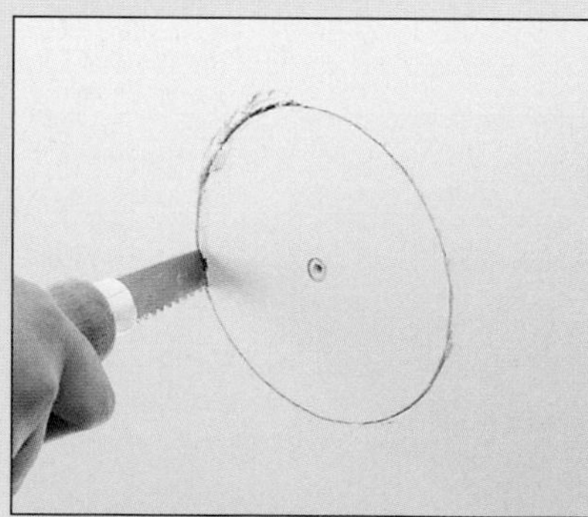

1 Trace a template of the box on the wall or ceiling surface, and then cut the opening for the box.

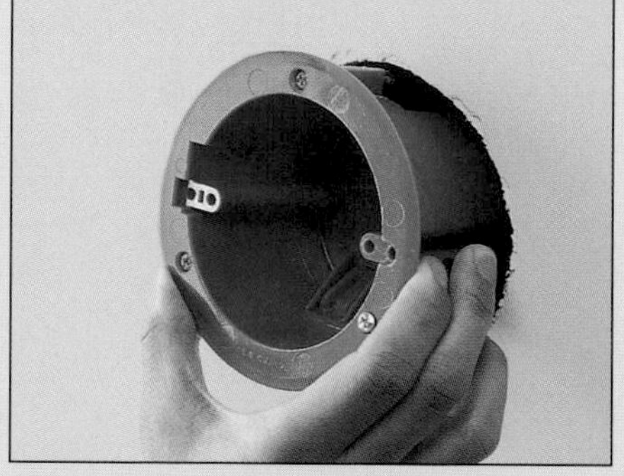

2 Insert the cut-in box in the opening, and then adjust the side wings against the back of the drywall.

3 Tighten the adjusting screws to bring the wings firmly against the back of the finished wall.

99 Faster Grounds

For safe grounding and electrical shock protection, all ground wires inside a box must be joined together. And in a metal box these wires must be attached to a green grounding screw in the back of the box. The traditional way to accomplish this is to use a pigtail wire and a common green-colored wire connector. You simply join one end of the pigtail to the other ground wires, twist on the connector, and then attach the other end of the pigtail to the ground screw. This isn't a hard job, but if you have lots of connections to make, save some time, some effort, and maybe even some wire by using ground wire connectors that have a hole in the top. To install them, cut one of the ground wires several inches longer than the others. Then slide the connector over the end of this long wire; twist it in place; and attach the end of the wire to the grounding screw.

In existing wiring, you're likely to come across the pigtail method of splicing ground wires.

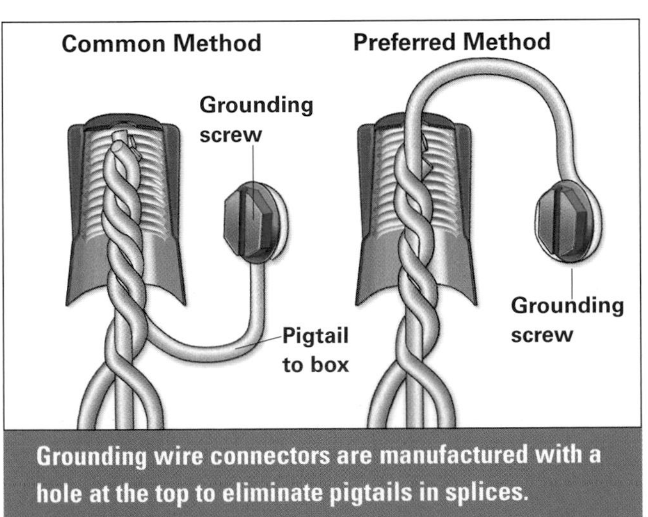

Grounding wire connectors are manufactured with a hole at the top to eliminate pigtails in splices.

100 Surface Solutions

Adding new wiring to a finished house is almost always difficult. If a major remodeling job is under way, cutting holes in the walls and ceilings to run cables and boxes isn't much of a problem. In fact, on most big jobs, all the drywall is removed as part of the demolition phase. But if you want to quickly add an outlet here and there or need to work on a concrete-block or other solid wall, surface wiring is a good choice.

When properly installed, surface wiring is code-approved and the components are easy to work with and reasonably priced. This photo shows a typical receptacle installation, but the same basic approach is used for switches and light fixtures. Using this type of wiring takes less time, and makes less of a mess than conventional methods.

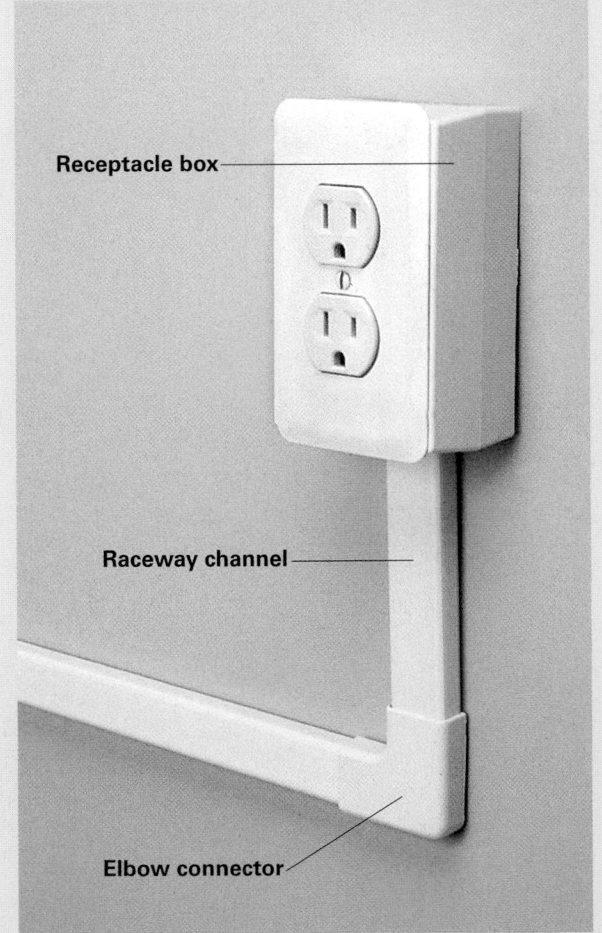

The raceway channels for this receptacle box protect exposed wire along the wall surface.

Greener Ways

101 Energy- and Money-Saving Occupancy Sensors

With record electrical rates and one switch often controlling a half dozen fixtures, forgetting to turn off the lights can mean a huge waste of power and money. One solution is to install occupancy sensor-equipped light switches. Choose a model that lets you turn on lights manually. The lights remain on until the infrared (or ultrasonic) sensor no longer senses occupancy and turns them off. You can program a switch-off delay of 30 seconds to 30 minutes. Switches cost less than $50, install easily, and often return your investment in one to three years.

102 How to Hide New Cables behind Baseboards

Fishing new circuit cables through finished walls is a difficult job that can drive even an experienced electrician a little crazy. Sometimes it's so hard to do that you have to cut small holes here and there to locate the fish wire and send it in the right direction. These holes, of course, have to be fixed later. A better path exists in the space behind the base trim. If you carefully remove these boards, you can cut notches in the studs and easily run new cable in the notches. Once you're done, cover up the cable with the old base trim and hide all your work with a little paint.

1 Mark the wall at the top of the baseboard. Cut along the joint.

2 Pry off the baseboard using a putty knife and shimming shingle.

3 Draw a cut line ½ in. down from your wall reference line.

4 Cut through the drywall along the cut line, and pull it away.

5 Run the cable in stud notches. Protect it with a metal shield.

6 Cover with the drywall; reinstall the baseboard; and paint.

Working Safer

103 Following the Code

The right way to install residential wiring is to follow the National Electrical Code (NEC). While the code itself can be hard to understand, many guides (including *Ultimate Guide: Wiring*, 2010, Creative Homeowner, ISBN: 978-1-58011-487-5) have been written in plain language that cover typical residential situations. Most of the code is concerned with safety and convenience, both when the system is installed and for years into the future. One case in point is the stipulation that when a white wire is used for a job that a black wire usually does, the white wire must be labeled with black tape or black marker. A typical example is the light switch shown here. When you install a switch like this, you know that the white wire is being used as a black wire because that's the only way a switch can work: it needs to be installed between two black (power) wires. But what you know now may not be what somebody 10 years from now will know when they work on this switch. The code calls for the labeling as a way to remind people of how a wire functions, instead of assuming the function based on wire color. These minor nitpicks are part of the reason that people lose patience with the NEC. But the smart move is to follow it exactly. Let the professionals cut the corners.

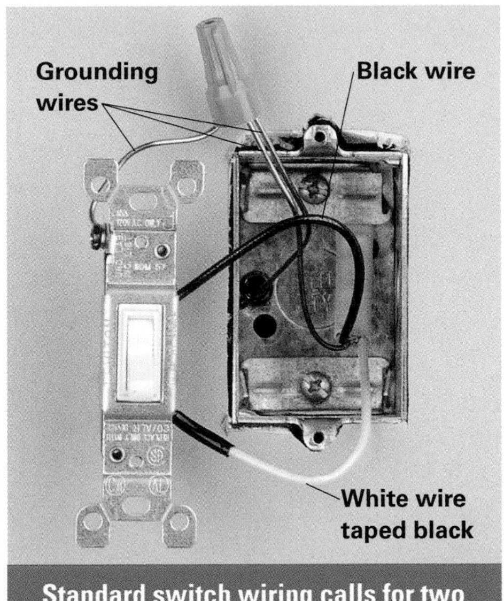

Standard switch wiring calls for two cable wires carrying power to be attached to the switch terminals and the cable's ground wire(s) to go to the switch and (with a pigtail) to the box grounding screw if there is one.

104 Easy Shock Protection

Shock protection is available for any circuit by just installing a properly rated ground-fault circuit-interrupter (GFCI) breaker in the service panel. The breaker isn't expensive, and the job usually takes only a few minutes. (See Tip 87.) But it does require working inside a service panel, which is a potentially dangerous environment by any standard. Not everyone wants to go there, and you may want to call in an electrician for the job. There is an easier and safer way to get point-of-use results. Replace a standard receptacle in a circuit with a GFCI *receptacle* wherever you need ground-fault portection. If a short occurs, the internal breaker will stop the current flow, and once the short is repaired, the device can be reactivated by pushing its red reset button.

A GFCI receptacle has both test and reset buttons. Push the former regularly to be sure the GFCI is working.

105 Testing a Switch

When you turn on a light switch and the circuit doesn't work, the problem may be with the switch itself. To test this, you'll need a battery-powered continuity tester like the one shown below.

Test Time Before you do anything else, turn off the power to the circuit at the service panel. Then remove the cover plate on the switch; hook the clip to one screw terminal; and touch the probe to the other. If the switch is good, the tester will light up, using the current supplied by its built-in battery. Turn off the switch, and test it again. If the tester doesn't light, the switch is good. If either step doesn't work as described here, the switch is bad and must be replaced.

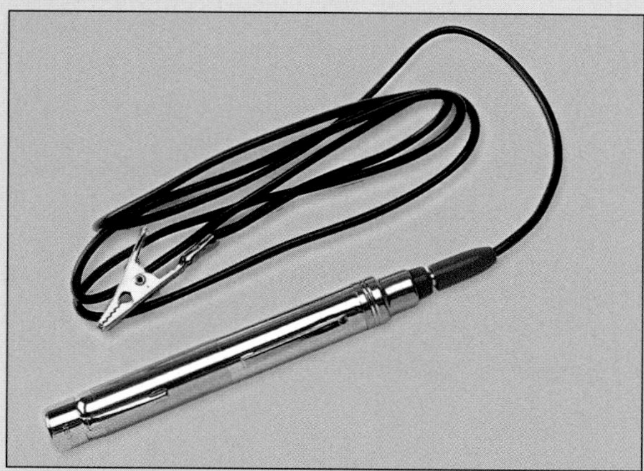

Do not attach a continuity tester, which is powered by its own battery, to live circuits.

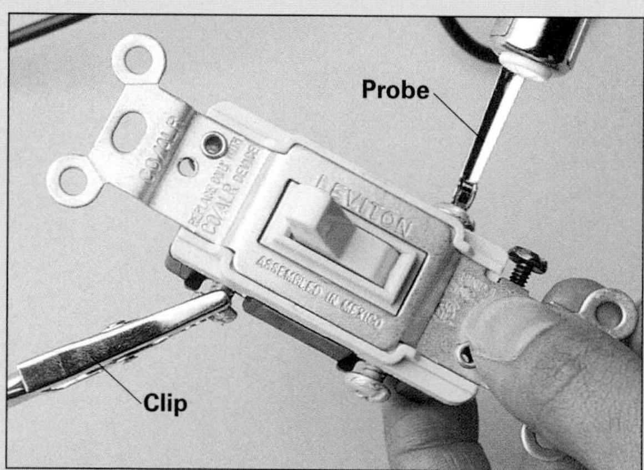

To test a switch, hook the clip onto one screw terminal and touch the probe to the other screw terminal.

Greener Ways

106 Energy-Saving Dimmers

Dimmer switches are an inexpensive way to change the mood of a room. Using them regularly will also save energy, reduce your electric bill, and extend the life of your lightbulbs. They're also easy to install if you're just replacing an existing single-pole switch. (You can add dimmer switches for fluorescent-only fixtures, but they're more expensive, involve more work, and require a new ballast.)

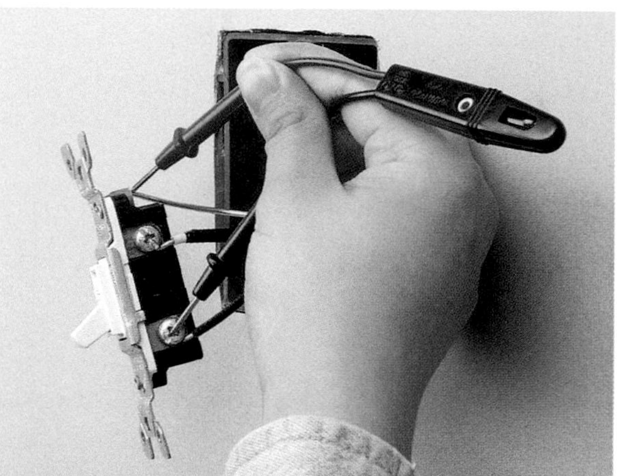

Turn off the power to the circuit, and pull out the switch. Check for current to be sure you've turned off the right circuit. Remove the switch.

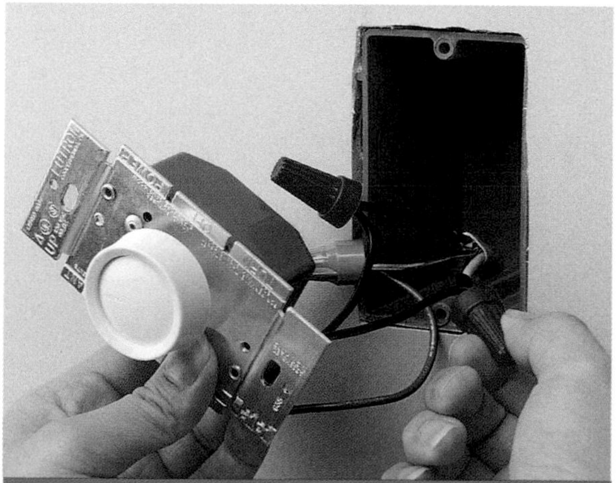

The dimmer has two power lead wires and a grounding lead. Connect these leads to the corresponding circuit wires using wire connectors.

107 Track Lights = More Light Where You Need It

Track lighting is a great way to add lots of light without lots of work. A track system can be used for general, task, or accent lighting—or any combination of the three. One of the most popular locations is above a kitchen island, though it's also used frequently over desks and workbenches. Locate tracks 12 to 24 inches out from the edges of wall cabinets to minimize shadows on countertops.

Installation The components are mounted directly on the ceiling; all that's required is a power source that's usually available from an existing light fixture. Once the track is installed, you can mount multiple light heads, turned in any direction you want, without the power being interrupted.

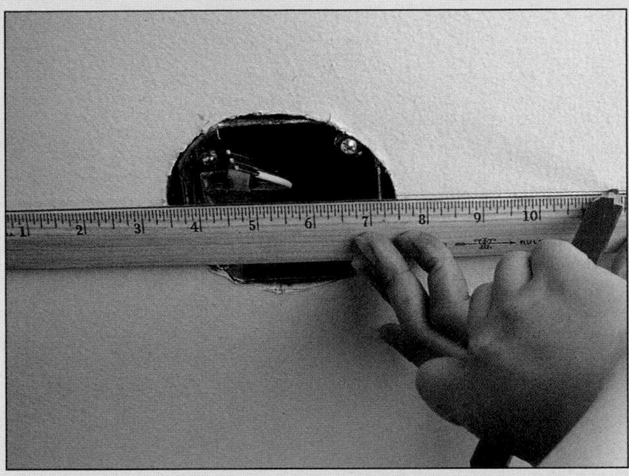

1 Turn off the power to the circuit; remove the old fixture; and mark the ceiling for the location of the tracks.

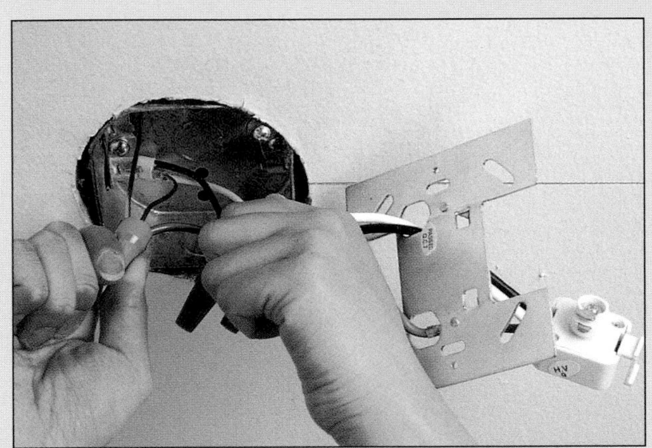

2 Thread the wires from the power connector through the mounting plate; then connect to those in the box.

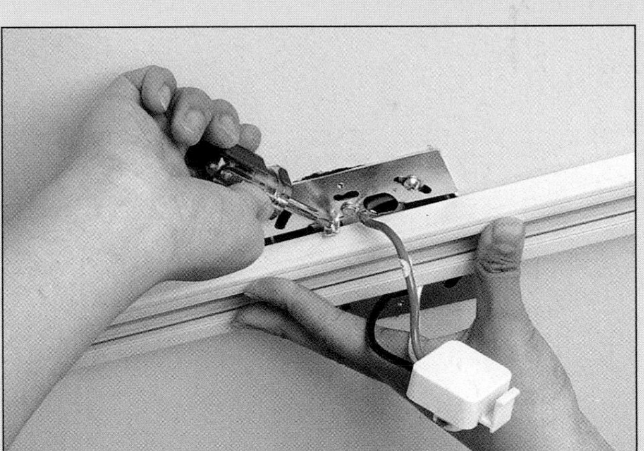

3 Screw the plate to the box; then slide a section of track between the wires and attach it to the plate.

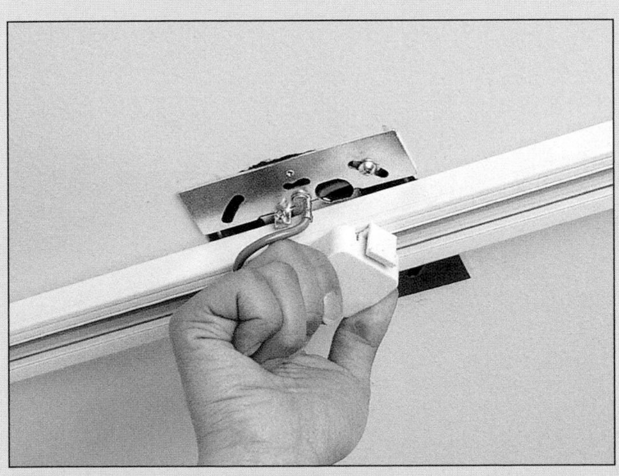

4 Push the power connector into the track, and twist-lock it in place.

5 Install the track tight against the ceiling; then slide the light fixtures onto the track, and lock them in place.

108 When You Have to Go Fishing

Fishing electrical cable inside closed walls and ceilings can be one of the most aggravating chores on any remodeling job. It's always better to work from a basement or an attic, but this isn't always possible. The next-best approach is to remove the baseboard at the bottom of the wall, cut out the drywall behind it (as described in Tip 100), and install as much cable as you can in this space. The third-best approach is to cut a box hole in the wall or ceiling and try to push a fish tape through openings in the framing members inside. Once the tape is pushed through, you attach the end of it to a piece of cable and pull them both back to you. When the two are disconnected, you have successfully fished an electrical cable through a closed space. This is very difficult to make work, but it doesn't make much of a mess either. The worst approach makes a big mess and requires significant repairs afterward—but it always works. It involves cutting a series of access holes in the ceiling or wall (or both) and using them to pull the cable through. The images below show the basics.

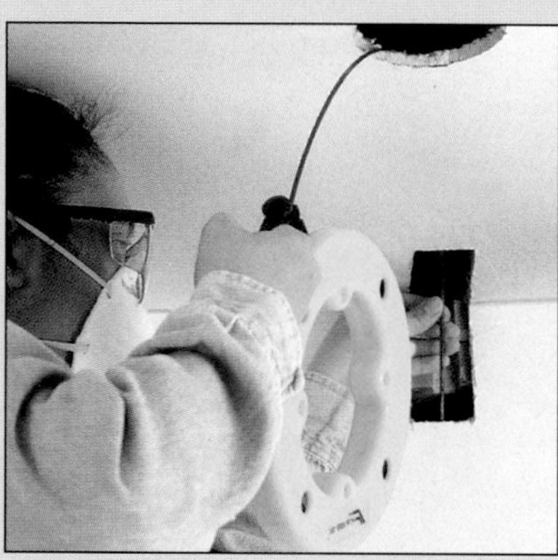

Fishing cable across a ceiling requires holes cut as shown and a notch in the top wall plate.

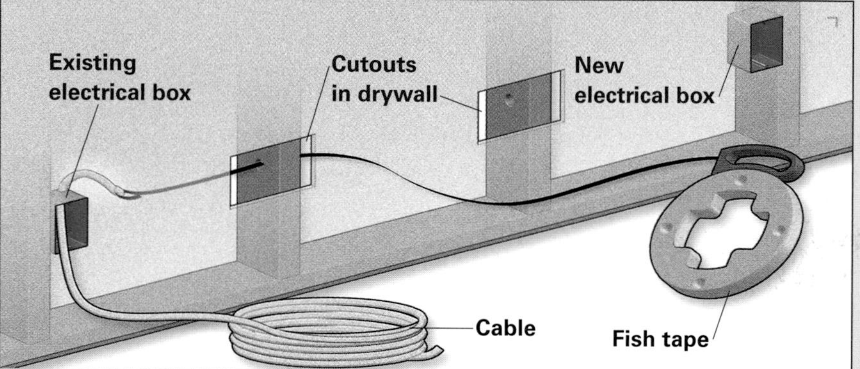

Fishing wire through a wall often requires making several cutouts so you can bore holes through the studs and fish the cable from the existing box to the new location. A long, flexible drill bit can minimize the number of cutouts.

109 Smarter Cable Trenching

Digging a trench without first knowing what is underneath the surface can be costly or even dangerous. You may unwittingly cut into a sewer, septic, or water pipe, or a telephone, cable TV, or electrical power line. Before you dig, have your local utility company mark the location of underground utility lines where you plan to dig. In most areas, you are required by law to inform your utility company and secure its approval before you do any excavating. Once you are cleared to excavate, you can dig your trench using a shovel, mattock, backhoe, or trencher. Keep your trenches as short and narrow as possible to reduce expenses and keep landscaping damage to a minimum. Also, when you run underground feeder (UF) cable in a trench, always be sure to leave a slack loop for expansion where the cable enters or leaves the pipe (conduit). Pulling the cable tight will result in damage or even a complete break because of the soil pressure against the cable.

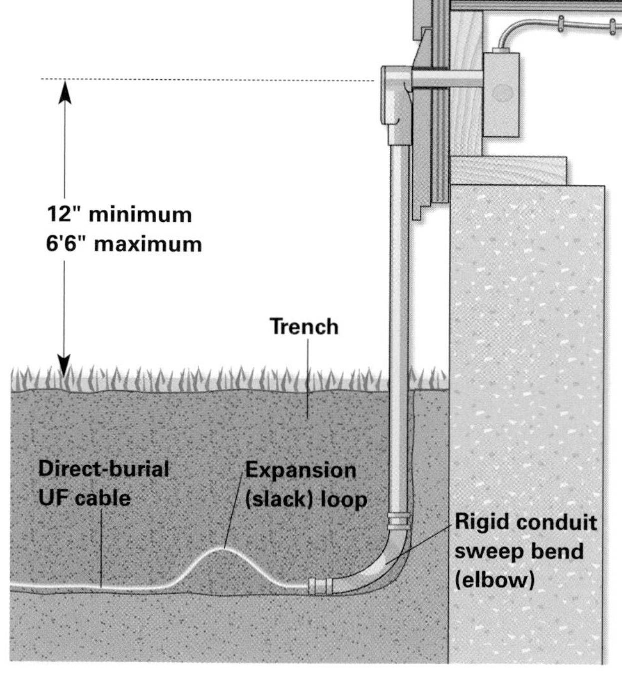

Working Safer

110 Reducing Fire Hazards from Recessed Lighting

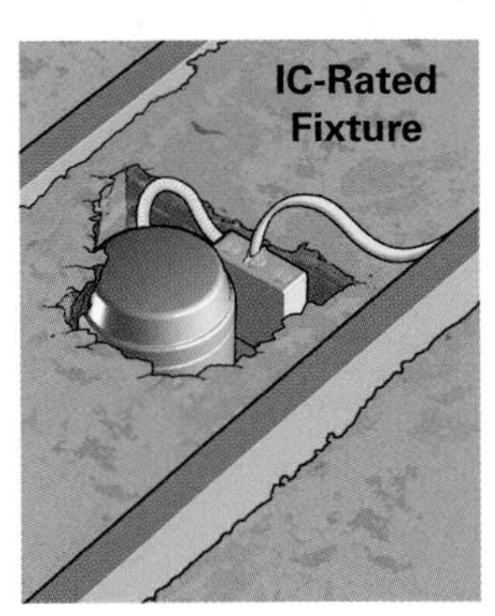

Most people like the way recessed lights look, but some models produce a lot of heat, so they can't be used next to fiberglass insulation because of fire concerns. Fortunately, some units are designed for this purpose. The fixture label will indicate whether it's approved for NIC (non-insulated ceiling) use or IC (insulated ceiling) use. The former can be used in an insulated ceiling, but the insulation must be kept at least 3 inches away on all sides. This prevents fires, but it also lets a lot of heat escape to the attic. IC units, on the other hand, can be installed in contact with insulation.

111 Better in the Weather

A typical exterior receptacle, mounted on the outside of your house, has spring-loaded flaps that cover the plug slots when they're not in use. This prevents water from getting into the receptacle and causing a short. This arrangement works well if you only use the receptacle once in a while, on dry days. But sometimes these outlets are used for longer periods, in good weather and bad. Under conditions like these, the chance of a short circuit is much higher. The safest way to make use of an exterior receptacle is by installing a weatherproof box. These boxes have a clear plastic, hinged cover that protects the electrical cord from falling and wind-blown rain and snow when it's plugged in.

112 Trenching under Slabs

If underground feeder (UF) cable must be run beneath a sidewalk or a driveway, the cable must be protected in rigid conduit. Run the trench for your direct-burial cable up to the sidewalk or driveway, and then continue it on the other side. To run cable between the two trenches, cut a length of rigid metal conduit 12 inches longer than the width to be spanned. Then flatten the end of the pipe, and drive it beneath the slab using a sledgehammer. Another way is to put a cap on the end of the pipe, and pound it through. Cut off the flattened or capped end, and push the cable through the pipe. (Also see Tip 83.)

When driving conduit with a sledgehammer, protect the end with a piece of scrap wood.

113 Lightning Protection Standards

Various useful standards are published regarding lightning protection systems. The National Fire Protection Association (NFPA) publishes "NFPA 780: Standard for Installation of Lightning Protection Systems." It provides requirements for the protection of people, buildings, and property against lightning damage. The Lightning Protection Institute publishes "Standard of Practice LPI–175," which establishes requirements for design, materials, workmanship, and inspection of lightning protection systems. Underwriters Laboratories (UL) sets guidelines for the certification of systems materials and components in its "Standard UL96A."

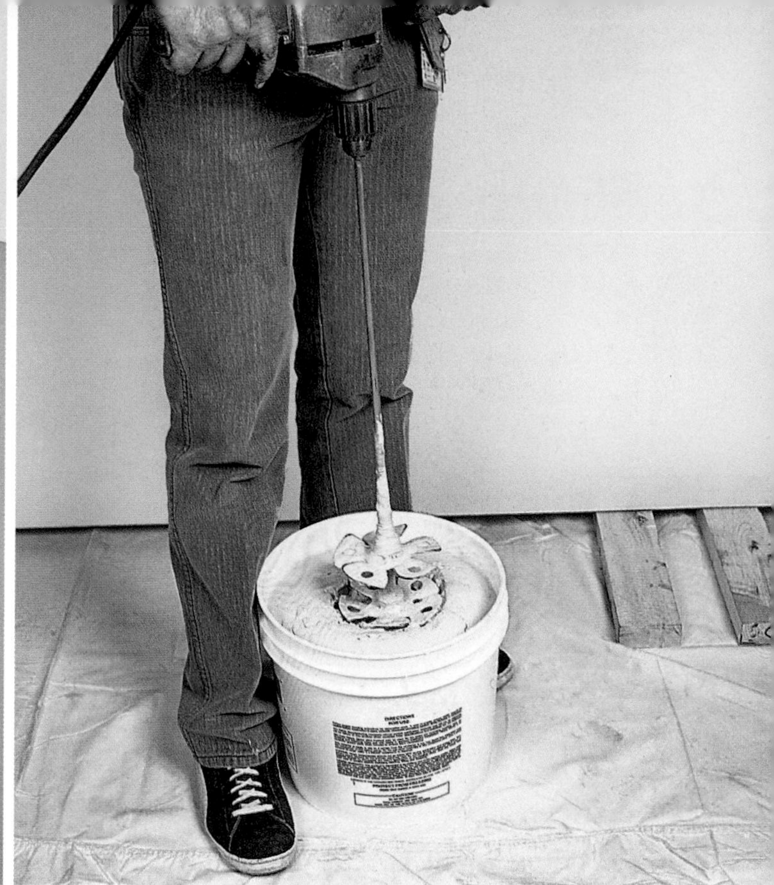

5 Drywall

• MAKING ACCURATE CUTS • EASIER PANEL HANGING
• BEST WAYS TO TAPE JOINTS AND FINISH FASTENER HEADS

114 Drywall Choices

Drywall panels are available in a variety of sizes. The standard for most residential work is the ½-inch-thick panel. It's what you should use for most jobs. Thicker, ⅝-inch panels are not usually used in houses because of the extra weight and cost. Thinner, ⅜-inch and ¼-inch panels are good for resurfacing work when a wall is so scarred that spackling cannot save it. The ¼-inch panels are the least expensive, but most pros don't like to use them because the sheets are very whippy and snap too easily during handling.

Know the Codes Check local building codes when planning a large-scale new construction or remodeling project.

Drywall panels are available in a variety of sizes, including (top to bottom) ¼ in., ⅜ in., ½ in., ⅝ in., and water-resistant ½ in.

Working Safer

115 Protecting Your Back

Drywall is heavy. A 4 x 8-foot panel that is ½ inch thick weighs about 55 pounds. One strong person can pick up a single sheet, but you'll want to recruit an assistant if you have to handle more than a couple of sheets. Don't attempt to move two-sheet units without help.

Window Delivery If you order 10 sheets or more, drywall is typically delivered on a boom truck with an articulated crane arm that can lift it to a second story if necessary. The crane cradles the drywall just outside the window for easy removal. Window delivery (especially if done before the jambs are installed) decreases labor, minimizes panel damage, and reduces the chance of back injury, a common hazard of carrying panels.

Saving Money

116 Just-in-Time Delivery

Drywall, until it's up and painted, is susceptible to damage. So wait until you are ready to use it to have it delivered —after the framers are done and the wiring and plumbing have been roughed in. Panels get damaged if stored on a job site for too long—especially if workers are walking through, carrying unwieldy tools, running extension cords, and so forth. Repairs will require multiple coats of joint compound, costing you time and money.

117 Storing Drywall

When storing drywall, distribute the panels throughout the areas where they will be used to spread the weight around. Fifty ½-inch panels weigh more than a ton. Estimate the number and types of panels each room requires; that way you can distribute them upon delivery and avoid double handling. In most rooms the ceiling goes up first, so off-load these panels last. This will place them at the top or front of the stack.

Where space is tight, stack panels on edge lengthwise against the wall that you will drywall last, with the good, or face, side out. (This way you won't have to turn the panels to install them.) Choose a location where the panels can sit perpendicular to the floor joists to help distribute the weight. If you intend to lay your stock flat, sweep the floor beforehand to remove debris that could cause a blemish or scratch, and lay the panels back side down.

118 Better Fastening

Drywall is attached to studs and joists with nails or screws. Screws have become the preferred fastener because they are easy to install, provide more holding power than nails, and don't disturb the framing or furring when applied. The pounding of drywall nails can shake furring loose, cause already-set nails to pop, and move studs out of alignment. Plus, screws can be removed should you need to remove and recut a panel, and screw-head depth is easier to control. Just set the screw gun clutch to release the drive once the screw has reached a desired depth. Nail-head depth, on the other hand, must be gauged correctly by eye and hand every time.

A few rules for installing drywall screws correctly:

- Fasten panels wherever there is framing.
- Keep screws at least ⅜ inch from the panel edge.
- Space the screws every 12 inches for ceilings and every 16 inches for walls.
- Drive screws squarely into the panels. Driving them at an angle will tear the paper and make finishing more difficult. It also reduces the screw's holding power and limits the sheer strength of the panel.

119 Where It's Wet

Moisture-resistant drywall, also called MR board or WR (water-resistant) board, is green or blue in color. It resists moisture but is not waterproof. It can withstand the high levels of humidity that often occur in bathrooms, kitchens, and laundry rooms. These panels make a good base for tile attached with mastic, but for a panel for use in areas that have direct contact with water, you should go with cement board. Unlike gypsum products, this material consists of a portland cement core sandwiched between layers of a polymer-coated glass-fiber mesh. Cement board provides excellent fire and water resistance and makes an ideal backing for tile.. It also offers a superior underlayment for use with slate and quarry tile.

From Side to Side Each cement board has a rough and a smooth side. Install the rough side facing outward when attaching tiles with a mortar or with the smooth side out when using adhesive or mastic.

Use waterproof cement board (below) behind ceramic tile in areas subject to constant or high moisture.

120 Using the Right Screw

Not all drywall screws are the same. In fact, three types of screws are used to fasten drywall to studs and joists: Type W (wood), Type G (gypsum), and Type S (steel). When fastening drywall to wood studs or joists, use Type W. Use Type G to fasten one drywall panel to another in double-layer applications, such as when soundproofing a wall. Use Type S for steel studs. The self-tapping variety makes the job go easier.

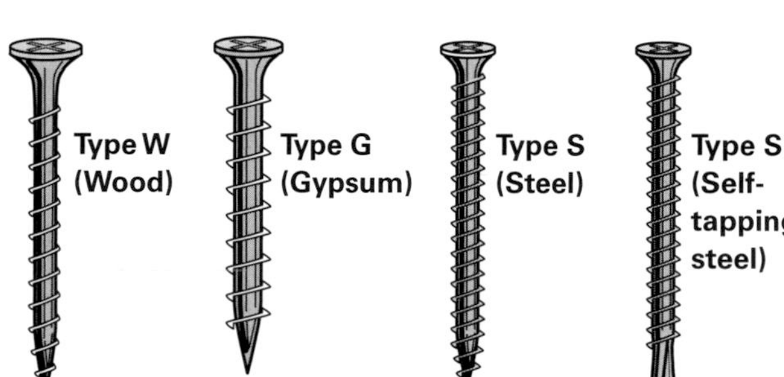

121 Going Paperless

The paper covering of drywall is an excellent breeding ground for mold when drywall is used in moist environments, so some manufacturers have replaced the paper with a glass-fiber mat to create a mold-resistant (and stronger) product. Others use a gypsum formulation that provides a smooth surface that also resists mold.

Worth the Price The new generation of paperless panels comes in standard sizes. Installation and finishing options are the same for paperless panels as they are for regular drywall panels. Unfortunately, paperless drywall is not available everywhere. It costs more than conventional products, too—but the peace of mind may be worth it.

122 Where There's No Nailer

Occasionally, you'll find an inside corner framed in such a way that it does not present a nailing surface. Nevertheless, panels meeting at corners must have a solid backing, so you'll need to install an extra stud. In cases where this is impossible, you can install drywall clips.

When There's No Base Drywall clips are L-shaped pieces of metal or plastic, with each wing measuring about 2 inches wide. They are used to provide a screwing base and backing on a drywall edge that doesn't face onto a stud, joist, or nailing block.

Several types are available. One has raised points on one face that are driven into the stud. Others get screwed in place. Either way, they support the drywall panel edge so you won't have to deal with corners opening up after the job is complete.

Use a drywall corner clip to support the panel edge when corner studs support only the adjacent sheet.

One side of the clip holds the panel, and the other has a tab that you nail into the adjacent stud.

123 Tape Types

Drywall tape is used as the base for the multiple layers of joint compound that will follow. Today many pros choose fiberglass tape, also called mesh, rather than paper tape. Apply this self-sticking material to a dry seam, and follow it with multiple coats of joint compound. There's no need to spread a base layer of joint compound before applying the tape to the seam, as you would have to do with paper tape. If you're a beginner drywaller, however, you'll have an easier time with paper tape. It resists wrinkling better than fiberglass tape and is easier to trim to the right length—just use the edge of your taping knife to cut it. Fexible metal tape is good for inside corners.

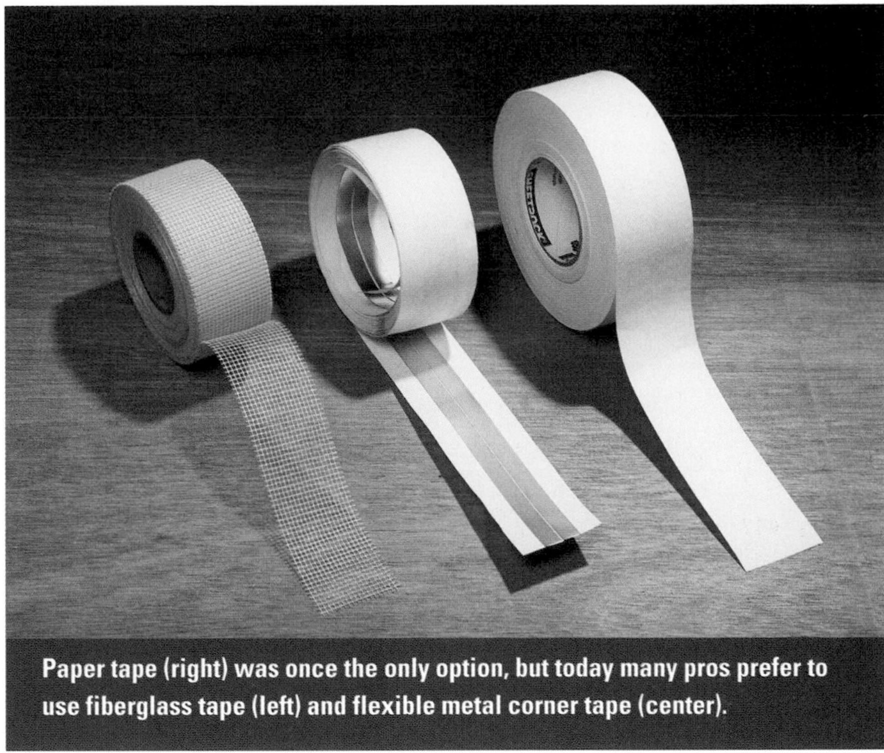

Paper tape (right) was once the only option, but today many pros prefer to use fiberglass tape (left) and flexible metal corner tape (center).

Working Safer

124 Avoiding Irritation, Pain

Gypsum drywall and the products used to install and finish it generally contain no toxic substances. The process does, however, generate dust that can irritate your eyes and lungs. To save yourself unnecessary aggravation, wear protective gear, especially when sawing and sanding. A disposable dust mask will do the job. If you're allergic or otherwise sensitive to the dust, you can also use one of the NIOSH- or OSHA-approved nuisance-dust masks, also called dust/mist respirators. The best of these have a reinforced molded shell and an exhaust valve.

Safety glasses are useful for installing and finishing drywall. During installation, when you're cutting panels with a utility knife and driving screws with a screw gun or drill, you put your eyes at risk. When hanging ceiling panels, you face the hazard of falling grit, and it's easy to flick a drop of joint compound into your eye during finish work.

You may hyperextend your lower back hoisting and positioning panels, so it's a good idea to wear a lower-back support, such as a brace or a wrap, even if you don't have back problems.

When positioning panels on a ceiling, you'll need both hands to load and drive screws. It sounds odd, but drywallers commonly use their heads to hold panels in place. If you have a construction hard hat or light helmet, use it during this part of the operation. Tape a sponge on top of the helmet, both to protect the panel and relieve strain on your head.

125 Choosing the Right Compound

Joint compound, sometimes called Spackle or mud, is available in two basic types. One is a vinyl-based drying compound, which hardens as the water medium dries. The other is a setting-type compound, which is hardened by a chemical reaction when catalyzed by water. The former is preferred by most do-it-yourselfers because it comes in a premixed, all-purpose form. The latter, preferred by many professionals, comes in powdered form only. It sets faster and harder than drying-type compounds and resists cracking better. With this type of compound, you can apply consecutive coats to the drywall in the same day. Be careful though: the powdered type is tougher to sand, so it pays to get a nice finish, or polish, during the application rather than depending on sanding.

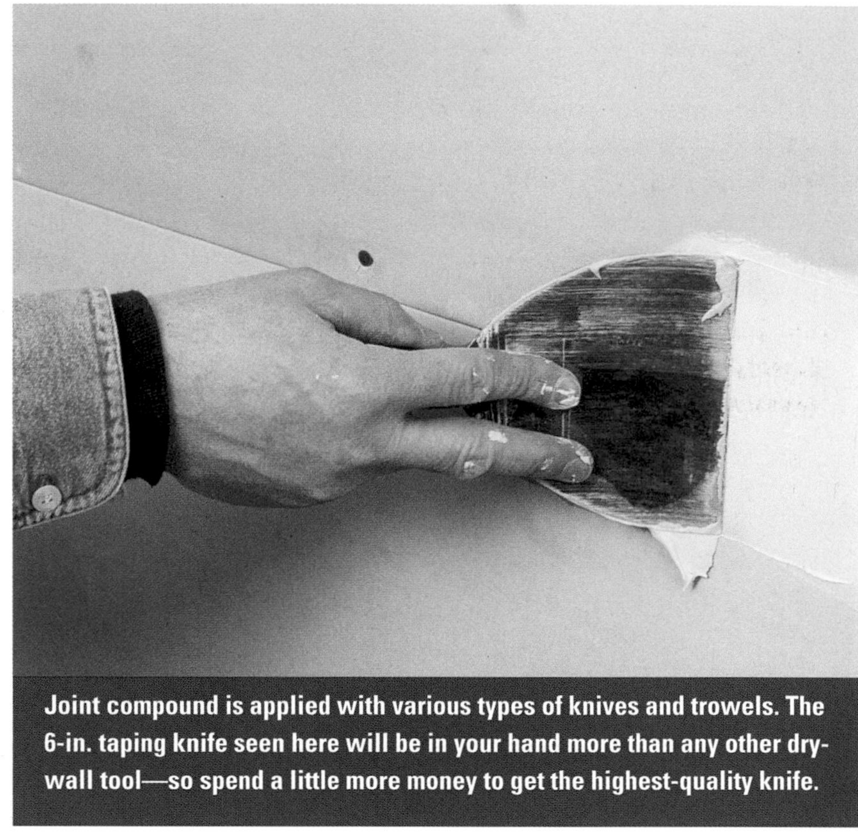

Joint compound is applied with various types of knives and trowels. The 6-in. taping knife seen here will be in your hand more than any other drywall tool—so spend a little more money to get the highest-quality knife.

126 Dust Control

Drywalling creates dust, so dust control is a major concern, especially if you are remodeling part of a finished house. Dust will drift invisibly through open doorways or even underneath a closed door. In addition to vacuuming every day and using floor protection on finished areas you're likely to traverse, dust curtains are critical. Commercial curtain walls and dust doors are available but costly.

Make It You can make a perfectly adequate dust-control system using furring strips, duct tape, and 6-mil polyethylene plastic. Trap a sheet of plastic against an unfinished wall over a door opening with furring strips, and then screw through the furring and plastic sheet into the wall. If you will need to use a doorway and can't block it off, slit the plastic wall down the center, and drape a wide plastic curtain over the slit.

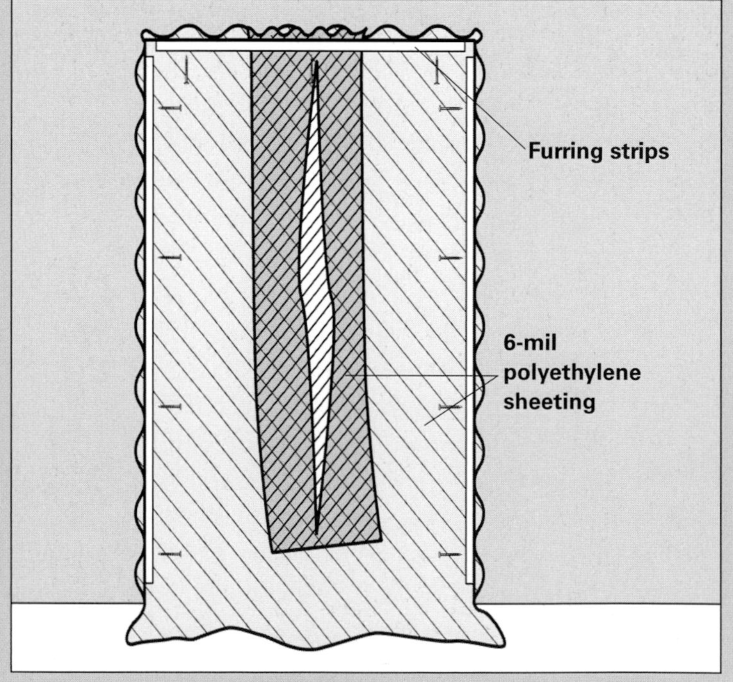

For improved dust protection, create an airlock by installing two of these plastic walls in tandem, 3 ft. apart.

Working Safer

127 Arm Extender

Although moving panels is a two-man job, one person can carry an 8-foot panel with the aid of a panel carrier. This tool hooks below one edge of the panel, giving you a handle to hold the bottom without hurting your fingers and allowing you to hold on to the other edge of the panel at shoulder level. To prevent back injury, avoid quick movements as you rise to a standing position.

128 Panel Lifter

A panel lifter makes it easier to make minor height adjustments to panel positioning—and accurate positioning means less finishing work later. The tool looks like a miniature seesaw. (See illustration at right.) By slipping the thin-lipped front end of the jig beneath a drywall panel and stepping on the back end, you can lift the panel as much as 2 or 3 inches. You can make a panel lifter in the shop from scrap wood. Notch one end of a 1×3 so that it will easily fit under a panel, add a fulcrum, and you're in business. In a pinch, you can use a pry bar and a block of wood for this purpose, as shown in Tip 135.

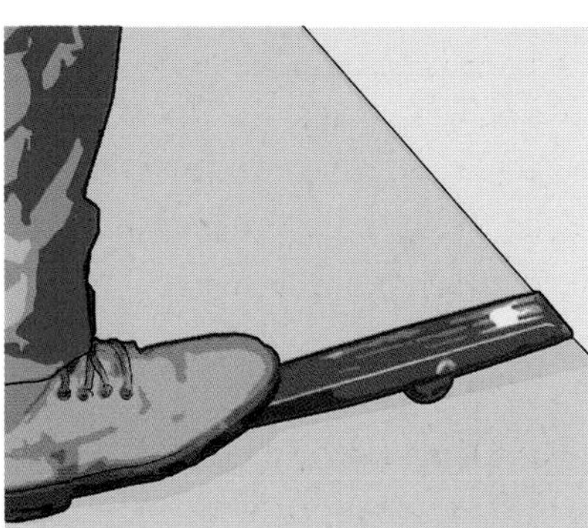

129 Gaining Height

On most drywall jobs, you will need to place some drywall panels with the aid of a ladder, bench, or scaffold—something to provide you and your helper with the extra height to reach the work area. Stepladders work well enough for small jobs, but if you are drywalling an entire room, the act of installing a panel and then moving two ladders so that you and a helper can lift the next panel into position will slow you down considerably. For large jobs, consider using a rolling scaffold. The scaffold allows you and a helper to work at a comfortable height and is easy to move. In addition, working on a scaffold is safer than trying to keep your balance on a stepladder while handling panels. You can rent scaffolds from a tool rental shop. Be sure to ask about assembly and safety cautions before leaving the rental agency.

Positioning a panel on a ceiling is a two-person job made easier with a couple of stepladders.

When working on the high reaches of walls, a rolling scaffold provides a safe work platform.

130 Hanging Panels on a Ceiling

Three is the ideal crew number for hanging drywall on the ceiling; two can hold the panel in place while the third drives the fasteners. Always hang ceilings before walls.

The Long and Short of It As with any drywall job, choose longer panel lengths to reduce the number of joints. Install the longest panel you can handle. For example, if your ceiling measures 10 × 12 feet, use three 4 × 10-foot panels rather than three 8-foot panels (with patches to fill the gaps). This will reduce the amount of finish work substantially.

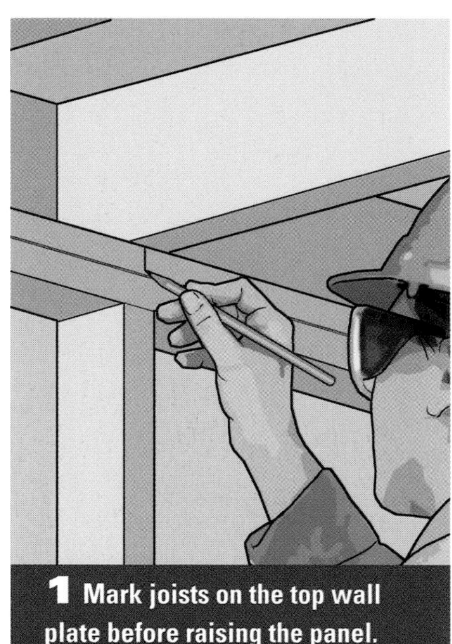

1 Mark joists on the top wall plate before raising the panel.

2 Apply adhesive to joists, and move the panel into position. Have fasteners ready once the panel is snug against the joists.

131 Drywalling Stairways

Stairways present a challenge because they often have angled surfaces. Then there's the added challenge of installing drywall panels over stairs. You can simplify the jobs by installing as many full panels as possible and then measuring and installing the odd-shaped panels last. The existing full panels will give you two of the three dimensions for each triangular panel, which makes it easy to find the length of the third.

To make a stairway scaffold, clamp one end of a wide plank to a stepladder and rest the other end on a step.

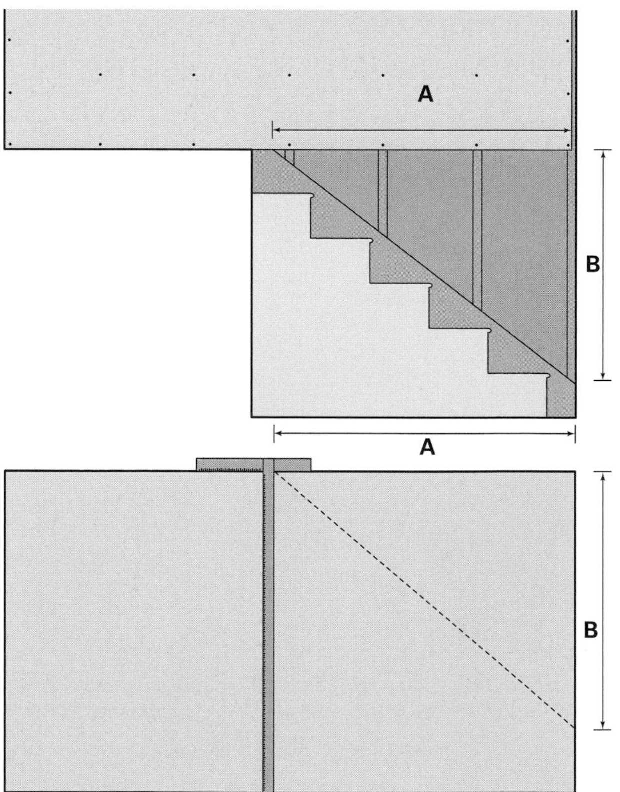

Before measuring for any odd-shaped panel, such as this one created for a stairway, install as many full and half panels as possible. Then measure the smaller space left un-drywalled. For a triangular area with one right angle, measure two of the three sides (A and B). Then transfer your measurements onto a full panel and cut out the irregular shape.

132 Three Ways to Raise Ceiling Panels

A "deadman," also called a T-brace or T-support, can be used to position and hold panels to the ceiling. It can be made in the shop with 2x4 lumber. Make the top member about 3 feet long, and make the post about 2 inches shorter than the distance from floor to ceiling. Glue carpet scrap or foam to the top of the T-support to protect the drywall panels, and staple a scrap of rubber to the post bottom to prevent slippage.

Using the Deadman If working with a helper, one of you can support the panel with the deadman while the other positions and attaches the panel (figure 3). If working alone, attach a temporary nailer to support one end of the sheet (photo A). Lift the sheet into position, and apply pressure with the deadman. Keep the crosspiece under a ceiling joist (photo B).

Heavy Equipment A panel jack (bottom right) is the safest and easiest way to raise drywall panels to the ceiling. It consists of an adjustable metal frame that cradles the panel so that it can be raised or lowered by cranking a handle. The entire jack is mounted on casters and maneuvers easily. Raise the panel into place, and the panel jack holds it until you've fastened it to the joists. This device also works well for mounting panels high on tall walls. Rent one at your local rental shop.

1 Build a T-shaped support out of 2x4s. The height should be slightly less than the ceiling height.

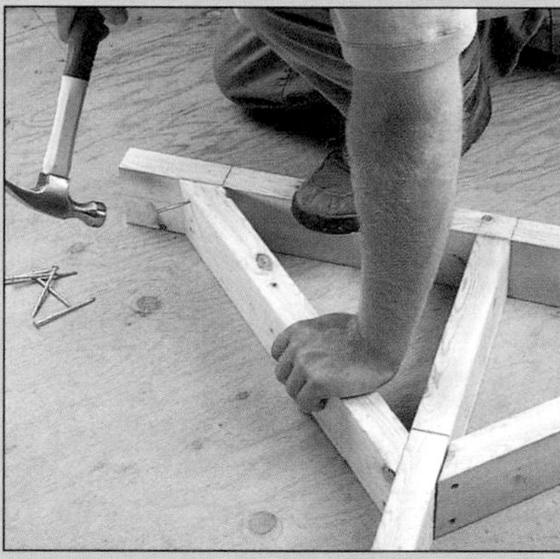

2 Keep the main support from wobbling by attaching angle braces made from 2x4s or lighter wood.

3 A deadman is used for panel support by wedging it between the floor and the underside of the panel.

A If working alone, attach a temporary cleat to support one end of the drywall panel.

B Raise the other end with the deadman. Keep applying pressure to prevent the panel from slipping off the cleat.

A panel jack is another option. It offers a safe way to raise panels into position on flat and sloped ceilings.

Greener Ways

133 "Serious" Drywalling

Drywall typically comprises a gypsum-based core sandwiched between two thick sheets of paper, and millions of tons of greenhouse gases are created each year in its production. A company called Serious Materials wants to change that, so it has developed a new board called EcoRock, which is produced without heat, making it simpler to manufacture—and using a lot less energy to produce. EcoRock contains 80 percent post-industrial recycled material—with no gypsum—and can be recycled. (It can even be used as a pH additive for soils.) It's also resistant to mold and generates less dust than traditional drywall. For more information, visit seriousmaterials.com.

134 Beware the End-Butt

Flush end-butt joints are formed wherever the untapered factory ends of drywall panels meet, where cut edges come together, or where an untapered end joins a factory-tapered end. Unlike the joints formed by factory-tapered panel edges, end-butt joints provide no recess for joint compound. Consequently, they must be carefully feathered over a wider distance to produce a smooth surface.

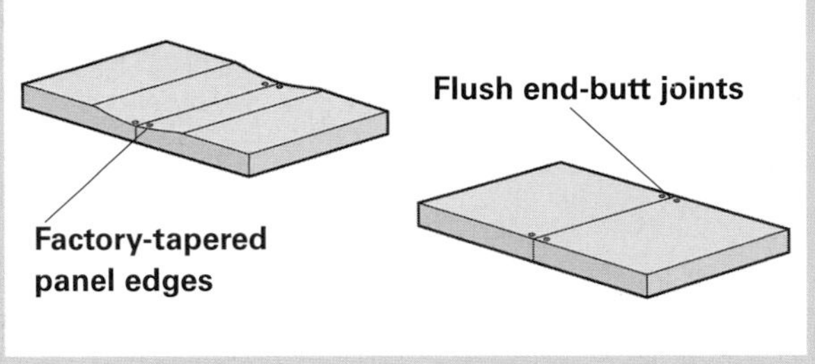

135 Hanging Drywall on a Flat Wall

Attaching panels to a flat wall goes more quickly than attaching to a ceiling. However, lifting and positioning the top row (or rows) still takes a good deal of energy and planning. It's only when you get to the bottom row that the job becomes relatively easy.

Whether you're covering a ceiling or a wall, the same principles apply:

- Install the largest panel you can handle.
- Hold the panel firmly against the framing before fastening it in place.
- When sizing a panel, cut it small enough to fit without binding but large enough that it doesn't leave a gap too wide (more than ¼ inch) to be taped and filled easily.

Raise the panel against the ceiling (or the panel above it), and press firmly against the studs before fastening.

A pry bar and block (or a panel lifter) is a useful tool for fine-tuning panel elevation on the floor level.

136 Making the Cut

The edges of drywall panels arrive square from the manufacturer. Buy yourself a T-square, and making perfect cuts will be a snap. Use a tape measure to get the dimensions of the wall area you intend to cover, and transfer them to the panel. Then slide the T-square along the edge or end of the panel until the edge of its blade lines up with the mark you made. Mark your cut line with a pencil. Repeat for the perpendicular cut, if one is needed. Using the square as a guide, score the face side (also known as the good side) of the panel to a depth of ⅛ inch. Always maintain a sharp blade to prevent time-consuming tears to the panel. Then use a quick motion to snap the panel along the cut line, and fold it back slightly. Use your utility knife to cut (not tear) the paper along the fold, and separate the panels.

1 Use the measurements you took from the wall, and transfer them onto the panel you intend to install.

2 Use a T-square to draw your cut line on the panel face, and then cut using a sharp utility knife.

3 Using one quick motion, snap the panel back along the cut line.

4 Use the utility knife to cut through the paper on the back of the panel, and separate the pieces.

137 Making Holes for Junction Boxes

You may measure for junction boxes and transfer those measurements to your panel, but this method is time-consuming. A quick, sure alternative for marking box locations is the hammer-and-block method. Place the drywall panel in position against the studs. Place a piece of scrap wood against the panel wherever a box is located, and tap the wood lightly with a hammer. The edges of the box should make a slight indentation in the panel's back face. Remove the panel, and cut out the openings. Reinstall the panel, and fasten it in place. If you're doing several rooms, you may find it worthwhile to buy a utility-box cutout locator. This device attaches to the utility box on the wall. When you press the panel into position, the locator (which has a sticky face) sticks to the drywall. You simply trace around the locator and then remove it.

1 An easy way to mark for a utility box is to position the drywall where it will be installed.

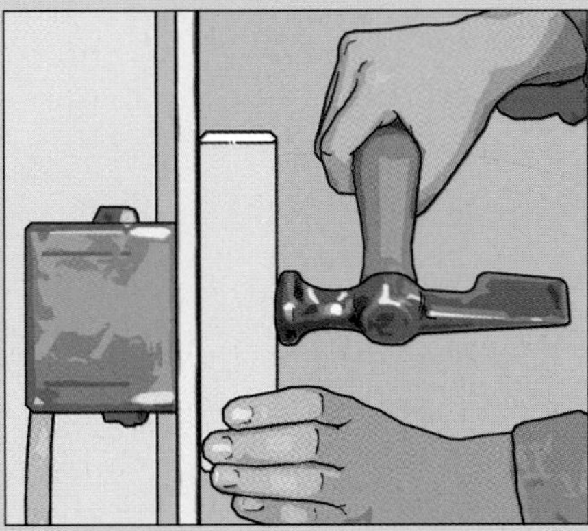

2 Place a wood block over the box's location, and gently tap. The box will leave an imprint on the panel back.

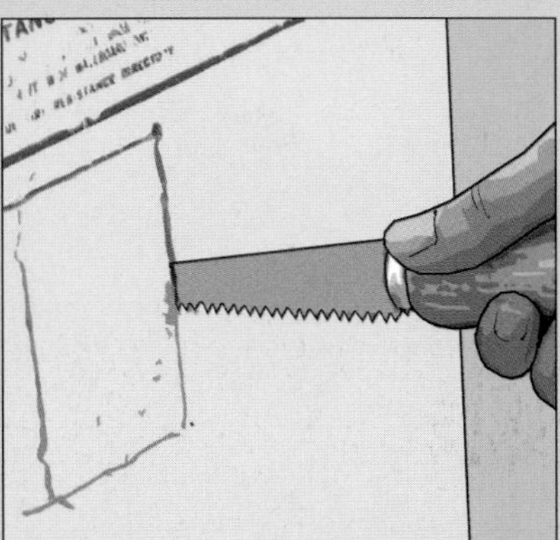

3 Turn the sheet around, and carefully cut around the imprinted box outline using a drywall saw.

138 Taping Prep

Taping can be a frustrating experience. To ensure good results, follow this checklist before starting.

- Ventilate the room with fans or by allowing a cross-breeze from doors and windows. This will lower humidity and accelerate the drying process.
- Double-check all panels to make sure they're firmly attached.
- Verify that cutouts have been made for all outlets, switches, and fixtures.
- Assemble tools, joint compound, and tape in one area. Double-check estimates to ensure that you have sufficient joint compound and tape.
- Prefill any gap more than 1¼-inch wide with setting-type joint compound, and then smooth the faces of the compound flush with the drywall face. Let this dry entirely before you start the taping procedure, and if necessary, scrape off any high spots.
- Clean and remove grit from all taping knives and trowels. Sand their faces smooth if necessary.
- Position ladders and scaffolds within easy reach.
- Make sure the temperature in the room where you'll apply joint compound remains at least 55° F for 24 hours following application.

Taping will help determine the final appearance of the drywall job.

139 Efficient Wall Taping

First, apply an even, ¼-inch-thick tape-embedding coat (if you're using paper tape) with a 5- or 6-inch knife. Cover the entire length of the joint, and make sure that you completely fill any gaps between panels. Cut a length of tape to the length of the joint, and press it into the wet first coat with your fingers. Make sure that the tape centers on the joint and that you don't create any folds or wrinkles. Using the 5- or 6-inch knife, apply light pressure to the tape, and draw the knife along its full length, squeezing joint compound out from beneath the tape as you smooth the coat. You should leave a thin layer of joint compound beneath the tape. If the tape blisters, you haven't left enough joint compound beneath it. Peel back the tape in just that section, and add joint compound before proceeding. Allow this coat to dry.

Before applying the second (filler) coat, use a drywall knife to scrape or knock down any burrs or high spots that you may have missed while the tape-embedding coat was still wet. Take care not to cause gouges. If you do, apply a thin layer of joint compound to this area. Apply the second coat with a 10- or 12-inch straight-handle knife. The coat should be as wide as the knife. Make it as smooth as you can get it, using repeat passes if necessary. Let the coat dry thoroughly. Again, use a scraper to knock down any burrs or high spots that you may have missed.

Apply a wide finish coat with a 12- or 16-inch finishing trowel. This should be a light skim coat. Move with long, steady strokes, pulling in one direction and feathering out both edges to create the smoothest possible transition to the drywall face. Sand the joint, when dry, if necessary.

1 Use a power drill and a mixing paddle to mix joint compound.

2 Apply a first coat of joint compound using a taping knife.

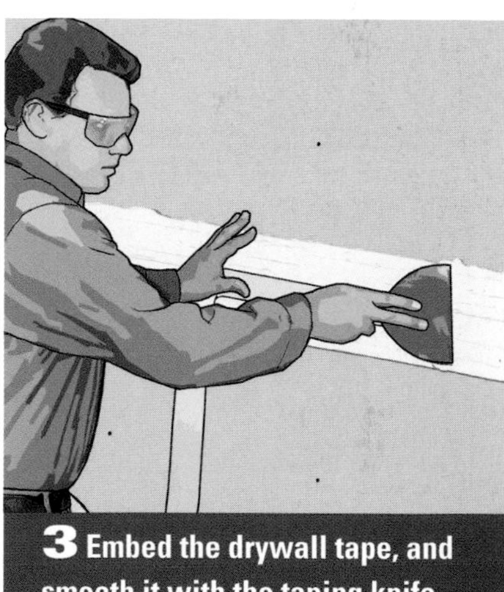

3 Embed the drywall tape, and smooth it with the taping knife.

4 Use the knife to remove the excess mud from the tape edges.

5 Apply the second coat with a 10- or 12-in. straight-handle knife.

6 Use a 12- or 16-in. finishing trowel to apply the finish coat.

140 Finishing Fastener Heads

The dimples left by screw heads or nailheads can be treated with a few coats of joint compound. Apply the first coat using a 5- or 6-inch knife over the fastener heads. This coat should merely fill in the dimples you created. The best way to do this is by covering an entire row with one pass rather than treating them one at a time. This will make the joint compound less conspicuous. When the first coat is dry, scrape off any burrs or high spots. Apply a second coat slightly wider than the first using a 10-inch straight-handle knife. Allow the coat to dry, and then scrape it smooth.

Apply the final coat with ta 12-inch staight-handle knife. It should cover the second coat entirely. Carefully feather the edges, creating a gradual transition to the drywall surface. Allow this coat to dry completely, and sand it if necessary.

1 Cover nailheads or screw heads quickly by using long swaths of joint compound.

2 The larger swath of joint compound is easier to feather and blend into the face of the drywall panel.

3 The final coat of joint compound should be feathered out so thinly that it appears flat.

141 Checking the Crown

It's easy to check a drywall joint for excessive crowns or recesses after you've applied the second or third coat of joint compound. Hold the straight edge of a trowel or wide drywall knife across the top of the joint and see whether you can detect a gap between the joint compound and the ends of the knife. Rock the trowel or knife from side to side. If the gap measures more than $\frac{1}{16}$ inch or so, you'll need to apply a wider swath of joint compound and feather it out more gradually.

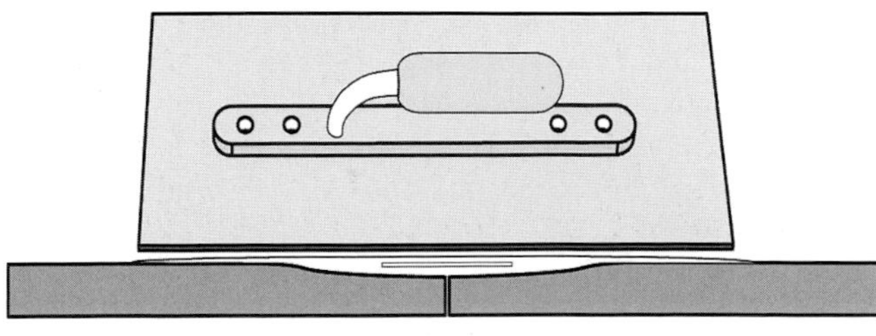

142 Cleaning Taping Tools

Joint compound cleans up easily using only water. Just spray the tools with a hose or faucet blast. Use one knife to scrape any stubborn spots from another. (Don't wash joint compound down the drain because the sediment can clog your pipes.)

Once you've cleaned drywall knives, set them out to dry so that water runs off the blades and doesn't have a chance to pool on them. Otherwise, the blades will rust quickly. If they do rust, or if you've missed some joint compound, simply sand the blades clean.

Knife Storage It's critical that you keep knife blades true and free of bends or nicks that might prevent a smooth finish on a future job. To ensure this, store knives where they won't be bent or bowed beneath the weight of other tools. Many knives have a hole in the handle so that they can be hung from a nail, which is a good option. A narrow shelf with a slot, into which you can slip knives, is also a good storage solution.

143 Sanding Techniques for a Finer Finish

Sanding drywall seams involves two steps: one pass with a sanding pole fitted with 120-grit sandpaper (or fine screen) and one pass with a hand-sander loaded with 150-grit sandpaper. If possible, seal off your work area to keep the dust from drifting into finished rooms. To accomplish this, set up a dust barrier of polyethylene sheets between the work space and all clean areas. Seal all four edges with masking tape. Keep in mind that joint-compound dust is very fine and can escape through tiny cracks between doors and jambs or around unsealed dust barriers.

Minimize the Dust A nearly dust-less alternative to this messy process is to wet-sand the drywall panels using a small-celled polyurethane sponge designed specifically for this purpose. Wet-sanding with one of these sponges does not yield as fine a finish as dry-sanding with 150-grit sandpaper, but in situations that don't permit dust, it makes a good substitute for the pole-sanding/hand-sanding technique. If you're particularly sensitive to dust, you can use a commercial sanding machine with a wet/dry vacuum attachment for nearly dust-free sanding.

1 When you need to sand drywall wall and ceiling seams, a sanding pole is the ideal tool.

2 Check the joints for smoothness with the palm of your hand, and sand down any bumps that you feel.

3 Hand-sanding may be required to get into corners. Using a sanding pole here may damage the seams.

Wet-sanding with a sponge doesn't result in as fine a finish as regular sanding, but it's virtually dust free.

6 Windows and Doors

• INSTALLING FULL-REPLACEMENT WINDOWS • WINDOW INSERTS
• INTERIOR AND EXTERIOR DOORS • TAKING ADVANTAGE OF THE SUN

Greener Ways

144 Placing Windows

Orient a door, window, or skylight to take best advantage of breezes and seasonal sunlight. Also take into account trees, shrubs, neighboring structures, and the potential view. Avoid placement that will cause overheating in the summer or excess heat loss in the winter. South-facing windows will allow heat gain in the winter when the sun's path is low in the sky but not in the summer, especially if it's shielded by a roof overhang, deep eave, or awning.

145 Checking R- and SHGC-Values

Solar-heat-gain-coefficient (SHGC) values range from 0 to 1. A low SHGC blocks sunlight from entering your home—a great thing if you're concerned about overheating or furniture-damaging UV light. A high SHGC allows more solar energy to enter your home, which is what you'd need for solar heat gain. The R-value, on the other hand, is a window's resistance to heat flow. The higher the R-value, the better the window resists heat loss in winter and heat gain in summer.

146 The Best Window for the Job

Five common types of windows exist. They can be used individually or combined in various ways.

Fixed A fixed window is simply glass installed in a frame that is attached to the house. It's the least expensive, admits the most light, and comes in the greatest variety of shapes and sizes. But it doesn't provide ventilation.

Double-Hung Double-hung windows have a traditional look that blends with a home's overall architecture. They consist of two framed glass panels, called sash, which slide vertically on a track.

Casement Casement windows, which are hinged at the side and swing outward, have a more contemporary feel. The better models provide maximum ventilation.

Sliding Similar to double-hung windows turned on their side, sliding windows work well where there is a need for a window opening that is wider than it is tall.

Awning Awning windows, which are similar to casements but are hinged at the top, can be left opened slightly for air even when it rains.

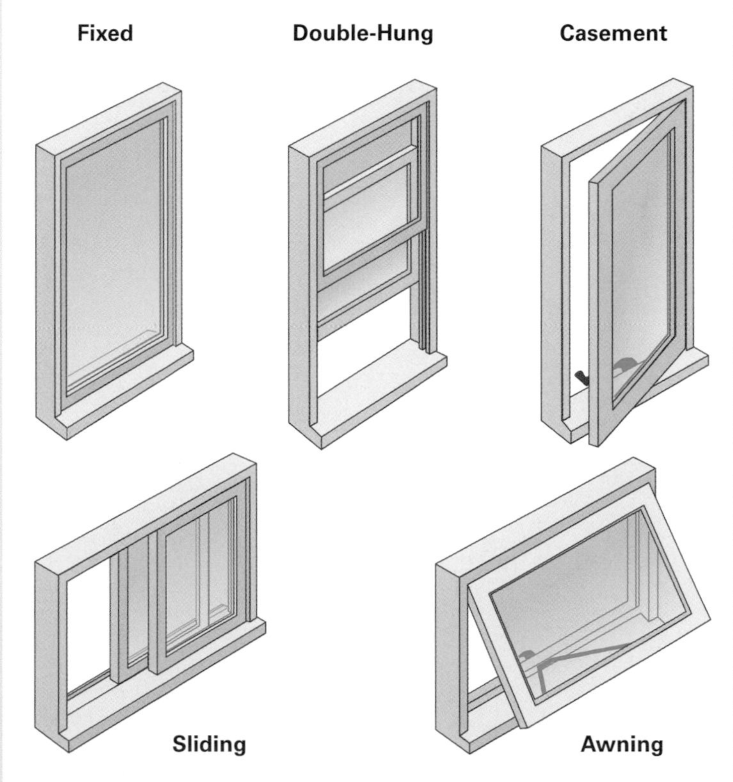

Choose a window type based on the style of your house and upon your needs. When making replacements, use the same type or change to ones that are more historically appropriate.

147 Installing a New Window

Installing a new window seems straightforward: cut away the sheathing to reveal the framed opening, pop in the new unit, nail it in place, and then get on with interior trim and exterior siding. In reality, proper installation requires care and attention to detail if the window is to perform well in the years to come.

Three Keys You must keep three key goals in mind: weather-tightness, energy-tightness, and smooth operation. To achieve the first, be sure to extend house wrap around the inside of the rough opening and to staple it in place. This will reduce drafts and help prevent heat loss. Also, pay close attention to drip cap (flashing) recommendations. A common reason for window rot is missing flashing that allows rainwater to seep into the wall around the window frame. Energy efficiency depends upon the installation as much as the R-value of the window unit. Be sure to apply caulk and to insulate according to the manufacturer's installation instructions. On a window with a flange, this means applying a thick bead of caulk on the backside of the flange and the insertion of insulation into any narrow gaps between the rough opening and jambs. Operation of the unit, not to mention good craftsmanship, depends upon a plumb installation. Use a shim to adjust the window so it's perfectly vertical before nailing it in place.

1 Fold house wrap around the framing members of the window opening, and staple it in place.

2 Run a bead of silicone caulk around the backside of the nailing flange to create a tight seal.

3 Set the window onto the rough sill, and tip the top into the opening. Tack in place for security.

4 Use pairs of tapered shims to adjust window on all sides in the opening, checking for plumb.

5 After installing the window, fill the gap between the jambs and the wall framing with fiberglass insulation.

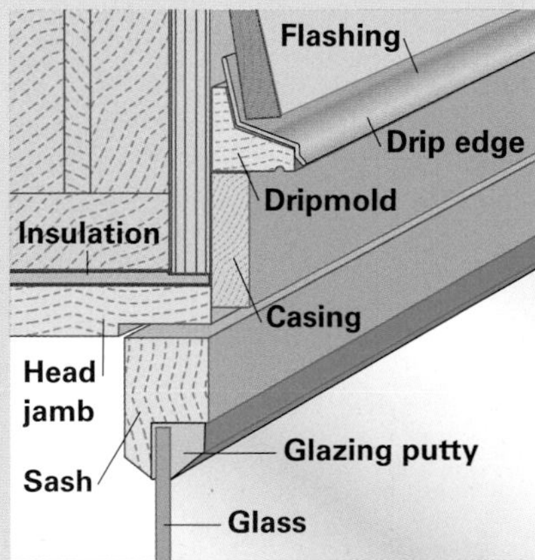

Details vary, but every window installation should include flashing at the top to prevent water infiltration.

148 Solar Tubes

Daylighting, the use of sunlight to provide illumination in homes, is tricky business. You can easily end up with too much light (glare), overheating, or excessive heat loss during the heating season. Moreover, light is often needed in dark interior areas not near windows.

Daylighting with a solar tube, also known as a solar light pipe, daylight pipe, or solar tunnel, solves all of these problems. The light it supplies is diffused and soft; it brings in more light and loses less heat than a window per square foot of opening; and it can be installed above dark areas of the home that would otherwise require artificial light even during the day. Solar tubes are offered by several manufacturers and are typically simpler to install than skylights.

Solar tubes transmit natural light to the room below and diffuse it for glare-free daylighting.

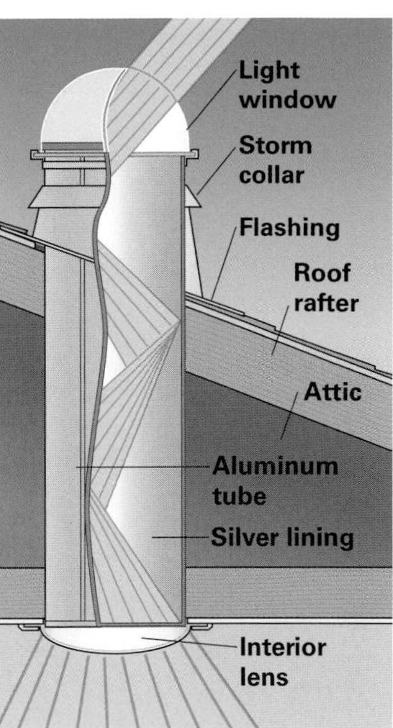

149 Avoiding Skylight Leaks

The extra natural light flooding through a skylight can dramatically change the look of a room. Don't try to skimp on the unit though. The smart approach to this popular home-improvement project is to install a fixed or venting glazed-type roof window warranted against water leaks. The best units have three layers of water protection: a preattached metal deck seal, a self-adhering underlayment, and flashing. Avoid old-style, plastic bubble units. They are trouble prone, and the labor to install one is not much different from installing a high-quality roof window.

Skylights can be added to rooms of a one-story house or on the top floor of a multistory house. It's a matter of mounting the skylight on the roof and building a short light shaft to the room. In an attic living space, the job is even easier—you don't need the light shaft. In some attic renovations, a skylight or two eliminates the need for a dormer.

1 After framing the opening, install the roof window. Then use a plumb bob and measuring stick to mark the ceiling joists for cutting.

2 Openings in both the roof and ceiling require double headers where joists are cut. Reinforce rafters and joists prior to removing them.

3 Working from below while standing on a ladder or scaffolding, finish the light shaft surfaces with drywall and white paint.

Saving Money

150 The Case for Storms

With so many high-tech alternatives, you may wonder why there is still a market for storm windows. They're old-fashioned, a nuisance, and easily replaced with energy-saving double-glazed windows.

In homes with single-pane glass, double glazing certainly makes a noticeable difference in your comfort and utility bills. However, you can also make a difference—for far less money and effort—by putting up storm windows. Many types are available, and in almost all cases, adding a removable storm window is less costly and less work than ripping out old window sash and frames and installing new units—with all the trim, touch-ups, and other work that goes along with opening a large hole in the side of your house. Aluminum combination storm/screen units are best.

Old-style, wood-framed storms require regular maintenance, such as replacing old, crumbling glazing compound (shown). Combination storms involve less work.

151 Sash-Only Replacements

The easiest way for do-it-yourselfers to replace an old window, assuming the window frame is in good shape, is with a sash replacement kit. Because only the sash get replaced, interior trim, exterior siding, and exterior trim are all unaffected.

Several types of replacement sash are available. Buy units that allow you to tilt both sash for easy cleaning—and don't forget to ask about screening options.

Out with the Old When preparing the old opening for the new sash, be sure to remove old sash weights and pulleys, if any, along with their cords or chains. Fill the void left behind with insulation. Avoid the use of expanding foam insulation because it may compromise the squareness of the window frame.

1 Remove window stops, old sash, sash weights, sash cords or chains, and pulleys.

2 Follow manufacturer's directions for measuring, cutting, and assembling the jamb liners.

3 Install top and bottom sash in the new jamb liners, and replace stop trim as required.

152 Installing a Replacement Window

Replacing the sash in old windows, as described on the opposite page, is the easiest and least-expensive approach to window replacement. Sash replacements, however, are not as energy efficient as replacement windows, which are custom-made to fit into an existing window frame (usually at no extra cost) and are not restricted to the standard sizes of most sash kits. Replacement windows have less glass area than the original ones that they replace, but if cost is a major consideration, vinyl replacement windows are the way to go.

New windows give you a wider range of options—you can go to larger sizes and different shapes—but the installation involves more work because you have to rip out the old window entirely. If the new one is only a little larger, you may be able to take advantage of extra space in the rough frame that was formerly occupied by the sash weights. For larger windows, it means cutting a bigger wall opening and installing new framing.

1 To remove an old window, use a pry bar, hammer, and chisel to pry loose the exterior trim.

2 Use the same technique inside to remove interior trim from old, single-glazed windows.

3 To release the window, cut through the nails that extend from the frame into the house-wall studs.

4 Once the nails are cut, you can pry out the window. You may need to release shims at the sides first.

5 Add felt paper or house wrap as required; check for level; and tack the replacement window in place.

6 Ensure that the window is plumb, using shims to adjust. Nail the window in place, and repair siding.

Greener Ways

153 Getting a Solar Boost

So your house was not designed to take advantage of the sun. You can do plenty of things to capture heat from the late fall to the early spring—and to prevent heat buildup in the summer.

If you have a sunroom or enclosed porch with a southern exposure, it can be used to collect tremendous amounts of heat. Use fans or natural convection to move air through a doorway from solar-warmed rooms to adjacent interior spaces. Just be sure to provide an opening for "return" air, such as an open window between the sunroom and the house, to ensure good air movement.

Even if you don't have a sunroom or sun porch, you can use blinds, shutters, drapes, or shades to control the sunlight. Blinds are often the best choice because they can be adjusted to let light in (or to keep it out) while maintaining privacy. Insulated shades and drapes are a better choice for areas with very cold winters.

Greener Ways

154 Getting "Awn" It

Don't waste energy and money to cool your house when you can keep the heat out with a simple device: an awning. Awnings reduce the amount of sunlight that gets through glass doors and windows. This reduction in solar heat gain keeps your home's interior cooler on hot days—by as much as 8 to 15 degrees—which means your air conditioner doesn't have to run as long or as hard.

Costs Awning prices vary. A stationary window awning may cost a few hundred bucks while an electrically powered retractable awning with wind and sun sensors can set you back thousands of dollars.

155 Built-up Colonial Casings

Using readily available stock, you can create a larger and more detailed Colonial casing that conveys a more nuanced sense of style than is available with an off-the-shelf profile. The process is not difficult; it uses 1×4 and 1×2 boards, and stock panel or base cap molding; 1×4 boards form the foundation of the casing. While you can certainly leave the edges of the boards square, or ease them gently with sandpaper, the casing will be more interesting if you add a molded profile to the inside edge. In order to do this, install an ogee or cove bit in the router, and use it to cut the profile along one edge of each 1×4 board. Other styles are possible using the same idea. Choose the style that best fits the decor of your home.

Colonial casing with panel molding and a backband.

Traditional-style casing with simple butt joints.

Neo-Classical casing suggests a Roman column.

Victorian casing between rosette blocks.

156 Deeper Jambs

Don't be worried if your new door and window jambs are an inch or two short of the wall surface. Instead of offering windows with different jamb widths, most manufacturers rely on the installer to install jamb extensions.

Use a small straightedge, held on the wall surface, and a tape measure to measure the depth of the required filler. Sometimes a window is installed so that it is not perfectly parallel with the wall surface, so check the dimensions at several spots around the window frame and use the largest measurement. Ideally, the jambs should be about 1⁄16 inch proud of the wall. Plane excess as required.

Align the inside surfaces of the jamb extension with the factory window (or door) jambs.

Screw the extensions to the jambs. If you center the screws, the casing will cover them.

157 Choosing the Right Door

Interior and exterior doors are offered in dozens of shapes, sizes, and materials. Some or the more popular styles are as follows:

Panel Doors Doors that have panels can be constructed with as few as 3 to as many as 10 or more solid panels. Sometimes, the bottom panels are wood and the top ones are glass. Exterior doors often have glass panels.

Flush Doors Generally less expensive, flush, or flat, doors come in a limited range of variations. You can enhance their simple looks with wood molding for a traditional appeal.

This French door provides ample amounts of natural light.

Sliders Sliding doors most often consist of a large panel of glass framed with wood or metal. Usually one of the doors is stationary while the other slides.

French Doors Traditional French doors are made of multiple framed-glass panels with either true divided lites or pop-in dividers.

Dutch Doors Dutch doors have independently operating half-sections, top and bottom. When locked, the two halves open and close as a unit. For ventilation, you can open just the top section.

158 Easy Mark

As a general rule, you are better off directly marking the size of a trim piece rather than measuring its length. Whenever you measure and mark a piece for length, there is an inevitable degree of variation in the way the dimension is transferred to the workpiece. By marking the size of a piece directly in its ultimate location, you reduce the opportunity for careless errors.

Mark the length of a trim piece in its ultimate location, using a pencil.

159 Combination Doors

When replacing an old storm door, consider a unit that combines both the storm glazing and screen in the upper half. Such doors allow you to slide the storm glazing down and the screen up when you want ventilation in summer. It's an easy task to reverse them again for added security when you leave on vacation or when a storm is expected.

The storm glazing and insect screen are stored in the lower portion of this combination door. They slide easily into place when you need to reverse them.

160 Strengthening Doors

To strengthen the connection between an existing doorjamb and house wall, start by removing the door stop trim. If you score the seam with a sharp utility knife first and pry it away gradually, you should be able to reuse it. Then drive several screws through the doorjamb into the nearest studs, particularly around the hinge and lock locations. This reinforcement makes it harder to pry the frame and release a latch or bolt from its keeper.

Use screws at least 3 inches long that can reach through the doorjamb, the shimming space around the frame, and well into the studs. Avoid driving them too deeply, or the jamb is likely to bow. You can now reinstall the door stop trim over the screws. You probably will need to do a bit of touch-up painting along the stop.

161 Installing a Prehung Door

If you want to add a door to a room, select a prehung unit to make the installation simple and quick. With a prehung door, you eliminate the need to fit the door to the opening, cut hinge and lockset mortises, and fit the door stops.

Getting Started To begin your installation, remove the door from the frame by knocking out the hinge pins. Stand the frame in the opening, and check that the head jamb is level. If one side is higher than the other, block up the low side until it is correct, and note the thickness of the blocking required. Mark the bottom of the high side jamb to remove that same amount, and cut it off. Place the frame in the opening again to make sure the head is level. Next, check whether the jack stud on the hinge side of the door is plumb. If it is, use 8d or 10d finishing nails to nail the top of the jamb to the stud. Then place the level on the edge of the jamb to make sure it is plumb in both directions. Adjust the jamb as necessary, and nail the bottom. Position nails near the top, bottom, and center of the jamb.

1 With the jamb plumb, nail the hinge jamb to the jack stud.

2 Pry the nailed jamb out slightly. Then install shims as shown every 16 inches.

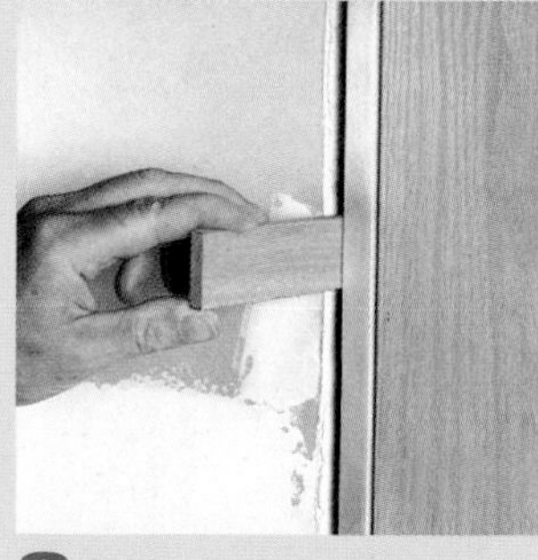

3 Rehang the door, and use it as a guide to adjust the latch jamb with shims.

4 Use a sharp utility knife to score and snap off excess shims.

162 Space-Saving Doors

Pocket doors save valuable space by sliding on a track directly into a cavity in the wall (the space normally filled with framing studs). They eliminate the need to swing a door through a room or hallway. They also save wall space. When you open a conventional door, it covers the wall and prohibits you from putting a chair or chest there. Not so with a pocket door. Install pocket doors according to the manufacturer's directions, and remember: the frame must be plumb for the door to slide smoothly on its track.

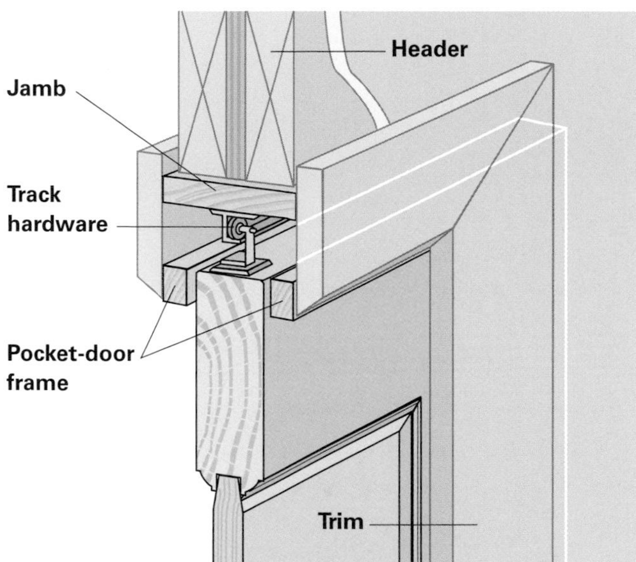

A pocket door looks like other doors when closed but slides open sideways into a cavity in the wall.

163 Replacing Thresholds

When replacing an exterior door, it's often necessary to replace an old, worn threshold as well. With the old door frame removed, this is a relatively simple task. Replacing an old threshold when you're not replacing the door is a bit trickier. Follow the photos shown below to make it easier. Tip: finish the underside of the new threshold prior to installation.

With an old threshold cut in two pieces, it's easier to split the sections with a chisel and to pry them out.

To keep water from seeping in, install threshold flashing and use a double bead of waterproof caulk.

Notch the threshold; slide in place; and fasten with countersunk screws. Then plug or putty the holes.

164 Casing a Drywall Opening

Many newer homes feature drywall jambs in passageways between rooms, but it's not difficult to add a wooden jamb to the opening. The first step is to use a flat pry bar to expose the metal corner bead and pry it away from the wall. Work your way up each corner and across the top of the opening. Pry off the drywall strips that line the inside of the opening, and trim any remaining drywall flush to the inside surface of the studs and header. Rip 1×6 pine stock to the necessary jamb width. Next, measure the width of the rough opening in several places along the jack studs. Take the smallest measure and subtract 1¼ inches to arrive at the length of the head jamb. Cut the side jambs about ¼ inch shorter than the rough opening height.

To join side and head jambs, make ⅜-in.-deep cuts in the head jamb. Remove waste with chisel.

Apply wood glue to the mating surfaces; square the frame; and fasten with finishing nails.

Build up molding on a passageway opening for greater visual impact and to match decor. **See style options in Tip 155.**

165 Vinyl and Metal Doors

Most door units are made of wood or wood by-products, though many are made of metal, stamped or embossed to look like wood. Purists may insist on real wood instead of synthetic substitutes, but both metal- and vinyl-clad exterior doors offer several advantages. They are stronger than wood and provide more security and durability. They don't have directional grain, so they are less likely to warp. The surfaces normally don't need to be refinished the way wood does. They won't shrink or swell when exposed to moisture or extreme temperatures. And many that have embossed wood textures can be stained or painted.

At Its Core When you shop for door units of any kind, make energy conservation a prime consideration. An energy-efficient door will keep your indoor air in and the outdoor air out. Steel and fiberglass doors with a polyurethane foam core are the most energy efficient. They insulate better than wood doors, which have a traditional look but are susceptible to the elements.

Although this entryway door looks like wood, it's made of steel.

Greener Ways

166 More-Efficient Garage Doors

In winter, garage doors contribute to heat loss, especially if the door to the house is not insulated or the garage is heated. Similarly, they contribute to heat gain in summer. When replacing old doors or building a new garage, choose doors with foam-in-place polyurethane cores and an R-value of at least R-11. Look for a flexible bottom door seal to stop infiltration on the doors you purchase as well.

167 Entryway Lighting

In addition to helping visitors find you, a well-lit entryway enables them to safely negotiate front steps—and allows you to see who's knocking. A ceiling fixture works, but two lanterns or sconces mounted on either side of the door, at or slightly above eye level, do the best job of illuminating visitors. Fixtures are available in styles that range from contemporary to Colonial. Choose ones that work with the style of your home—and that will not cause glare for you or your neighbors. When in doubt, go with a simple design. Some lighting retailers will allow you to borrow the fixture so you can hold it in place and see how it looks. When buying entryway lights, be sure they are UL listed for use in wet or damp locations.

Entryway lights are now fitted with LEDs for low-cost operation and long service.

168 Weatherstripping a Door

Not ready to invest in a new high-efficiency front (or back) door? Improve its energy efficiency with weatherstripping. Manufacturers offer many types for both the jambs and sills. Keep in mind that gasket-style weatherstripping lasts longer than foam types, and the nail-on products stay put better than the self-adhering types.

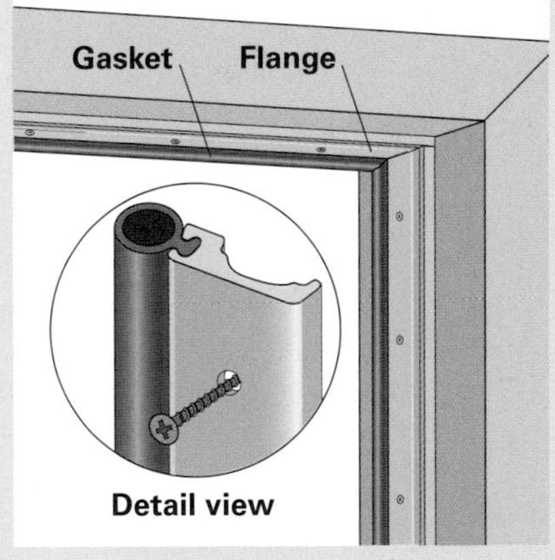

Adjust the location of weatherstripping so that when the door closes, the gasket compresses only slightly against the door.

169 Going Glass, Staying Safe

Exterior doors provide a way into the house. Exterior glass doors provide a way for sunlight to enter the house as well—and sunlight brings cheer and sparkle to any room. However, these types of doors—with their large glass panels—are also more vulnerable to break-ins. To minimalize your risk, you can use tempered or safety glazing, which is harder to break. (Double glazing is also more resistant than single glazing.) The problem is that by breaking the glass, a burglar can simply reach inside to undo the locks. To prevent that easy entry, use glass panels on top of the door or small panes that don't allow access to the locks.

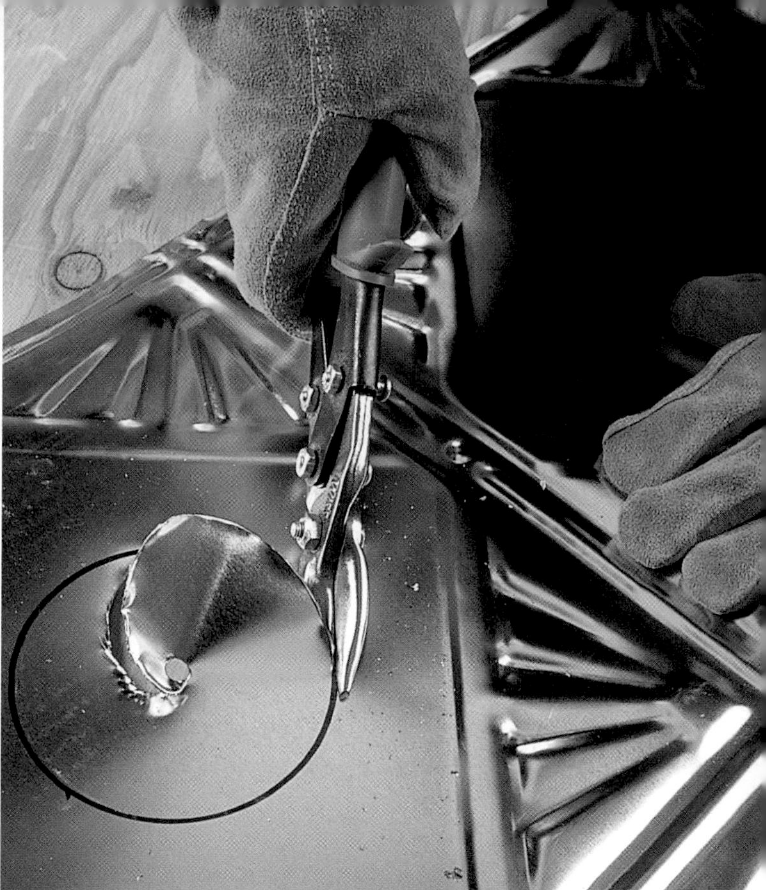

7 Floors, Walls, and Ceilings

- CHOOSING MATERIALS • PREPPING FOR THE JOB
- HANDLING WALLPAPER • HIDING IMPERFECTIONS

Saving Money

170 The Look of Stone for a Lot Less

Want the look of stone without the hassle or cost? Installers have devised ways to pour thin-but-strong layers of acrylic-fortified concrete over various substrates, including wooden subfloors. They then use dyes and chemical acid stains that create stone- or tile-like effects and colors on the smooth concrete surface. Contemporary one-of-a-kind designs are also possible. Once polished, these floors require little maintenance and are unaffected by moisture. When coupled with radiant heat in the floor, cold floor temperature is no longer an issue. No getting around it, these floors are hard, but they are also cost effective. Basement rooms and garages are the most popular rooms for decorative concrete flooring, but they are also being used in kitchens, baths, and laundry rooms.

171 About Engineered Wood

Engineered wood generally comes in 3- to 6⅛-inch-wide prefinished planks of single or random lengths. Overall thickness ranges from ¼ to ¾ inch, depending on the manufacturer. Plies range from 2 to 10. The more plies, the more stable the product, but the key issue when buying engineered wood products is the thickness of the veneer layer. If it's too thin, it can't be refinished. Look for a product with at least a ⅛-inch veneer. You'll be able to refinish it two or three times.

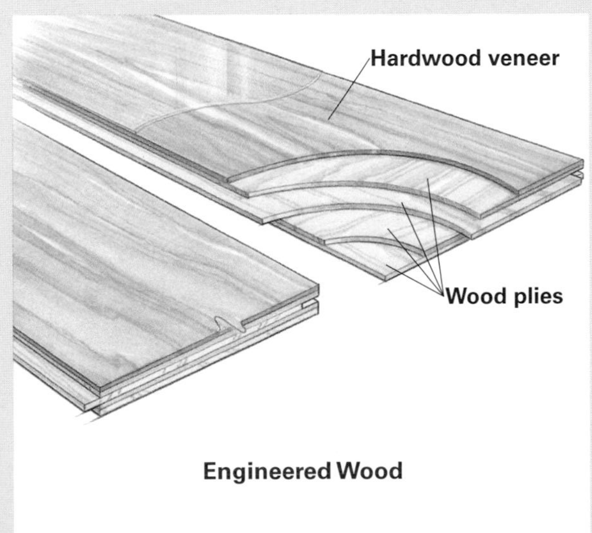

Engineered Wood

172 Subfloor Preparation

New planks of wood flooring may look as though they will hide all the sins of the subfloor, but they probably won't. Careful preparation is the secret to any professional-looking result. If the subfloor is uneven, the new wood floor will be, too. Voids left under the floor will result in squeaks later on. If your subfloor has minor humps or if the plywood is slightly raised around the edges, rent an edger (a powerful sanding machine) to level them. Minor dips may be shimmed with 30-pound roofing felt. All loose boards should be secured with deck screws. If your subfloor has more-severe problems, it may need to be shimmed with plywood, feathered to meet the existing subfloor—a job best left to a pro.

Underlayment panels should be attached with screws driven through the subfloor. Panels attach to the floor joists, not just the flooring.

Working Safer

173 Dealing with Asbestos

Asbestos was used in many building products until it was banned in the 1970s. Old floor tiles and floor adhesives that were made with asbestos are best left in place. Such floors can only be removed by a licensed asbestos-abatement company at considerable expense. Save by covering the old tiles with the new flooring—and avoid the risk of releasing asbestos fibers into your home.

174 Grout-Joint Widths

Allow a large enough joint gap when laying floor tile to accommodate variances in tile size. If the difference between the largest tile in the carton and the smallest is ⅛ inch, allow at least a ¼-inch joint. If the variance is greater than ⅛ inch, you may want to allow a ⅜- or ½-inch joint. Otherwise, the variations will be noticeable in the final result. Having slightly wider joints will also allow you to accommodate small height differences between tiles by sloping the grout.

175 Handling Old Flooring

When replacing old vinyl, asphalt, or linoleum flooring, particularly in kitchens and baths, don't presume that you can install the new floor over the old. If the height of the old floor plus the new floor and the recommended underlayment will be ½ inch or more higher than adjacent floors, it's often wiser to remove the old floor to avoid creating a tripping hazard at thresholds. If the old floor is damaged or uneven or has structural problems, you will need to tear it up and make any needed repairs to the subfloor before putting down the new surface. Leave old flooring in place if it is raised only ¼ or ⅜ inch above adjacent flooring, is smooth and solid, and is not easily removed.

If you must transition from one surface to a lower surface, consider reducer moldings. The reducers shown below illustrate common transitions from wood flooring and from tile to lower floors.

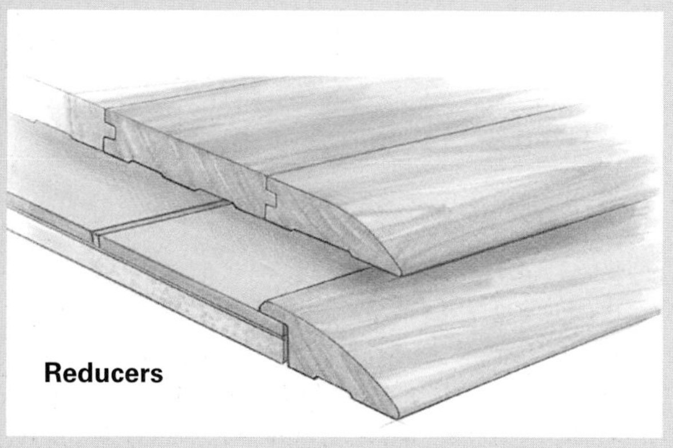
Reducers

Saving Money

176 Flooring with Character

Solid wood flooring is available in a variety of grades, with the better grades costing more because they're scarcer. Grades, however, do not affect performance; all are sound. Clear oak will not last longer than common grades. So if flooring with more "character" (knots and color variations) suits your taste, you can save significantly on the cost of materials. Dark stains, currently very popular, can be used to mask variations in any case.

177 Buying Better Padding

Padding or carpet underlay is generally recommended for installation under carpeting. Available in various thicknesses, from ¼ to 7⁄16 inch, it serves two purposes. First, it makes carpeting more resilient and consequently more comfortable on which to walk. Second, it helps to preserve the carpet by preventing fibers from being crushed.

Upgrade Carpet dealers often throw in an inexpensive padding with your purchase if you have them do the installation. In the long run, it makes more sense to upgrade to a better padding, even if you have to pay for it. Better padding will improve carpet performance and prevent spills from leaking through to the flooring below. From good to best, paddings include rebond (a high-density foam), slab rubber, fiber (made from jute or synthetic fiber), and frothed foam (high-density polyurethane).

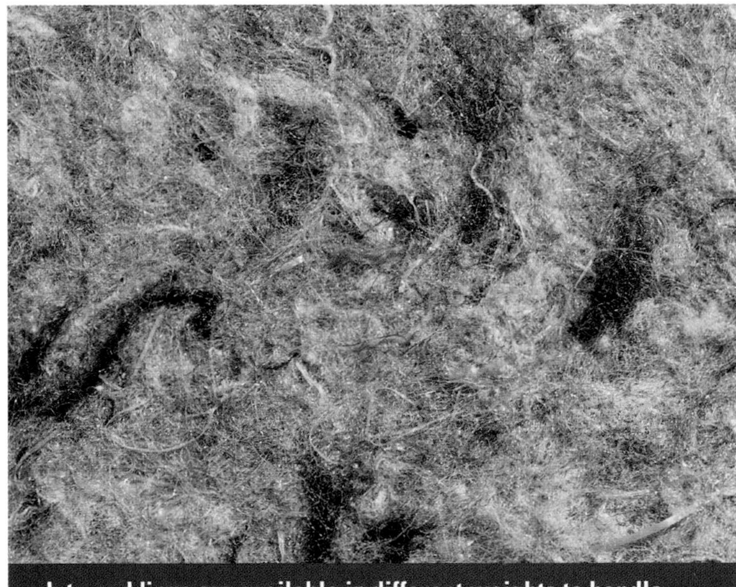

Jute paddings are available in different weights to handle low-, medium-, and high-traffic situations. Install waterproof padding to preserve your wood floors underneath the carpet.

178 Solving Problems with Furring Strips

Horizontal furring strips make installing paneling, such as the wainscoting shown here, easy. They do two things: allow you to level an uneven surface, and provide a nailer to which you can fasten the paneling.

How-To Instructions Begin by snapping horizontal chalk lines at 16- or 24-inch intervals. Then install the furring strips, but fasten them only at the ends. Using a string that is offset from the wall with identically sized blocks, determine where the wall protrudes or recedes. At receding (low) spots, insert shims behind the strips. For large gaps, use two shims inserted in opposing directions. At protruding (high) spots, shave the furring slightly. Lastly, drive nails or screws through the furring strips and shims into the studs behind the wall. Furring can be used on masonry walls, such as those in a basement, wavy plaster, drywall, and bare framing.

Nail horizontal furring strips to the wall, and fill any hollows behind the strips with shims.

Slide the groove of each board over the tongue of the previous one. Drive nails diagonally at the base of the tongue.

The exposed tops of wainscoting boards must be covered with trim. Cut a piece, and nail it into the

179 Easier Wallcoverings

When buying wallcoverings, choose the prepasted variety and save yourself a lot of time and mess. You just have to dunk it and hang it. There are still some pitfalls to overcome, though. Using patterned papers, for example, can be tricky. You may want to dry-match patterns by laying out sheets on the floor or by sketching on graph paper how the sheets will fall.

Also, some papers should be set aside for a short time after soaking. When this is specified, be sure to keep the interval consistent from sheet to sheet because the paper may expand a little once it's wet. If you hang one strip right away next to a sheet that had a long soak, you could get a noticeable gap in the seam.

Sheets of prepasted paper get dunked in a tray of water.

180 Avoiding Bubbles

To successfully hang wallpaper, you'll need to use a smoothing brush, shown below, to remove any air bubbles from under the paper. Work from the center of the paper toward the edges in slow, firm strokes. But don't bear down so hard that you distort or tear the paper.

181 Foolproof Paper Hanging

There is a discipline to successfully hanging wallcoverings. Work with a sharp utility knife: change the blade after every few cuts, or sharpen it frequently with a sharpening stone. Keep your worktable clean and free of paste or adhesive. Make sure the outside of each strip of paper is clean before you hang the next piece. Handle the wallcovering gently. And always establish a plumb starting line on each wall that you plan to cover.

1 Draw a vertical, floor-to-ceiling, starting line that's the width of the paper from a corner, minus ½ in.

2 Folding, or "booking," the paper as shown makes it easier to handle than trying to work with long strips.

3 To align the strip to the drawn line, position it slightly away from the line and gently push it over to it.

182 Handling Inside and Outside Corners

Walls, especially in older homes, are often not plumb. This means that corners may not be plumb either. To avoid noticeably crooked wallcovering patterns, remember to always draw a new plumb line on the second wall. Locate this line a distance from the corner that matches the width of your last cutoff strip. Use this cutoff to begin the new wall.

On the Outside For wrapping outside corners, use the same procedure, but add ½ inch to the measurement. Place the paper in position, but before wrapping it around the corner, make small slits in the waste portions near the ceiling and baseboard. The cuts will allow you to turn the corner without tearing or wrinkling the paper. Hang the remainder of the cut sheet so that it overlaps the first portion.

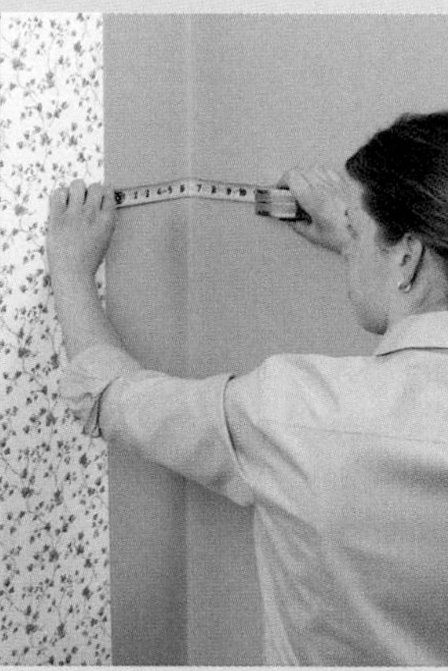

1 Cover wall remainder with a strip that's wide enough to turn the corner by ⅛ in.

2 Resume hanging paper from the corner with the strip left over from the previous cut.

183 Getting Neat Borders

Trim the strips of wallpaper to length by first pressing a taping knife against the wall to create a crease. Then cut along the edge of the taping knife using a sharp utility knife, as shown below. Use the same technique to cut the top of the paper against the ceiling.

184 Perfect Pattern Matches

Matching the running pattern on wallcovering sometimes requires that you overlap the two pieces until the pattern aligns. Keep in mind that the paste doesn't set up immediately. You have time to manipulate the paper to make adjustments. Use a utility knife with a new blade to cut through the center of the overlap. Discard the top piece; then lift the seam, and pull out the other cut piece from underneath. Cutting both pieces like this creates a perfect seam. Roll the cut seams flat using a wallpaper roller. Use a damp sponge to wipe away any paste or adhesive from the surface. Also clean away any adhesive from the base trim or the ceiling that may have rubbed off the paper.

On wallpaper pieces that overlap, use a sharp knife to cut through both strips at once. Get rid of the top piece. Then lift the seam, and pull out the other cut piece from below.

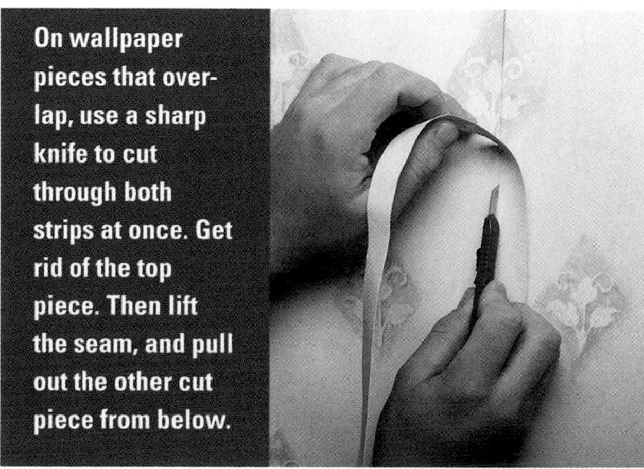

Greener Ways

185 More Natural Paint Options

Try natural paints the next time you paint a wall or ceiling. They are made from natural substances such as plant oils, minerals, beeswax, and milk. Natural paint options include:

Natural Clay Paints Made from naturally occurring clays, these paints can be applied to most surfaces, including masonry and drywall.

Plaster A traditional paint alternative made from natural clays, plaster can be tinted and troweled on to any surface that absorbs water. New drywall and previously painted surfaces typically require priming first.

Milk Paints Used in Colonial times, milk paints are made from milk, lime, and natural pigments. Milk paint does not flow out, as do conventional paints, so your brush marks will remain visible and give the surface texture rather than a smooth finish. Milk paint can be used outdoors as well.

Whitewash Similar to milk paints but usually without the milk, whitewash is made with lime and water and can be tinted with natural pigments. It, too, can be used indoors or outdoors.

186 Working on "Open Time"

When installing tile, be sure to read the container label on your adhesive to find out what its "open time" is. This refers to how long the material can be exposed to the air before it starts to dry out and won't hold the tile. The best approach is to start by applying the adhesive to a small area—a 2 × 2-foot square, for example—and noting how long it takes you to get the tile in place. If you are well within the open-time limitations, enlarge your working area for the next stage.

Use a notched trowel to apply the tile adhesive to the wall. Cover a wall area no bigger than what can be comfortably completed before the adhesive dries.

187 Supporting Wall Tiles

Tile adhesive is formulated to prevent tiles from sagging while it dries. But when installing wall, it's a good idea to support the bottom row of tiles anyway.

Your Options You can screw a straight board to the wall and place the tiles on the top edge of the board. Or you can drive two drywall nails for each tile in the wall, as shown below.

Gently push each tile into the adhesive, twisting it slightly to ensure complete contact. Note how the first course rests on drywall nails.

188 Going Glass

Glass-block walls and windows add a distinctive element to any room, and they allow filtered light in without sacrificing privacy. These blocks aren't difficult to install, though the framing in the room may need to be beefed up to support the additional weight.

Design your installation so that it uses only full blocks, which makes the job easier. Begin by mixing some mortar and adding an expansion strip and joint anchors to the wall. Then spread a bed of mortar on the floor. Lay each block in this bed, and then start the next course, working upward course by course. Finish by smoothing the joints.

Glass blocks are set in place above a curb (optional) or floor using joint anchors, mortar, and spacers.

When the wall reaches the ceiling, slide the blocks for the last course in place. Don't distort mortar joints.

189 Real Brick and Stone Facings, Fast

If you like the look of brick or stone and would like to use it inside your house, consider products called facing brick and facing stone. These materials are much thinner and lighter than the full-size versions, so they can be installed just like ceramic tile, using either thinset mortar or mastic adhesive. No extra wall or floor support is required.

Not Always Authentic These products are usually real brick and stone, but some manufacturers offer composite products that look like the real thing.

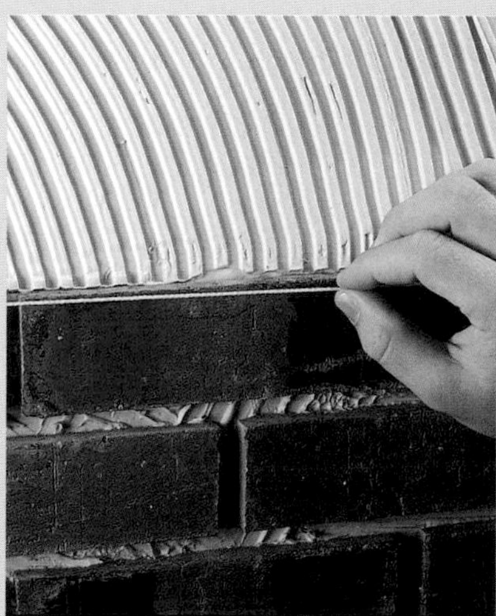

String can be used to ensure that bricks pressed against the adhesive are straight and level.

A piece of ¼- or ⅜-in.-thick plywood helps to create proper joint spaces before the adhesive sets.

Once the adhesive sets, you'll need to fill a grout bag and use it to squeeze grout between the bricks.

190 Hiding Blemishes

Textured finishes on walls and ceilings can be used to enhance the decor of a room—or to hide imperfections. Pros do the job by spraying a popcorn-like material (polystyrene or vermiculite) on surfaces. You can achieve similar orange-peel texture without a sprayer. Simply use a paint roller to apply watered-down joint compound. If the roller produces the texture you want, allow it to dry as is. If not, knock down the half-dry surface by lightly drawing a finishing knife across it.

Orange-peel texture can be applied using a paint roller (shown before the knockdown technique).

191 Paneled Ceilings

There is no load on ceiling planks; they just have to stay attached to the rafters or ceiling joists, so you can use material that is ½ inch thick or less. A standard ceiling installation has planks that interlock with a tongue and groove. This configuration is available in a variety of materials, including exotic hardwoods and plain pine.

Weight Issues Several manufacturers offer packages of thin, lightweight material in cedar or pine. The individual planks are extremely flexible but firm up once you lock the joints together and add nails. Always check the manufacturer's installation instructions. On some thin material you may need to add a layer of strapping to provide more frequent support than standard rafters or ceilings joists set 16 inches on center.

192 Tips for Hanging Suspended Ceilings

Suspended ceilings are a great way to hide pipes, ductwork, and electrical cables in a finished basement. When you need access, it's simple to pop the ceiling tiles out of the way.

Most suspended ceiling systems include four components. The first are the L-shaped metal edge strips that are installed on the perimeter of the room. The second are the T-shaped metal main runners that rest on the edge strips and are aligned perpendicular to the joists. The third are the metal crosspieces that are hooked between the main runners. And the fourth are the acoustical ceiling panels that are supported by the metal structure. A variety of designs is available for both the framework and the panels.

1 Below the height of all obstacles, draw a level line around the room. Then install metal edge strips.

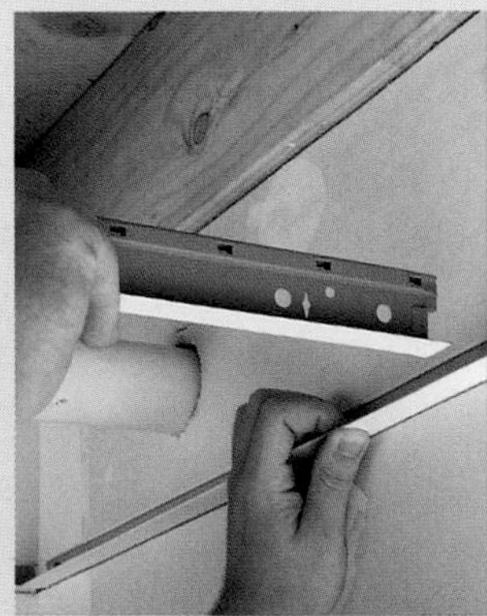

2 Cut the main runners to length, and then place them on top of the edge strips.

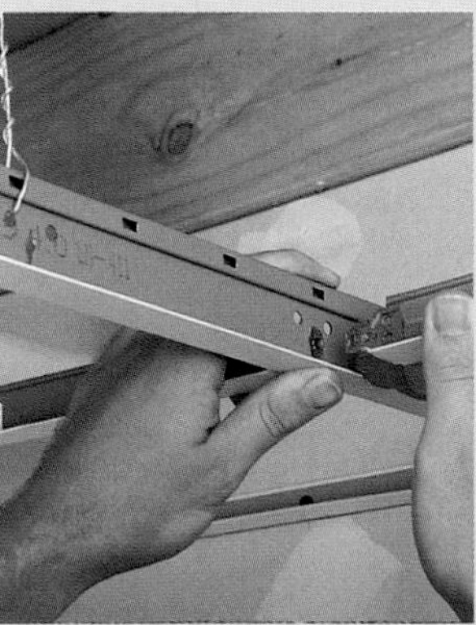

3 Once the runners are level, install the crosspieces by snapping their ends into the runner slots.

4 Slide cut tiles over the metal grid, and drop them into place. Remove to reach pipes and cables.

193 False Beams

False beams can be installed for decorative reasons, but they're also useful if you have something to hide, such as a pipe. The beams are easy to make. Just glue and nail three boards together. Installing them isn't much harder. Just attach a cleat to the ceiling, being sure to screw through to a joist, and hang the beam from this board.

1 The three boards that form the false beam are joined using wood glue and 4d finishing nails at all the mitered edges.

2 Cut a board so that it fits just inside the beam. Screw this board to the joists so that it is located where you want the beam to be.

3 Lift the false beam up to the ceiling, and fit it over the nailing board. Nail the beam to the board with finishing nails.

194 Tin Ceilings

Tin ceilings are making a comeback these days, more than 100 years after their widespread popularity. Many of the patterns available today are exact reproductions of original designs. These panels can be installed directly on the surface of a flat ceiling, if ⅜-inch-thick plywood is installed first. But if the ceiling isn't flat or if it's damaged, install furring strips and shim them until they are flat. Then attach the tiles to the furring. Ceiling panels and trim pieces can be cut to fit using tin snips.

Nail blocking between furring strips; then nail on tin panels with 10d common nails.

Working Safer

195 The Right Gloves

When working with many materials and tools, it helps to wear the right hand protectors. For latex paint, lightweight cotton gloves are fine. Vinyl or latex gloves are best with solvent-based products. But when you must handle rough, heavy materials, such as timbers or masonry, or sharp materials, such as tin or metal flashing, heavy-duty leather gloves are a must.

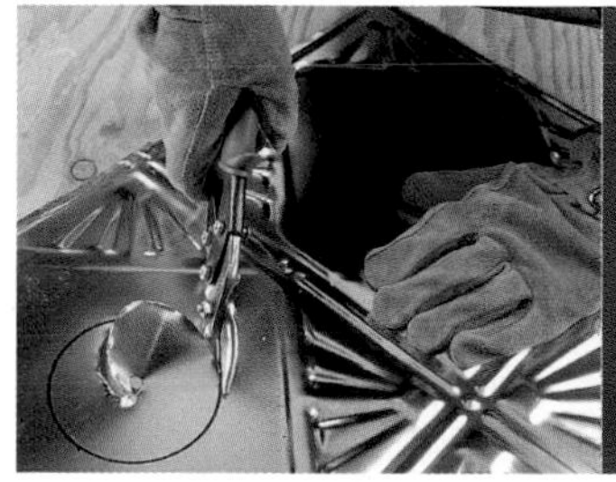

When cutting tin ceiling tiles, it's best to protect yourself with a pair of leather work gloves.

8 Paint and Other Finishes

- CHOOSING COLORS • EASIER PAINT PREP
- MORE EFFICIENT PAINTING • SPEEDY JOB CLEANUP

196 Proper Prep

Before you paint over a place where the drywall paper covering has torn, use a sharp utility knife to cut away all torn edges, and peel away the damaged paper covering. Don't think you'll be able to sand the problem away! Once the torn paper is removed, apply several thin coats of all-purpose joint compound with a wide trowel. When dry, sand the patched area with 150-grit abrasive, and apply primer. This last step is important. If you skip the primer, the dried joint compound will suck moisture from the finish coat and leave a dull spot. You're now ready to apply your top coat and can expect a blemish-free finish.

Use a utility knife to remove all torn drywall paper before applying any joint compound. Be sure the knife has a fresh, sharp razor blade.

197 A Wiser Way to Choose Interior Colors

Nothing is more wasteful of time, materials, and money than choosing the wrong color and having to begin the job over. Avoid this sort of nightmare by taking a little extra time when deciding about colors, especially if you intend to repaint several adjoining rooms. Experts recommend that you find an "anchor" color that you like first. Check out the many color chips and swatches available at paint stores and home-improvement centers. Be sure to examine your choices in different types of light, including natural light at different times of day for interior and exterior paint jobs, and in varying levels of artificial light for interior jobs. From there, a seasoned salesperson can help you select a full scheme of colors for walls, trim, doors, and the like.

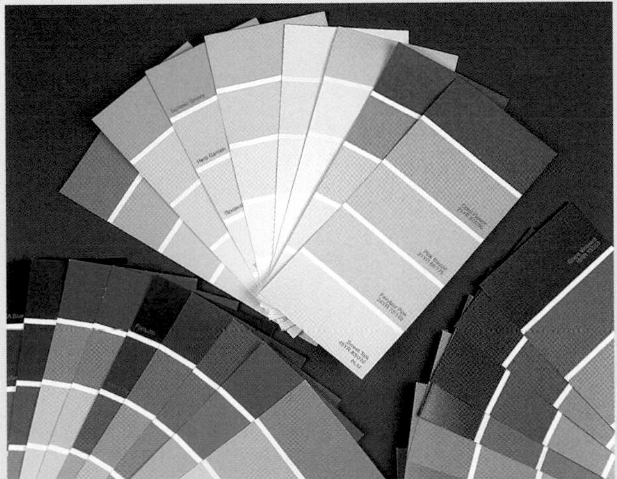

Color swatches at home-improvement centers and paint stores provide a good starting point.

Don't Forgo Trial Follow up by buying samples of the colors you are considering. They're usually sold in small jars. Paint 2- by 3-foot poster boards with them. Place them in the rooms you intend to paint and observe them in different lights and near carpets and furniture. Keep in mind, however, that the size of the area being painted will affect your perception of the color. The larger the surface area, the darker the color will appear. If you're painting a large room, you may want to select a color that is two shades lighter than the one you originally selected.

Another useful tool when choosing color is your computer. Several paint manufacturers offer software that allows you to "prepaint" a room before you lift a brush. See "A Wiser Way to Choose Exterior Colors," Tip 218.

198 The Right Brush

The advice about how the right tool makes the job easier is true for paintbrushes, too. Flat brushes have a tapered edge and are the most versatile of brushes. A 3- or 4-inch-wide flat brush can cover large areas, produce sharp cut lines, and be used to "lay off," or smooth, paint that's just been applied. As with other bristle brushes, flat brushes are available with synthetic or natural bristles. Use synthetics with latex or oil-based paints. Use natural-bristle brushes only with oil-based paints. Sash brushes have angled heads, making them ideal for making crisp lines on trim, molding, and window muntins. Stain brushes have shorter, wider heads. The stubby design is meant to counteract the tendency stain has to drip. Foam brushes are cheap and disposable. They may be useful for touch-ups and for painting window trim.

When Buying a Brush Tug on the bristles. If any pull out, leave the brush behind. Next, bounce and wiggle the bristles in your palm. A good brush feels soft and springy, and the bristles are thick. Finally, check the metal ferrule that secures the brush head to the handle. It should be substantial, not flimsy, and well secured to the handle.

From left: one flat and two sash brushes (all synthetic), two foam brushes, deck stain brush (natural bristles).

199 Loading Paint like the Pros

When loading a roller or brush with paint, you want to pick up as much paint as possible without picking up so much that it will drip and create a mess. For rollers it's relatively easy. Dip the roller in the reservoir of a roller tray, and roll it over the ridges of the tray to shed the excess paint and distribute it evenly on the roller cover. With brushes, dip the bristles about an inch deep into the paint, and then tap them on the rim of the container to knock off excess. Dip too deeply, and paint may harden in the heel of the brush near the ferrule. Wiping the bristles across the edge of the container removes too much paint and slows the job.

Before loading a roller or brush, remove loose fibers and bristles. Tape does the trick with rollers.

As an extra precaution against drips, place the roller pan on a piece of cardboard, such as an open pizza box.

Load paint as shown to prevent drips, splatters, and accumulations of hardened paint in the brush heel.

200 Picking the Right Paint-Roller Cover

Choosing the right roller will improve the look of the finished job considerably and may save you some time, too. The key rule to remember is to choose the roller based upon the degree of surface texture. The smoother the surface, the shorter the cover nap should be; the rougher the surface texture, the longer the nap. For example, if you're painting drywall, use a short-nap roller cover. If you're painting stucco or brick, use a long-nap roller. Manufacturers offer about a half dozen different cover nap lengths and typically rate them from "very smooth" to "very rough." If you were to use a short-nap roller on a rough surface, it would take a long time—and may be impossible—to complete the job. A long-nap roller on a smooth surface would produce lumpy, unacceptable results.

Natural vs. Synthetic The material with which the roller cover is made can make a difference in the results, too. For the most part, choose a good-quality polyester or nylon cover. Both can be used with latex or oil-based paints. Natural fibers, such as sheepskin, woven wool, and mohair, are also available. The natural fibers hold more paint than synthetics can and therefore speed the job. Sheepskin covers generally are long-napped and naturally very dense, so they hold a lot of paint. They are best for rough surfaces. Mohair covers are usually short-napped and are useful when super-smooth results are desired, such as when applying a semigloss or gloss enamel on woodwork. Most natural fibers are meant to be used with oil-based, not latex, paints—although polyester-wool blends can be used with either type of paint. Whatever material you choose, look for high fiber density and well-secured fibers. Note: foam rollers can be used to apply smooth coats of paint, at less cost than natural-fiber roller covers.

Choose a roller handle with a female fitting in the handle. It will allow you to attach an extension pole that will speed your work, whether you're painting walls, ceilings, or floors. Choose a large-frame roller for large jobs.

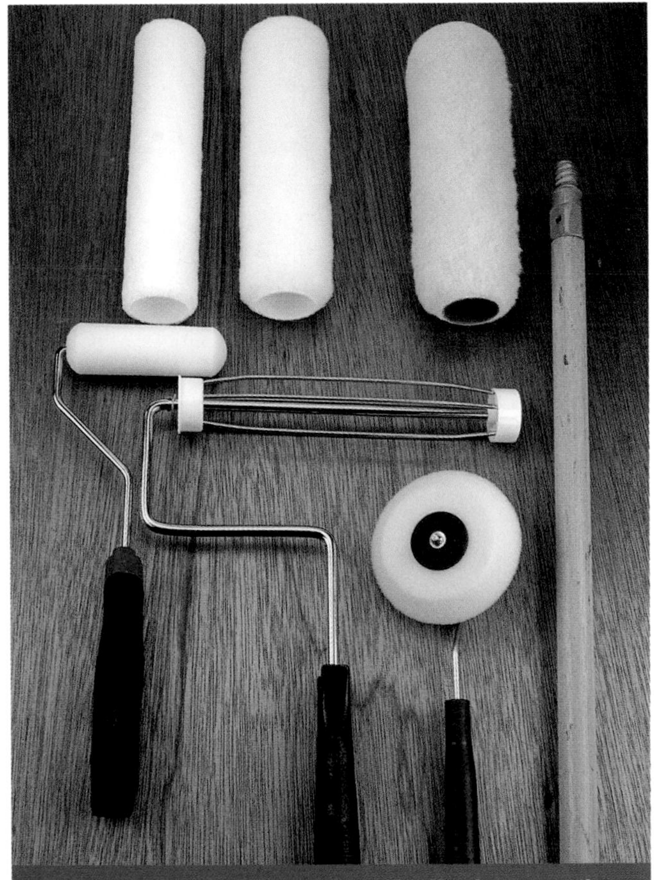

Pictured here is an assortment of roller frames and roller covers, along with an extension handle.

When on the job, you can keep paint in a roller pan (bottom), a bucket (top), or a can (right).

201 Finishing Cabinets

Painting or staining wood cabinets is much easier if you first remove obstacles such as shelves, drawers, and hardware. Next, prep by sanding and cleaning the surfaces, and follow a work sequence that allows you to "back out" of the cabinet as you brush on the finish. This will help minimize both marring already finished surfaces and excessive brushing.

For Best Results Remove the doors and finish them with a sprayer. You can also spray-paint cabinet exteriors while they are still in place if you're careful about protecting surrounding areas from overspray. A good spraying job will produce glass-like smoothness, whereas brushing will inevitably leave some stroke marks. Practice on a piece of scrap wood first because sprayers take time to get used to. If you're not careful, you'll apply too much paint. You can also have the cabinets painted at a professional shop; this provides the smoothest and longest-last-

Greener Ways

202 Taming Alkyd Finishes

If you're used to today's latex finishes, alkyds are, put simply, nasty to use. The odor, drying time, cleanup, and eco-guilt with which you have to deal are unwelcome, to say the least. Sometimes, however, using alkyd paints and the solvents that go with them are necessary. Perhaps you need to prime or recoat old alkyd-based paint, or you prefer highly durable alkyds for coating woodwork that must be cleaned regularly.

Handling Leftovers When you must use alkyds, buy only what you need. Leftovers are considered toxic waste and must be handled as such. Save leftover turpentine and mineral spirits in cans or jars. After a few days, the solid matter will settle to the bottom of the container, allowing you to pour off the clear solvent and save it for reuse.

Working Safer

203 Removing Paint from Woodwork

Using paint removers to lift layers of old paint from woodwork, such as windows or doors, is messy and often caustic—or worse. The best tool for removing paint is a heat gun. Hold the nozzle a few inches from the old paint. When the paint begins to soften and bubble, use a scraper to remove it. Keep the gun's nozzle moving to avoid scorching the wood or setting the paint (or insulation in the wall) on fire. Caution: if you suspect that any layer of paint was applied before the mid-1980s, test for lead before you begin. Easy-to-use testers are available. Visit the National Lead Information Center (NLIC) at epa.gov/oppt/lead/pubs/leadinfo.htm for additional information.

The Preferred Tool A heat gun is also the preferred tool for removing paint from exterior surfaces. Use a push scraper or putty knife to remove softened paint from flat surfaces. Use a molding scraper, which conforms to various contours, for scraping irregular surfaces. Do not strip paint using a blowtorch, and do not let anybody else do it on your house. Blowtorches are more likely to ignite a fire than heat guns.

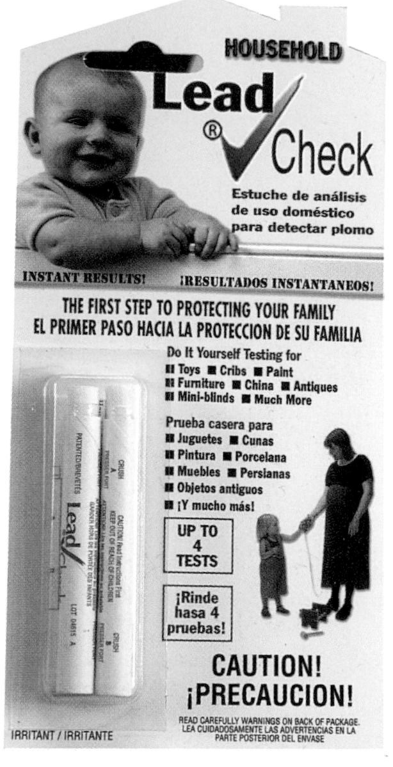

204 Shining More Light on the Job

You'll paint faster and more effectively in a well-lit room. "Holidays," or areas that you miss; drips; and other imperfections will be easier to spot. Work lights come in a variety of sizes with different bulb types. Incandescent bulbs in a plastic or metal cage are inexpensive and serve most jobs very well. You can clamp the fixtures to a ladder or chair or use them as a handheld "wand" to inspect the paint after you have applied it. If you need more light, try halogen lamps. They are very bright but give off a great deal of heat, which can be a problem in small rooms if it causes paint to dry too quickly. Fluorescent lights don't give off much heat, but they sometimes make colors look different from how they look in natural or incandescent light. The nice thing about fluorescents is that the bulbs are long lasting.

205 Getting Better Coverage

In most cases, you will not be able to remove everything from the room, so you must protect what remains. Place all movable furniture in the center of the room, and cover with canvas drop cloths. Don't be tempted to use newspaper because paint will seep through. Cover hanging light fixtures in plastic. Remove or tape door hardware. (See Tip 211.) Mask the trim that you do not plan to repaint (such as base trim and door and window casing). Be sure to use painter's tape. Regular masking tape is too sticky and will remove finishes when you pull the tape off the surface. Buy the best painter's tape you can find. It will pay off with neater results and less touch-up later.

Put an old sheet or plastic sheeting over chandeliers and ceiling fans. Unscrew the ring at the top of the chandelier, too, and lower the canopy to ease painting.

Saving Money

206 Preserving Paint

The smartest way to avoid wasting money with leftover paint at the end of a job is to be careful when estimating your needs. Every paint can has information about coverage printed on its label. A good wall paint, for example, may state that you'll be able to cover 400 to 450 square feet with one gallon. All you need to do is determine the area of the wall, floor, or ceiling that you're painting.

Another good practice to avoid waste is to be diligent about labeling the can with the date, color, and location where it was used. You are more likely to reuse a labeled can in the future.

Careful storage of paint will help preserve it for future use as well. Store cans out of the sun, and protect them from freezing. The lid should be tapped in place with a hammer.

Finally, when pouring paint from a can, always pour so that drips, should they occur, won't obscure important information printed on the label, such as recommended coverage, surface preparation, suggested primers, drying times, temperature limitations, and the like.

A tight-fitting lid will help preserve paint. To keep the lid clear of dry paint buildup, punch a few holes in the channel to allow the paint to drip back into the can.

Salvage a fouled can of paint by straining the contents through a sieve fashioned from cheesecloth.

207 Drywall Primer

If you have experience painting new drywall, you're already aware that you should prime it before applying the finish coats. Otherwise, painted areas that were covered by drywall joint compound will have a different texture than those covered by drywall paper, giving the job a splotchy look. Choose a primer specifically made for drywall to solve the problem. While you're at it, have the paint store tint your primer to a shade that matches the tone of the finish color you've selected. This will reduce the number of top coats needed for good coverage (sometimes to only one), saving both time and the cost of additional paint.

Use a primer to cover patches, unpainted drywall, stains, and any wall area that has been damaged and repaired.

208 From the Top, Down

Save yourself extra work and paint by painting rooms in a logical order. Begin with the ceiling. Cut in with a brush around the perimeter, being sure to cover the entire wall-ceiling joint, and then start rolling. If some paint gets on the walls while you're cutting in or rolling, it won't matter because you'll be painting the walls next.

Allow the ceiling paint to dry, and then carefully cut in at the ceiling, corners, and baseboard. The easiest way to cut in is to begin with a paint-heavy stroke about ½ inch from the joint. Use a second stroke to bring the paint to the joint. Then roll the walls. Most people leave the woodwork until last. Do it earlier, and it's bound to get splattered. Apply tape to the wall before painting the trim so that the leading edge slightly covers the molding. In this way, paint is less likely to seep under the tape and get on ceilings, walls, or floors.

When to Paint Woodwork Some pros prefer to paint woodwork first because the edges of moldings and casings are often extremely narrow, and it is difficult to paint them without getting paint on the adjacent surfaces. In rooms with lots of woodwork, such as crown molding and chair rails, this may be the better approach because it's easier to cut a clean edge on the wall or ceiling surface than on the molding.

1 Use a small brush to cut in around the ceiling edges. This covers areas the roller cannot reach.

2 Roll on paint working from the ceiling edge back. Use an extension handle to save time and effort.

209 Two Paint-Rolling Techniques

Rolling paint on a large surface area, such as a ceiling or wall, can be done in a couple of ways. One is to apply paint in a zigzag M or W pattern. The idea is to apply enough paint on the surface to cover a 3- by 5-foot section before needing to reload the roller. Then fill voids by rolling out the paint you've just applied. Work from top to bottom (photos 1–3).

Maintain a Wet Edge When one section is complete, reload the roller and begin the next, overlapping the just-painted area and maintaining a wet edge. (If the lead edge of your paint job dries, the overlaps will be noticeable, so don't stop until you reach a natural break, such as the corner of the room or, at the very least, one edge of a doorway.) Every 4 or 5 feet, lightly roll sections of wall or ceiling that have been completed. Roll vertically, from top to bottom, without lifting the roller off the surface. Keep the roller rotating in the same direction as you proceed. Overlap the previous smoothing roll by an inch or two. This technique will help keep the "grain" of the applied paint consistent. Avoid re-rolling areas that have become tacky. Doing so causes an "orange peel" effect that may not blend in when the paint dries.

Instead of applying paint in zigzag patterns, you may also paint two vertical parallel strips as shown in the bottom photos. Fill in the gaps by connecting the strips with perpendicular strokes (photos A–C).

1 Pour the paint into the roller pan, and dip the roller in the paint.

2 Apply the paint in a zigzag W pattern.

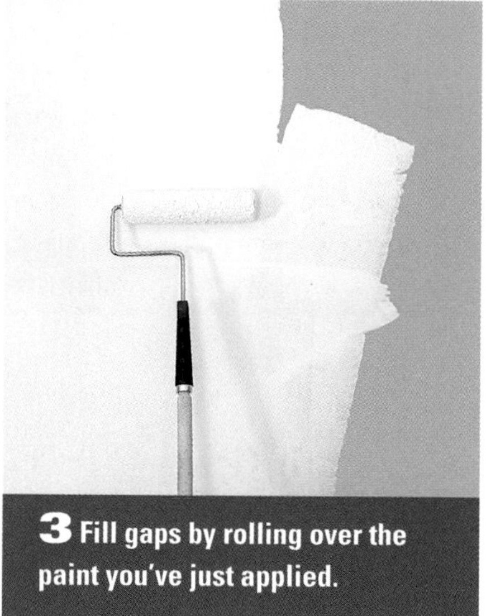

3 Fill gaps by rolling over the paint you've just applied.

A Use an extension pole to make painting walls easier.

B Use horizontal strokes to connect painted areas.

C Apply light pressure as you move the roller across the wall.

210 Putting a Job on Pause

If you need to pause a job for an hour or two when painting with a brush, there's no need to waste time cleaning it. Instead, wrap the brush in plastic wrap, and put it in a cool place, out of the sunlight. The plastic will keep the paint from drying. Close the paint can, and place it out of the sunlight as well. To put a brush job on hold overnight, wrap the brush in plastic and put it in the refrigerator.

To pause a roller job for an hour or two, dip the roller in the paint you're using so it's thoroughly loaded. Lay it in the tray, and cover the tray with plastic wrap. To stop overnight, double-wrap the fully loaded roller in plastic wrap and store it in the refrigerator. Professional painter Ken Ulliano says that the plastic sleeves in which roller covers are packaged make excellent storage wrappers. Tie off the open end and the roller will stay moist for weeks.

211 Prep Shortcut

Removing hardware before you paint windows, doors, walls, and ceilings is the time-honored way to do the job right. If you go this route, put the parts in a plastic bag and label them. This will save time later.

Professional Trick A faster way to get good results is to tape over switch plates, doorknobs, latch plates, and the like instead of removing them. Use a sharp box cutter to slice off excess tape, and then brush, spray, or roll away. Professional painter Davon Hansard says it's important to buy top-of-the-line masking tape and to replace the razor blade frequently to ensure sharp, crisp edges.

Tape over hardware, and use a box cutter or utility knife to cut away the excess. Burnish tape edges to ensure a good seal; paint; and then remove tape.

212 Painting Secrets for Double-Hung Windows

There's a simple trick for getting fast, neat results when painting double-hung windows. First, raise the lower sash and pull down the upper sash before you begin to paint. If the upper sash has been painted shut, run the blade of a utility knife at the joint between sash and track to free it.

Reversing the Sash With the sash in reversed positions, paint as much of the lower half (3 or more inches at least) of what was the upper sash as you can. Then reverse sash positions again, leaving them open a couple of inches at top and bottom. Finish painting the upper sash, and paint all of the lower sash.

Proceed to painting the inside surface of the side and head jambs, starting with the left-side jamb and working clockwise to the right-side jamb. Do not paint the tracks in which the sash slides. If they are unsightly and made of wood, coat them with an opaque stain. This will prevent paint layers from building up and causing the sash to stick. If the tracks are vinyl or aluminum, do not paint them.

On to the Trim Finish by painting the casing (molding around the window) and stool and apron (molding beneath the window). Begin with the outer edge, apron, and stool underside. Then paint the casing face. The trick is to remove all excess paint so there will be none to cause sags and runs. Paint the stool top and front stool edge last.

1 Pull the upper sash down a couple of inches, and paint the top rail and as much of the sides as you can.

2 Push the upper sash down and the lower sash up. Finish painting the parts of the upper sash.

3 Paint the lower sash. Move both sash up and down periodically to keep the paint from sticking.

4 Use a straight-edged razor to remove any paint that gets on the window glass.

213 Pro Tips for Painting Panel Doors

The common error made by many paint-it-yourselfers is to allow drips to form when painting doors. Once hardened, they are difficult to remove and remain an unsightly reminder of your mistakes.

The Correct Painting Sequence Professional painters know that painting in the correct sequence can help reduce or eliminate these blemishes.

Remove or mask the door hardware before you start. Paint the door edges first using a 2-inch sash brush, and then proceed to the recessed panel areas with the same brush. The best sequence to follow is to work left to right, top to bottom. Brush away from, not toward, recessed corners. This will help prevent any paint buildup and drips.

Rails and Stiles Next When all the panels are painted, paint the rails (horizontal members), again working from the top to the bottom. Then move on to the stiles (vertical members), working from the left to the right. Remember to always make your final smoothing brush strokes with the grain of the wood (or the material that's made to simulate wood). This sequence should minimize buildup at the base of recessed panels, but check for drips when you're finished painting, as well as 10 minutes later.

1 Paint the door edges first. To make the job easier, remove or mask the hardware before you begin.

2 Using the same brush, proceed to the panels on the door, working from left to right and top to bottom.

3 Paint the rails next, working from top to bottom. Apply the paint in the direction of the wood grain.

4 Finish by painting the stiles, working from left to right. Check for drips when you're done.

Working Safer

214 Glove Etiquette

It's a good idea to wear rubber-coated or latex vinyl gloves while you're cleaning up, especially with oil-based paints (right). Otherwise, toxic solvents can be absorbed by your skin. Some people like to wear cotton or vinyl gloves at all times while painting, whether they're using oil-based or "safer" water-based paints. Doing so saves time washing hands later. Cotton gloves are the most comfortable; vinyl gloves will cause your hands to sweat in warm weather. If you're stripping paint using heat or a chemical stripper, wear gloves, a shirt with long sleeves, and long pants to protect yourself while you work.

215 Clever Brush Cleaning

The fastest and least wasteful way to clean a paintbrush is to wipe as much paint or finish off it first. A rag works best, but you can also use newspaper. Regardless, this simple step simplifies cleanup immensely.

If you're using latex paint, the next step is to wash the brush in a bucket of warm water. You can add a drop of dishwashing liquid to speed the job. Lastly, rinse the nearly clean brush under the faucet or with a garden hose outside. You may use a brush spinner to force the rinse water from the bristles.

If you're using a solvent-based paint or finish, wipe off as much as you can with a rag, and dip the brush in a bucket containing the appropriate solvent. Then wipe the bristles thoroughly again with a rag. Repeat as necessary. It's wise to wear impermeable rubber or vinyl gloves and to work outside or in a well-ventilated area.

Roller covers are usually not worth cleaning. Extend their use as long as possible between pauses in the job as described in Tip 210, and toss them when the job is complete.

Rinse a brush used with latex paint under running faucet or hose water.

Spinning a brush in a large bucket forces the rinse water from the bristles.

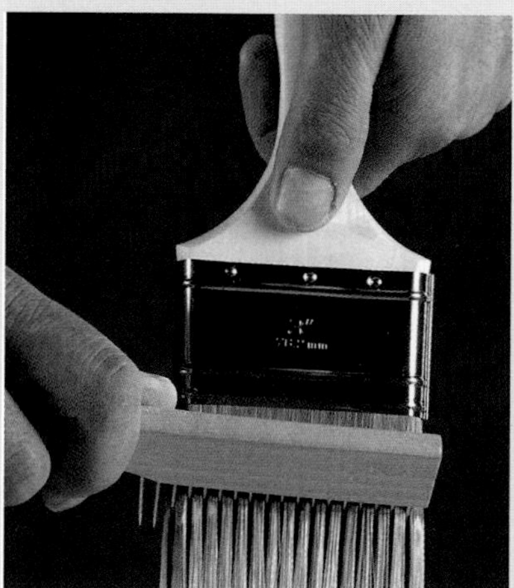

Remove paint from the bristles using a brush comb.

216 Painting Woodwork

Whether you're painting built-in cabinetry, window and door casings, baseboards, windows, or doors, the goal is to achieve as smooth and texture-free a finish as possible. To do this, first apply paint to surfaces across the grain. Then smooth the paint with strokes that run in the same direction as the grain. If you make your finish stroke against the grain, you'll create an unsightly crosshatch effect. Use a light touch with your final stroke for the smoothest results. If you're applying two coats, a light sanding between coats will ensure smoother results.

Keep a rag handy when painting to wipe away any dust you may have missed during prep.

217 Preserving Paintbrushes

Good paintbrushes are expensive, so it makes sense to take an extra couple of steps to maintain them. After cleaning the brush, comb the bristles with a clean brush comb. Comb from the ferrule toward the tips of the bristles. The idea is to return the bristles to their original form—straight and parallel with one another. Some painters wrap the bristles in the original wrapper or newspaper, secured at the ferrule by a rubber band, to help the bristles retain their shape as they dry. Wrapped or not, store brushes by hanging them from the handle.

Wrap the brush bristles in the original wrapper or newspaper so the bristles retain their shape.

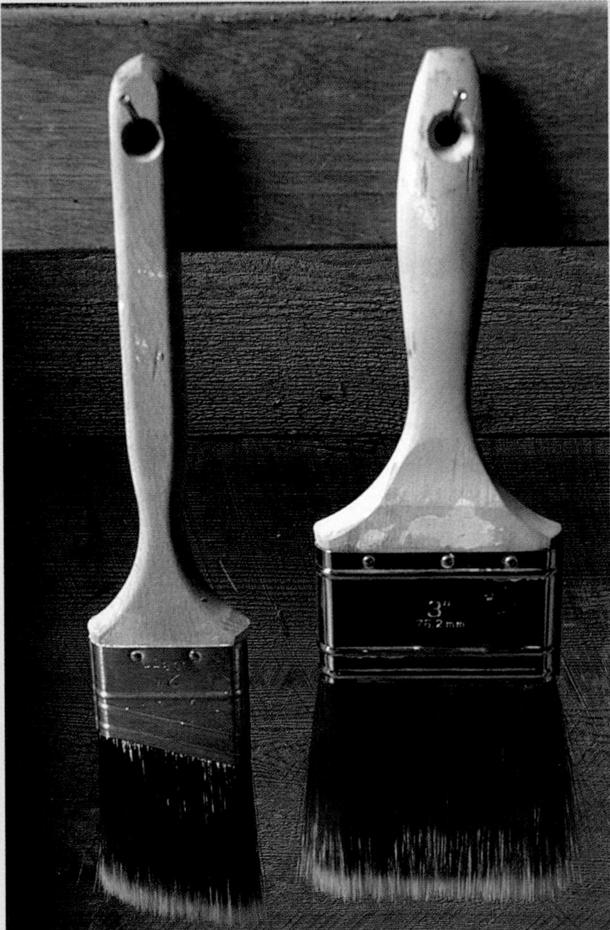

To preserve bristles, it's best to store brushes by hanging them from their handles.

218 A Wiser Way to Choose Exterior Colors

Choosing exterior colors for siding, trim, and doors can be complicated. Be sure to view color chips in natural light, even if you have to step out of the paint store to do it. You will also have to factor in things you can't or won't change, such as the roof color, nearby plantings, masonry work, and the color of your neighbors' houses. Many paint stores and some paint manufacturer Web sites offer hundreds of color combinations to get you started. Once you've narrowed down your preferences, several manufacturers' Web sites offer ways to "prepaint" an image of your house. You simply download an image of the room or house exterior you're painting and apply your color choices until you're satisfied with the combination.

Useful Guidelines When it comes to choosing colors for exterior architectural elements, the possibilities are limitless, but here are some guidelines to consider. Select a trim color that contrasts with the main color; it's common to paint the trim a color that is lighter than the body of the house. You can provide a striking effect by adding an accent color at the front entrance. (A white house with a bright red door is a good example.) Casings around windows and doors should all be the same color, or the house will seem too busy. Porch ceilings are often painted a light color to keep a sense of airiness, while porch floors are usually painted a dark color so that they won't show dirt and tracks as readily as a light-colored floor would.

219 The Stain Alternative

Stain is a smart alternative to paint for wood-sided houses, fences, and decks. Translucent stains allow the wood grain to show and provide a handsome, natural-looking finish. Opaque stains look more like paint, but they're easier and faster to apply. In addition, stains don't peel, so it's much easier to prep a stained surface when it's time to recoat it than it is to prep a painted surface. The only downside to stains is that they don't wear as long as paint—assuming other problems don't cause the paint to peel prematurely.

Opaque stains go on easier than paint and require less prep work when it's time to restain.

Stains come in latex and oil-based formulas. This translucent stain allows the wood grain to show through.

Opaque stains do a better job of protecting wood against damage from the sun's ultraviolet rays.

220 Painting Rules of Thumb

If your preparation has uncovered bare wood, you must prime it before proceeding with the top coats. (You do not need to prime over sound, well-adhered old paint.) Then begin applying the finish coat from the top down. There are two reasons for this. The first is the standing construction trade rule about doing the hard work first. Paint from ladders and scaffolds when concentration is best and before fatigue begins to set in. Second, paint drips down, so you can remove drips as you proceed with the job. Personal preferences may cause you to bend the rules. In the summer, for example, you may want to stay out of the sun.

When working across the face of a wall, work from left to right if you're right-handed and from right to left if you're left-handed. Apply paint up to natural break points. For example, finish off a whole gable before moving on to a new area. Plan your workday so you make it to a break point before quitting time.

With bare wood, begin with primer. Brush primer in the direction of the wood grain for best results.

221 Finishing Decks

Every wood deck needs protection, especially if it has a sunny exposure. To protect your investment, it's wise to apply paint, stain, or a clear protective coating every couple of years. High-quality wood decks are usually not painted. The wood used on these surfaces, such as redwood or an imported hardwood, is too beautiful to cover with paint. Use a stain or a clear protective finish. Pressure-treated wood, however, can be painted. Nothing in the treatment prevents paint from binding with the wood; however, the manufacturing and treatment process depends on water, and often the treated wood has a high moisture content when you purchase it. You should allow it to dry. For good measure, clean it with a diluted soap and water solution using a soft brush, and allow it to dry thoroughly. Once stained or painted, keep the surface swept to prevent dirt and traffic from grinding away the finish.

Saving Money

222 Epoxy for Wood

While prepping for an exterior paint job, it's common to discover pockets of rotted wood. It is especially common on windowsills and moldings. Replacing the damaged boards is often an expensive and time-consuming job. Often, however, the damage can be repaired. Many patching products are available, but for a long-lasting job, choose a two-part epoxy. Even severely damaged wood can be repaired this way. First, remove any very loose material. Material that is damaged but still attached can remain. Then pour a thin liquid that comes with the epoxy onto the rot-softened area to harden it. Lastly, you mix the patching material from two supplied components and apply it to the void using a disposable putty knife. You can sand, drill, and work epoxy patches with power tools. Then prime and paint as you would with wood.

Working Safer

223 Ladder Laws

The distance between the base of the ladder and the structure should be one-quarter the distance from where the ladder contacts the ground to where the ladder rests against the structure. For example, if the ladder spans 16 feet, it should be about 4 feet away from the wall. Always rest ladders on level surfaces. Slight irregularities can be accommodated by placing one or two ¾ x 3 x 3-foot pieces of plywood under the ladder leg that needs support. For sloped surfaces or stairs, consider a ladder leveler. It consists of two legs that you can set to different heights and allows you to have a stable ladder on a sloped surface. Avoid the use of rocks and odd pieces of scrap lumber to prop up a ladder leg. It's unsafe.

More Safety Other safety tips include not reaching too far to paint while on the ladder, not using a ladder on a very windy day, not climbing the ladder when tired, not working when it's dark, inspecting the ladder before using (especially if it hasn't been used in a while), keeping both feet on the ladder at all times, not wearing anything (such as a big belt buckle) that may get caught on the rungs, and not leaving a ladder unattended—and available to inquisitive children!

224 Making Ladders Better

Ladders are a necessity for most paint jobs. For a modest investment, you can improve the effectiveness of the one you own with a ladder standoff, which is a U-shaped bracket that attaches to the top of a ladder. Rather than have the side rails of the ladder in contact with the building, the stand-off is in contact. This allows you to set the ladder in the middle of a window so you can reach the entire window frame. No more reaching to the side to paint the middle of the window.

Scaffold Brackets To speed your job along even more, rent a pair of scaffold brackets, or ladder jacks, and a second ladder. Scaffold brackets hook on the ladders and can be used to support 2×10 wooden planks or an aluminum platform. There are two kinds of ladder jacks: inside-bracket and outside-bracket types. Inside ladder jacks suspend a plank or working platform beneath the ladders. Outside ladder jacks support a plank on the front face of ladders.

The entire window frame is within easy reach when you use a U-shaped ladder standoff.

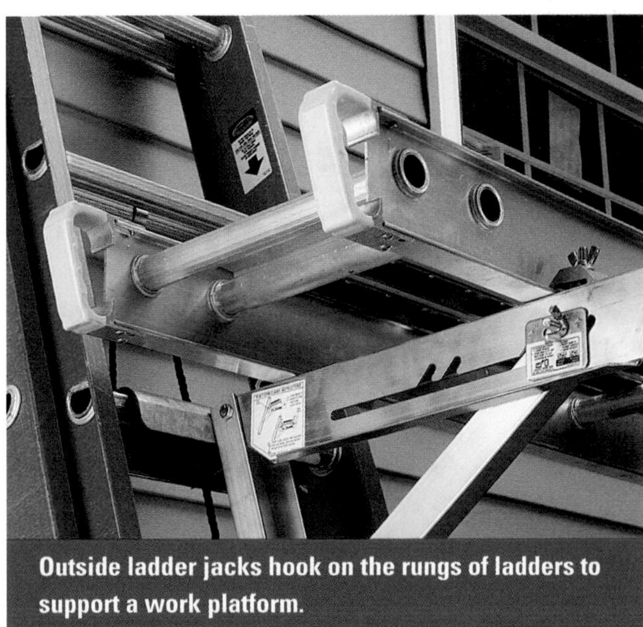

Outside ladder jacks hook on the rungs of ladders to support a work platform.

This man is standing on a stable, level platform that is supported by scaffolding you can rent.

9 Trim, Roofing, and Siding

- INSTALLING EXTERIOR TRIM • BETTER ROOFING AND SIDING METHODS
- STOPPING MOISTURE AND AIR INFILTRATION

225 Getting Rake Trim Right

The rake trim, or rake board, that follows the roof line on a typical gable roof is designed to protect the top of the siding boards and the end of the roof sheathing from exposure to the elements. There are several ways to do this besides the one that's shown here.

Rake Trim Options One of the most common ways is to construct an overhang, or soffit, on the rake (Tip 227) similar to one that's often installed on the eave sides of the roof. But building rake overhangs costs money and takes time, so they are often left off newer houses. As the illustration shows, when the house is being framed, the roof sheathing extends over the top of the wall sheathing, and then a furring strip is nailed to the gable end to cover the roof sheathing and to hold out the rake trim. Then the siding is installed so it fits below the furring, and the rake trim is nailed to the furring and the siding. Once the trim is in place, a drip edge is installed over the top of the board and the roofing shingles are nailed in place.

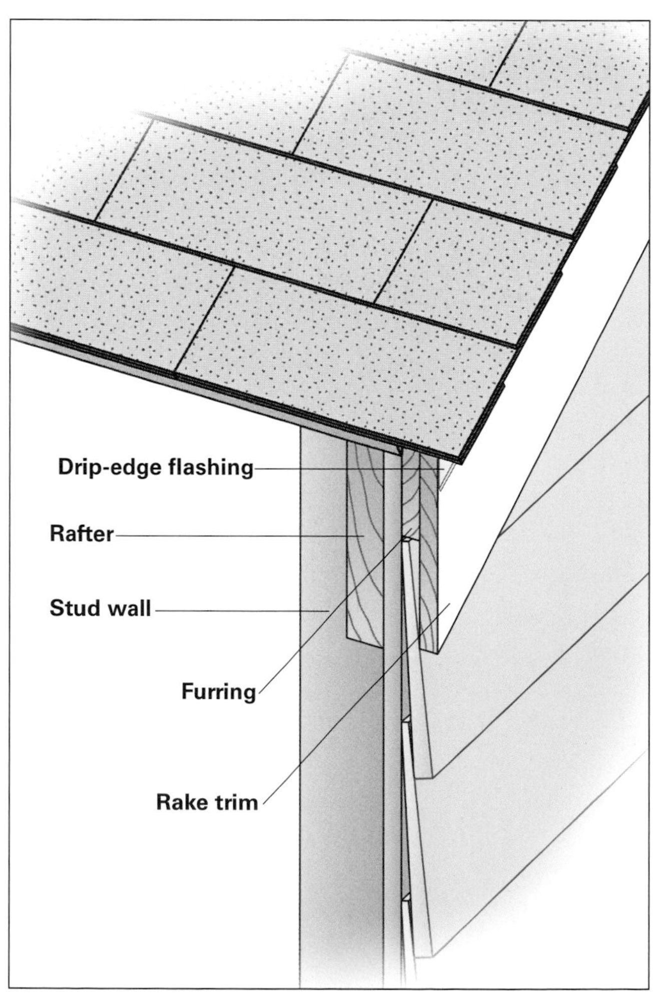

Saving Money

226 Plastic Trim Materials

It's not for the purist, but high-density plastic trim is a good alternative to wood when installing exterior trim. These moldings and boards are usually made of polyurethane. They are manufactured in most of the same nominal sizes as standard pine and cedar trim and are available in many decorative profiles. Installed costs are less than for wood, but the real savings come later with many years of low-maintenance, rot-free service.

227 Overhanging the Rake

Gable overhangs, or soffits, are usually installed at the same time that the roof is being constructed. They can be built in place or as a finished unit on the ground that's lifted up and attached to the gable. The latter approach is faster, but it increases the chance of making measuring and cutting mistakes. As the illustration below shows, the soffit is attached to two nailers; a trim board is nailed to the outside; and this assembly is joined to the top of the gable wall. At this point, the roof sheathing is usually installed, so the panels form an unbroken cantilever over the top of the overhang. When the roof sheathing is nailed to the trim board, it supports the weight of the whole assembly. The end of the sheathing is covered by a small trim board that is, in turn, covered by a drip edge when the roofing is installed.

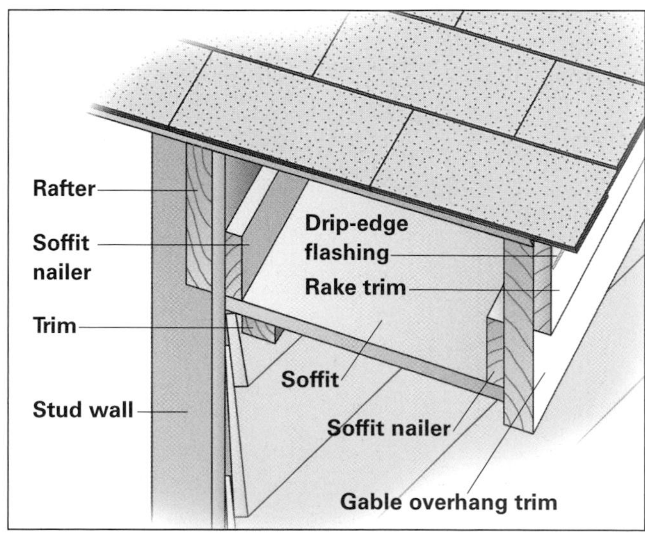

228 Picking the Right Corner-Board Detail

Whenever you install new siding on a house or addition, you must decide what the exterior trim is going to look like. Around windows and doors, this is largely an issue of how wide you want it to be. If you don't know, just take a drive around town and pick a size you like on a neighbor's house, and then duplicate that on yours. The width of corner boards also has to be determined, but here appearance isn't the only issue. You also need to decide how the boards are going to be installed. Three options are shown below. For an inside corner, you can install two wide boards (3 to 4 inches) that form an L shape where the walls meet, and then butt the siding boards against these boards. Or you can choose a square board, like the one shown here, to fill the corner. It's usually about 1 inch wide on a side, and it presents a more tailored look. Outside corners, on the other hand, can be constructed with the corner boards covering the end of the siding boards, as shown in the middle illustration. Or they can be attached so that the siding boards butt against them. Both arrangements work well as long as the joints between all the boards are sealed with a high-quality exterior caulk.

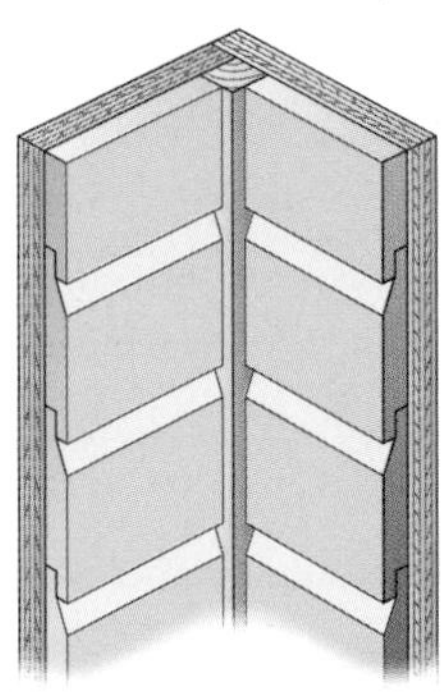

Butted Inside Corner

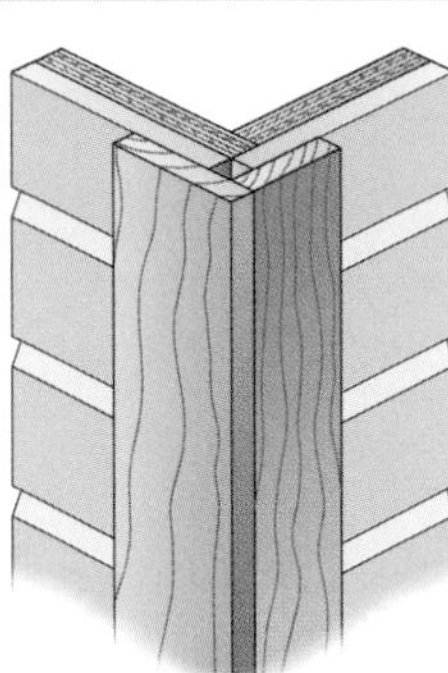

Applied Outside Corner

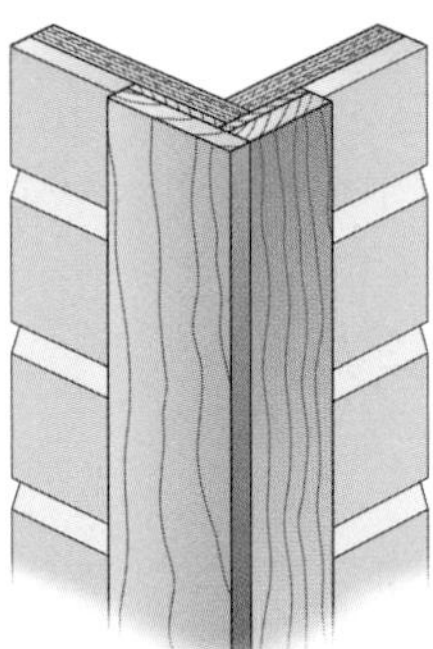

Butted Outside Corner

229 Choosing the Correct Caulk

It seems like a modest product, but caulk plays an important role in all sorts of exterior jobs. From reducing air infiltration around windows to blocking water penetration along corner boards and water tables, this simple, easy-to-apply substance is one of a remodeler's best friends. The number of different caulks at the home center, however, can be daunting. Your best choices are as follows:

Acrylic Latex Inexpensive and easy to apply, latex degrades in sunlight and adheres poorly to porous surfaces. (Siliconized versions work better, last longer.)

• **Drying skin:** ½ hour • **Curing:** 1 week • **Life:** 5-10 years

Butyl This caulk has better adhesion and stretching ability than acrylic, but it costs more and takes longer to cure. It also degrades in sunlight.

• **Drying skin:** 24 hours • **Curing:** 6 months • **Life:** 5-10 years

Polyurethane Expensive and more difficult to apply than latex and butyl, this caulk lasts longer, can cover a wider gap (up to ¾ inch), and stretches farther.

• **Drying skin:** 24 hours • **Curing:** 1 month • **Life:** 20+ years

Silicone Although silicone has good stretching ability and can cover a 1-inch gap, it can't be painted and adheres poorly to plastic and wood.

• **Drying skin:** 1 hour • **Curing:** 1 week • **Life:** 20+ years

Acrylic latex caulk applies easily.

Butyl is also called butyl rubber.

Greener Ways

230 Picking the Right Wood

Real wood siding is a renewable, eco-friendly product, unless it is being overharvested. When purchasing siding, check for certification by the Forest Stewardship Council or the Sustainable Forestry Initiative. Also consider wood alternatives. Products made from recycled wood fiber are often more stable than natural wood. They also tend to hold paint better and cost less. Fiber-cement siding is another option. It looks like wood but is made of cement, sand, wood fiber, and clay. Be skeptical if someone suggests that polyvinyl chloride (PVC) siding is a green building material. It's not. In fact, during its life cycle, from manufacture to disposal, it's extremely toxic and difficult to recycle.

231 Providing Edge Protection

After the roof sheathing is in place, there's usually a rush to get the roofing felt installed so that the building has some protection from the rain. The best way to do this is to roll out the felt and staple it to the sheathing, overlapping it at least 4 inches at all seams. Then cut it flush with the edge of the sheathing, and immediately nail the drip caps along the rake edges of the roof. This will help keep the wind from getting under the felt and tearing it off. Normally, you can keep the felt in place with the drip cap for a couple of weeks before you install the actual roofing.

Install felt and drip edges as soon as the sheathing is on.

232 How to Save Time: Premade Decorative Parts

Some of the most attractive ornamental features that make a house stand out can take a tremendous amount of time to build, even if you have all the necessary equipment. For this reason, most of these elements, such as porch columns, window shutters, and roof cupolas, are premade in factories and shipped directly to your house or local home center. Others offer kits, such as the cupola shown here, which need some assembly on site. The kit approach is especially attractive because you can save some money on construction and transportation while making the job easier: the smaller components are lighter to carry up on the roof.

Cupolas in kit form are available at many home centers and lumberyards.

A cupola can be used to ventilate a building, or it can be installed as a purely decorative element.

233 Sealing with Water Tables

A water table is an exterior trim component that consists of wide horizontal boards installed at the bottom of the framed walls. The first course of siding on each wall rests on top of the water table. Typically 8 or 10 inches wide, these boards have several purposes. First, they cover the joint between the foundation and the framed house wall, which stops air infiltration and discourages insects from entering your house. Second, from a design perspective, the strong horizontal statement they make clearly defines the bottom edge of the walls. Third, they are less likely than shingles to be damaged when struck by a wheelbarrow. Lastly, when topped with a drip cap, these boards direct water that's coming down the side of the house away from the foundation below.

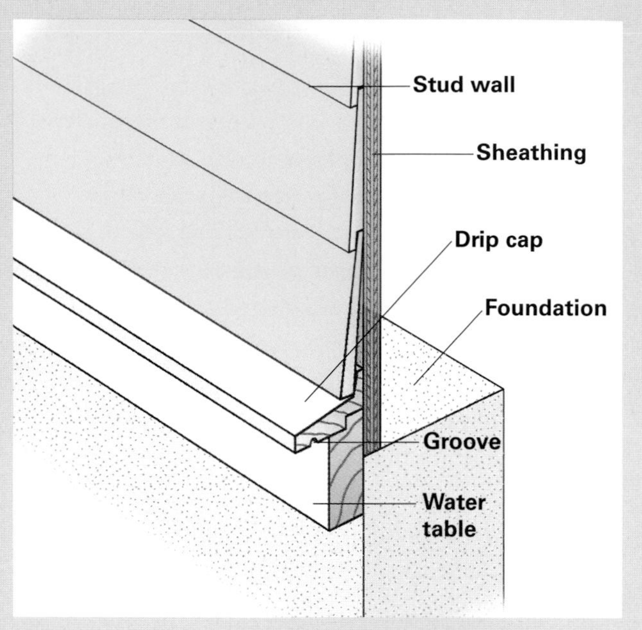

234 Cutting Asphalt Shingles

Cutting asphalt shingles before they're installed is mostly a matter of common sense. Mark the shingle length you need on the backside; lay the shingle face down on a piece of scrap plywood; and score to a depth that's just shy of the granule coating. Then give the shingle a backward bend so that it snaps on the score line. Carry a sharpening stone to sharpen your knife blade to reduce blade changes.

Cutting asphalt shingles once they're installed is a bit more difficult. Use hooked roofing blades instead of the straight variety. They're good for cutting shingle overhangs along rakes and valleys. Because the cutting edge wraps the thickness of the shingle, there is less chance of accidentally damaging the flashing or roofing paper below.

Use shears or a hooked utility knife blade (shown) when trimming shingles along a rake or along the run of a roof valley. Use a piece of metal flashing as a cutting surface.

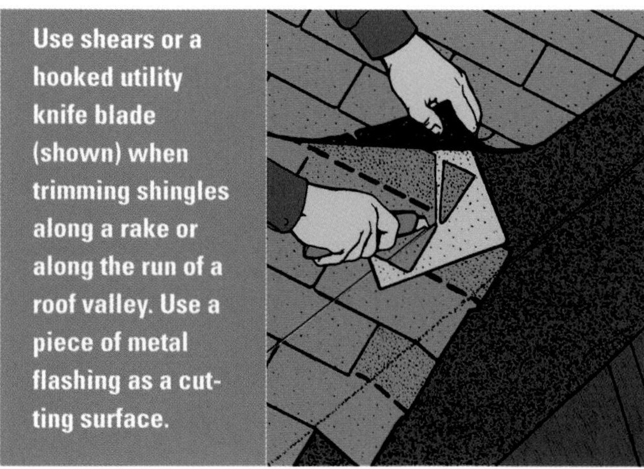

235 Air Power for Roofing

Three-tab fiberglass/asphalt shingles are among the most common roofing products used on homes today. They are inexpensive, long-lasting, and easy to install. That is, the individual shingle is easy to install, but after you nail a few hundred of them in place, you'll be interested in anything that makes the job go faster.

Air Speed One of the best ways to speed things up is by using a roofing air nailer. A roofing nailer works in the same way that other pneumatic nail guns work. The nails come in clips that you load directly into the gun. When you press the tip of the tool against a shingle and pull the trigger, an air-activated plunger drives the nail. A rubber hose that is attached to a compressor supplies the air. In the hands of a professional roofer, these tools can nail an entire shingle in less time than it takes to drive one nail by hand. For nonprofessionals, the speed is almost as fast. It only takes an hour or two to feel comfortable with the tool, and then the speed increases very quickly. If you adjust the air pressure at the compressor and the nailer properly, the gun will drive the nails perfectly. The gun, hose, and compressor are standard rental items.

236 Preserving Your Roof by Improving Attic Ventilation

Roofing products such as asphalt, fiberglass asphalt, and some architectural shingles start to wear out after a couple of decades. Unfortunately, many don't make it that far because of poor attic ventilation. If there's inadequate air movement through the attic, summertime temperatures can make the space so hot that the roof shingles are damaged from below. To improve airflow, the best ventilation designs feature continuous vents along the roof ridge and the soffits along the eaves. If you are having a new roof installed, the contractor will probably put in a continuous ridge vent without you saying a word. Retrofitting an existing roof with continuous soffit vents is much more time consuming, and for this reason is often "forgotten." Easy-to-install alternatives are the rectangular and plug vents shown here. You just locate the center point between the rafters (or trusses); drill or cut a hole in the soffit; and push (plug) or screw (rectangular) the vent into place.

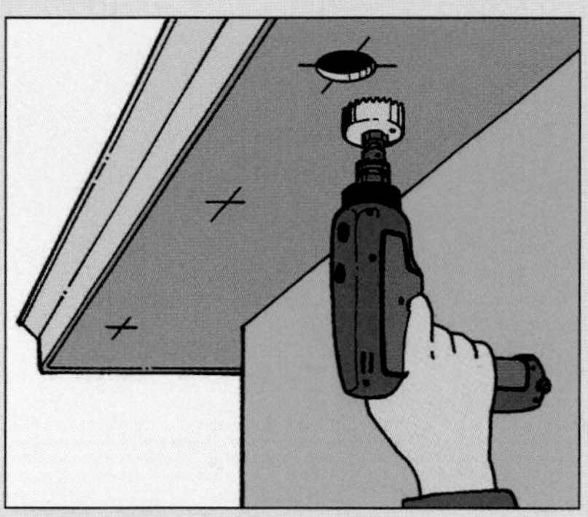

Cut a hole in the underside of the soffit using a drill and hole saw.

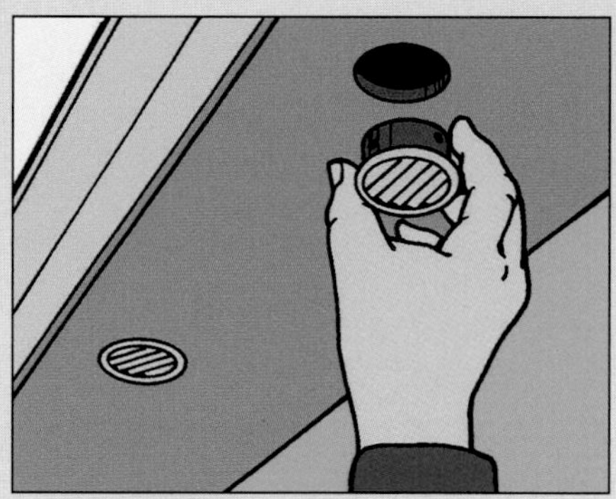

Then push the plug vent into the hole until its lip hits the soffit panel.

Installing a rectangular soffit vent is another option.

Working Safer

237 Easier Shingle Transport

Typical three-tab roofing shingles weigh about 200 pounds per square, and each square contains three bundles of shingles. This means each bundle weighs about 70 pounds. If you have a fairly typical 1,200-square-foot roof, it will take 12 squares of shingles (at 100 square feet of coverage per square) to do the job. This means you'll have to carry more than a ton of shingles up an extension ladder. Fortunately, you do have some options. One is to have the shingles delivered by a conveyor truck. This vehicle backs up to the building and extends an electric-powered conveyor up onto your roof. Then the driver loads the shingles, one bundle at a time, onto the bottom of the belt, and it carries them up to the roof. These trucks aren't available everywhere, and sometimes they can't get close enough to the house. In these circumstances, the best choice is to rent a "ladderveyor" machine. This tool is basically an extension ladder with an electric-powered sliding platform that moves up and down. One person on the ground loads a bundle onto the platform, and another person on the roof takes it off.

A ladderveyor works on standard 120-V household current.

238 Simplifying the Soffit

Soffit trim is some of the most complicated carpentry that occurs on the exterior of most houses. These overhangs are designed to do several things. First, they are supposed to direct rainwater from the roof away from the house, at least if the wind isn't blowing. Second, they provide a place for installing vents that will greatly improve the ventilation throughout the attic space and prolong the life of the roof sheathing and the roofing itself. And third, they create an attractive shadow line along the eaves that makes the roof look bigger and more substantial.

Installation Like the overhang trim that was discussed in Tips 225 and 227, soffit trim is usually installed when the roof is being constructed. A soffit nailer is attached to the end of the rafter and a ledger is attached to the house wall. Short lookout blocks are nailed to the side of the rafters and between the ledgers and soffit nailers. Then vents are installed in the soffit panels, and these panels are nailed to the underside of the nailers and lookouts. Next, a fascia and trim cover the front of the soffit and a trim board hides the area where the soffit and siding meet.

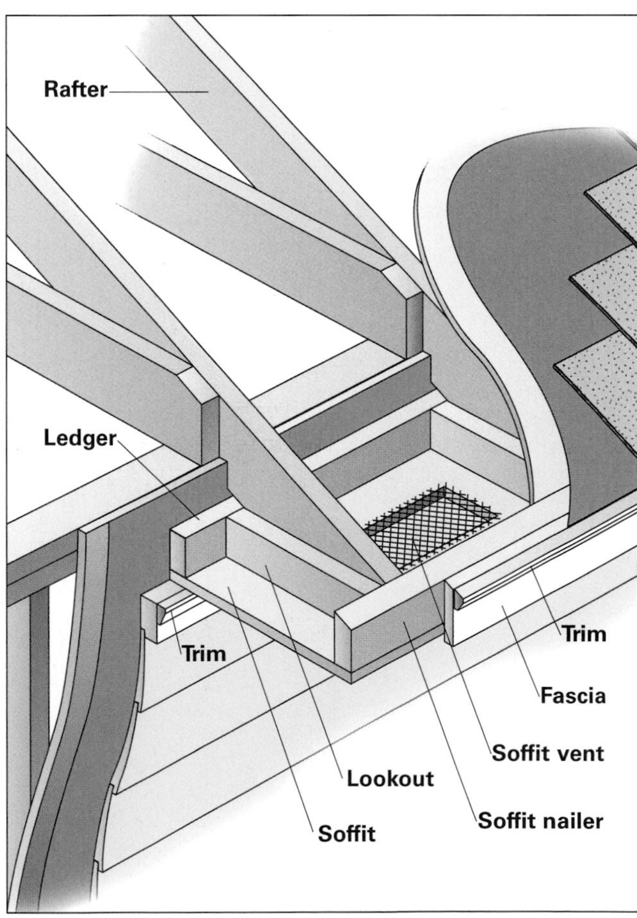

239 Proper Porch Roofs

Many porch roofs are built with a shallower pitch than the main house roof. This means that water doesn't run off as quickly. And when water lingers, it can cause trouble. If these roofs were installed on a backyard storage shed, their shallow pitch wouldn't make any difference. But they are almost always installed against the side of a house wall, and if they are not built—and flashed—properly, the joint between the house and the porch may leak and cause a lot of damage. This illustration below shows how to install the roofing and flashing so water can't penetrate the house. If you are building a new porch, remodeling an old one, or installing new siding on your house, make sure to follow these construction details.

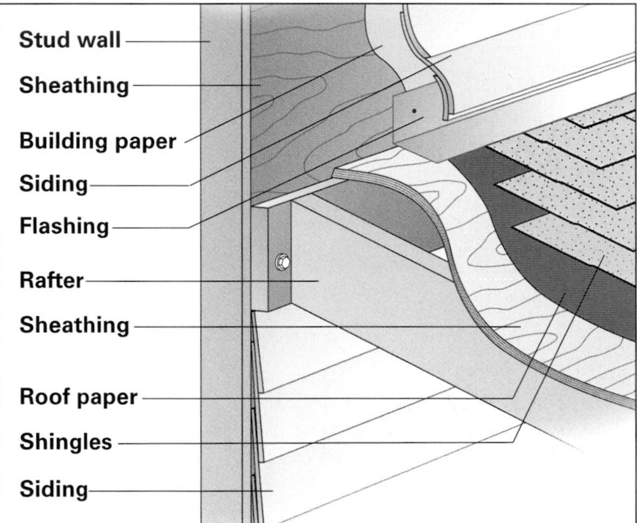

Greener Ways

240 Eco-Friendlier Roofing

Ideally, a roof needs to meet a variety of criteria: it should be long-lasting to minimize demolition waste, made of recyclable materials, and lightweight enough not to need extra structural support or extra fuel for transportation (or be locally produced), and it must not leach toxic materials that could contaminate collected rainwater. Roofing materials that meet most or all of these criteria include metal, clay and fiber-cement composite tiles, slate, and "green," or vegetated, roofs.

Saving Money

241 Low-Cost House Dressing

Installing a frieze board, with a dentil molding along the top edge, is a great way to dress up a house without spending a lot of money. When it's applied in the course of installing new siding, it only takes a couple of hours and is worth every minute of that time.

What Is It? The illustration at right shows that a frieze is nothing more than a wide horizontal board that's installed over the top of the last siding board and under the edge of the roofing. It's nailed in place, and then dentil molding is added along the top edge. You will have a choice of different dentil designs, but all of them are applied the same way.

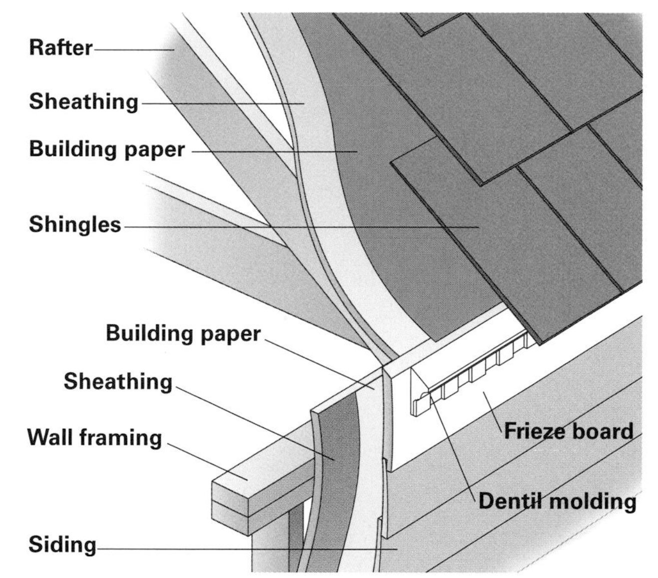

242 Reducing Wind Damage

The typical roof has two areas that are more vulnerable to wind damage than the rest of the roof: the areas along the rakes and eaves. Strong winds can catch and bend these shingles up. If the wind is strong enough, it can tear the shingles off. For this reason, it's a good idea to glue down each rake shingle with a dab of plastic roof cement. You can buy this material in a standard cartridge and apply it with a caulk gun. This approach will fortify the rakes. And though you can do the same along the eaves, two approaches supply more protection. One is to cut the tabs off standard roofing shingles and nail the resulting tab-free shingle along the eave edge of the roof, as shown here. Make sure to put the asphalt seal strip facing up, and be sure that the strips are just shy of the roof edge. This provides sticking area for the first full course of shingles.

Starter Strips Another approach is to use a self-sticking membrane for a starter strip. These strips are designed to seal the eave edge of the roof and reduce the chance of leaks caused by ice dams in the winter. If you live in a cold climate, a membrane is a good substitute for inverted shingles.

Cut the tabs off the first course of shingles; invert the tab-free strips; and position them along the roof edge.

243 Tear Off or Reroof?

The first step when reroofing a house is to check to see how many roofing layers there are. Once you determine the number of layers, check local roofing codes for the maximum number of roofing layers allowed—the figure will be different depending on the type of roofing and pitch of the roof. For asphalt shingles, codes usually allow the original plus two layers of reroofing.

Attic Inspection All rotten boards under the old roofing must be replaced. Go to the attic and examine any suspicious spots, including voids and separating plywood. Check for rot by poking with a screwdriver or awl. If rot is limited to a few places, you need only remove the old roofing and replace the boards in those spots. Where necessary, build up the roof above the replacement sheathing with extra layers of shingles to make a flush surface for the new roof.

If your roof has curled, brittle shingles like this, it's time to replace it.

244 Guarding against Ice Dams

Ice dams form as snow on the roof melts and then refreezes along the eaves. Even in houses with insulation in the ceilings, enough heat can rise through the blankets or bats to gradually warm the bottom of the roof over the attic. Under the right conditions, the heat causes the snow blanket to melt from the bottom up, and water trickles down toward the gutter. It may be cold outside, but the trickle is protected from freezing by the snow above. When the melted water reaches the roof overhang, there is no longer a heat source from below because the overhang is outside the exterior wall. That's where the water begins to freeze. It forms a dam, and the water above can back up under the shingles.

Here are four ways to keep ice from forming:

- Draw enough outside air through the attic so that heat rising through the insulation in the ceiling will be diluted before it can warm the roof and melt snow. (Venting also helps in the summer, Tip 236.)
- Push back ceiling insulation near the exterior wall so that it does not block soffit vents.
- Keep gutters and leaders clear of debris and free-draining so that any melting water won't be trapped.
- Install a rubberized barrier under the shingles on the overhang. This self-sealing membrane closes around nail shanks and protects the overhang from water that may back up and seep under the shingles.

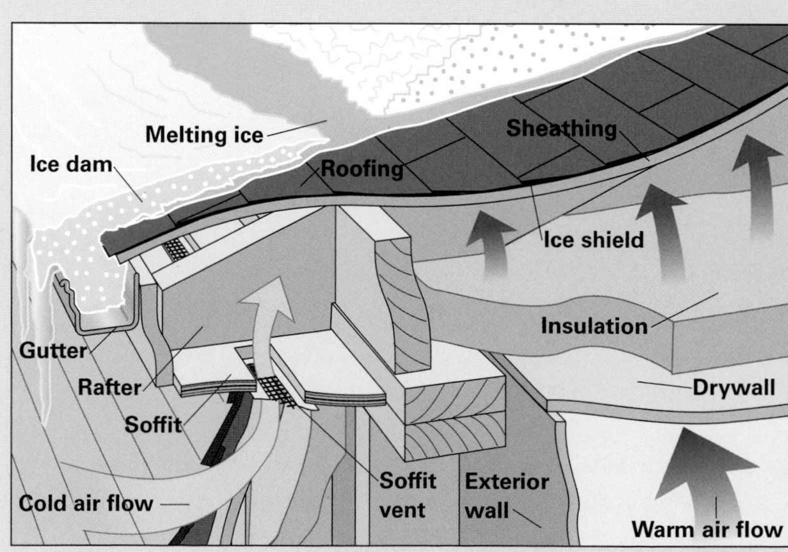

To install an ice shield, peel the paper backing off as you roll the shield in place.

Greener Ways

245 Stopping Air Infiltation

No matter how careful you are when you build a new home or frame an addition, there will always be small gaps here and there. None of this will impact the strength of the structure in the least. But the gaps can provide easier pathways for air infiltration and, as a result, reduce the overall energy efficiency of the building. The best way to close these gaps is to install house wrap over the sheathing on all the walls before siding. You simply staple the wrap in place around the perimeter walls. Then cut the window and door openings, and nail the wrap to the inside of the jack studs. You should seal tears or bad cuts with tape. When you install this wrap with a plastic vapor barrier on the inside of the wall, very little (if any) air can move through the walls. No air movement means less heat movement—and usually lower energy bills.

Staple house wrap to walls, beginning at the bottom. Then cut the wrap at wall openings.

246 Unexpected Remodeling Problems: Repair or Replace?

Remodeling jobs always bring a lot of decisions to the forefront, especially ones that you may not have considered. A typical example is when you are repairing or painting the siding on your house and you discover a partially rotted windowsill or a leak around the exterior window trim that is causing damage inside the wall. You may have to replace the window, even though the cost for doing this is not in your budget. But you should also consider making a repair. This probably won't last as long as a new window, but it can work for several years, at which time you may be able to afford the replacement. These triage decisions help you stretch your remodeling dollar without hurting your house. As the illustrations below show, temporary repairs can be pretty simple, so they don't have to interrupt the work flow or break the budget.

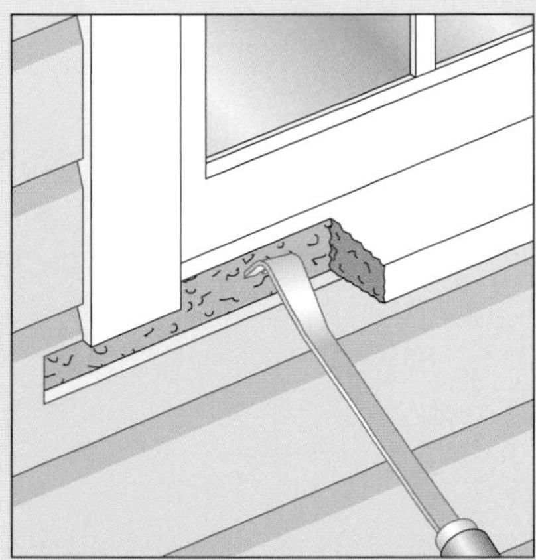

1 Remove the damaged wood. Use a pry bar or an old chisel to remove the loose material.

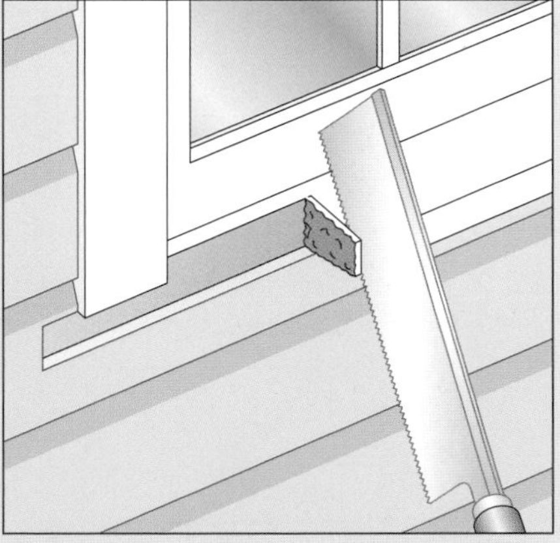

2 Square off the area to be replaced using a backsaw. Use a chisel to reach recessed portions you can't saw.

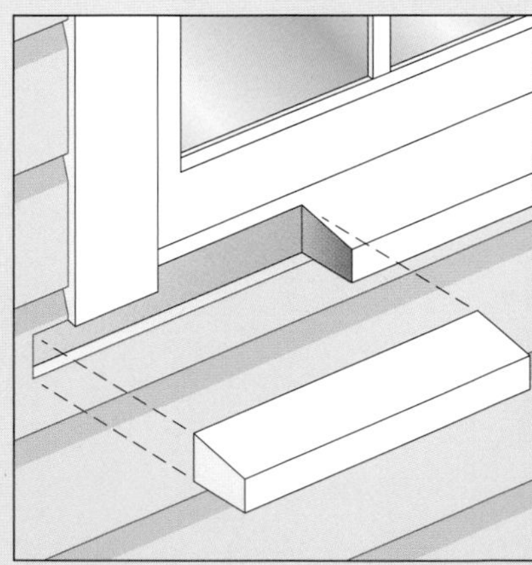

3 Cut a new section, and install it using exterior epoxy glue. Then sand, caulk, and paint.

247 Clapboard Secret: Priming

Wood clapboards are widely considered to be a first-class siding material. When properly installed and maintained, they can last indefinitely, often improving in appearance as they age. Also known as "beveled" or "lap" siding, the individual boards are cut in a tapered profile and are installed so that each row overlaps the one below by about an inch. This siding is commonly available in pine and spruce for paint finishes and in cedar and redwood for natural or stained finishes.

Proper Installation Of course, these features come at a substantial cost, as both the material and installation costs are relatively high when compared with other products. That's one reason why proper prep work and installation are key. Keep in mind that the most important installation chore is to prime every surface of every board. On painted jobs, this means you should apply a high-quality primer to the front and back faces, top and bottom edges, and both ends. For stained or clear finishes, you should coat the same six sides with sealer or wood preservative.

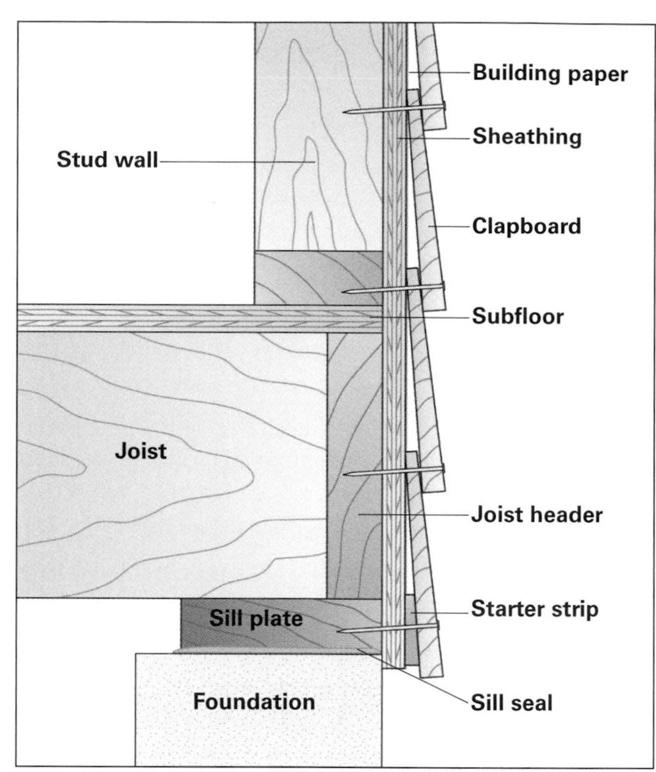

248 Solving Common Cedar-Clapboard Problems

All common wood clapboards are pretty thin and tend to split when they are nailed in place. Sawing them can often cause an unsightly splintery edge, and if you don't use the right fasteners, your new siding will be blackened by staining. Here's how to solve all three problems:

When nailing, a small split here and there isn't a cause for concern, but you never know whether a split is going to be small or large until it happens. It's much better to be safe than sorry. Drill a pilot hole for every nail you drive, and you will rarely split a board.

Before sawing a cedar board, score the cut line with a utility knife. A power miter saw makes fast crosscuts; use a saber saw for notching or making short rip cuts.

Use aluminum or stainless-steel fasteners for cedar siding because tannins in the wood react with iron and cause black stains. Even galvanized fasteners will eventually form a dark ring around each nail.

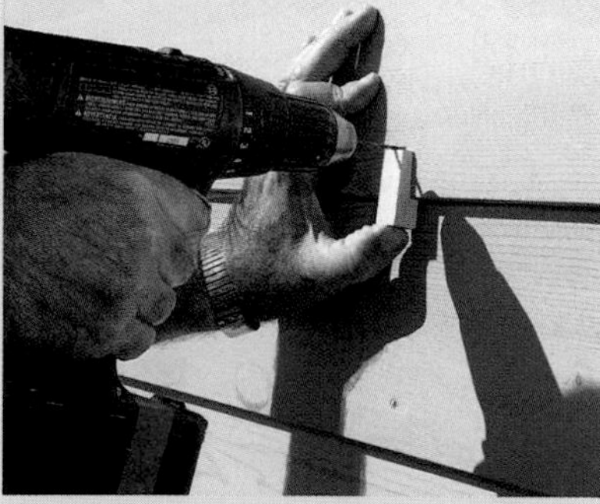

A nailing gauge makes drilling pilot holes easier. Drive nails so that the head just touches the board's surface.

Score cut lines using a utility knife. A saber saw is useful for notching and for making short rip cuts.

Use aluminum or stainless-steel fasteners when putting up cedar siding to prevent staining.

249 Spacing Jig for Speedy Siding

You can speed up the installation of clapboard or shakes and increase the overall accuracy of the project at the same time by relying on a simple siding jig that you can build yourself. (Jigs save time on clapboards, shakes, and any siding installed in horizontal courses.) The idea is to create a movable measuring tool that duplicates the overlap on each course. Every few rows you should still measure back to the base course, and check the current course for level. But you won't have to stop work and check each piece if you use a jig.

Building the Jig To construct the jig, screw a small cleat to a rectangular piece of wood in a square T-shape. (1×4s work well.) Use a square to check alignment, and then clamp the pieces and screw them together. Be sure to use screws that won't protrude through both pieces and scratch the siding underneath. To use the jig, slide the cleat section along the bottom edge of the last piece of siding you installed, and make a pencil mark, or simply set the next course in position on top of the jig. The long riser of the upside-down T will gauge the amount of exposure on the next piece and keep your clapboard installation uniform.

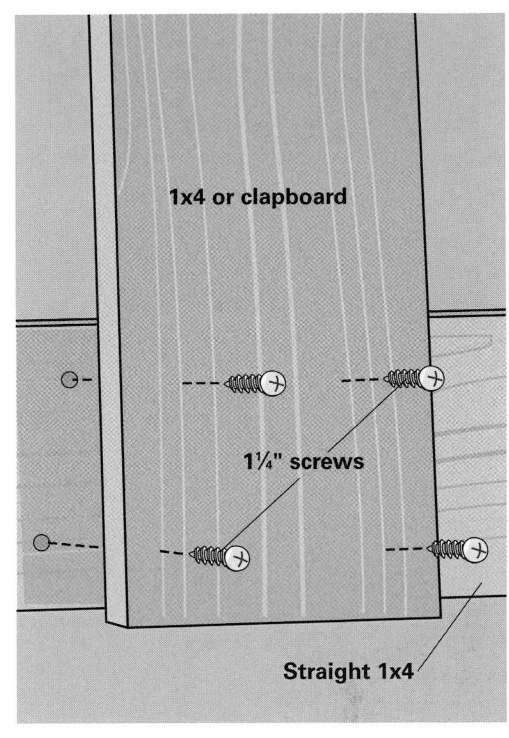

250 Panel-Siding Advantages

Because labor accounts for so much of the final bill in a re-siding job, plywood panels can be an attractive, cost-saving alternative. Typically, just two workers can panel an average-size house in about a weekend, and the skill needed is within the range of many DIYers. Also, panels are often available in 4×9- and 4×10-foot sheets that reach from foundation to roof edge.

Many lumberyards carry one of the most popular plywood panels, called Texture 1-11. These sheets have grooves cut into the face 4, 8, or 12 inches apart to simulate separate planks. But many other styles and surface treatments are available. Not all plywood can be used for siding, however: only sheets rated for exterior use, assembled with special adhesive that can withstand the exposure, may be used in such applications.

While the panel surface will be coated with stain or paint for appearance and protection against the weather, panel edges often are not coated. They are the weak links because layers of thin plywood laminations are exposed along the edges. If they soak up water, the panel is likely to delaminate, which can pop nails and create an array of repair problems. You can protect against this deterioration by brushing a primer coat on the edges prior to installation or by concealing the edges with trim, such as vertical corner boards. It's also important to caulk or flash seams around windows and doors and on two-story projects where one sheet rests on top of another.

Panel installation is a two-person job. Here, one makes sure the sheet is plumb while the other nails into studs.

10 Masonry

- CONCRETE • BUILDING WITH BLOCK
- BRICK AND STONEWORK • RETAINING WALLS

251 Mixing Options

For small jobs, less than 10 cubic feet or so, you can mix concrete in a sturdy wheelbarrow by hand, or you can rent a small power mixer. For large jobs, have the concrete delivered by a concrete truck. When you order ready-mix concrete, the trucks come with a front- or rear-mounted chute that extends 15 to 20 feet and can swivel from side to side. This makes placing the concrete where you want it a lot easier. These trucks can also deliver concrete on the hottest days and on some of the coldest ones, as long as additives are mixed in to keep the concrete from freezing before it starts to cure. Don't forget that ready-mix concrete is sold by the cubic yard. Measure the length, width, and depth of your job, and take this information to the concrete supplier. The supplier can quickly calculate how many yards you need and tell you how much it will cost.

Trucks with extension chutes deliver ready-mix concrete right where you want it.

252 Mixing Concrete to the Right Consistency

If you have a big concrete job to do, such as pouring sidewalks, patio slabs, or outbuilding foundations, you'll probably have mixed concrete delivered to your house in a big truck. For smaller jobs, buying concrete in dry mix bags and adding the water yourself is easy and inexpensive, and it may be your only choice. The bags contain portland cement, sand, and crushed stone.

Making Your Mix To make these ingredients into concrete, pour them into a wheelbarrow and add clean water at the proportion recommended on the bag. This should yield a good, strong mix. Avoid the temptation to just add water from a hose until "it looks right." What looks right in the beginning will almost never turn out right in the end. Remember, if your mix is too dry, just add a little water; if it's too wet, add some more mix from another bag.

1 Pour the contents of the bag into a wheelbarrow, and then use a garden hoe to mix in water.

2 If the concrete mix is too wet, ridges made in it with a trowel won't hold their shape.

3 If the concrete mix is too dry, a trowel can't form ridges and the mix is very hard to work.

4 When the mix is right, it will be wet, not soaked, and a trowel will leave firm ridges on the surface.

Saving Money

253 Estimating Concrete

To calculate the volume of concrete you need for rectangular footings, walls, and slabs, or for cylindrical piers, you only need a bit of math. For the former, multiply length by width by thickness (all in feet or fractions thereof) and divide by 27 to obtain the total volume in cubic yards. For a pier, multiply the square of its radius (in inches) by pi (3.14); multiply the result by the height (in inches); and divide by 1,728 to get cubic feet.

To calculate volumes of irregular shapes, break them down into rectangles, triangles, and portions of circles; make your calculations; and then add the results together. To allow for waste and irregularities in concrete thickness, add about 5 percent to your order. Falling short can ruin a job.

254 The Right Proportions

Concrete-mix proportions vary depending on the intended use of the concrete and the weather conditions. Especially important is the water-to-cement ratio. Too much water will weaken the concrete, and too little will make it unworkable. Site-mixed concrete is typically 1 part cement, 2½ parts sand, 3 parts coarse aggregate, and about 5 gallons of water per bag of cement. But there are exceptions to the rule. For example, add more water on hot, dry days to prevent the wet mix from drying out prematurely.

Always measure out the dry ingredients carefully in a clean container, and mix them thoroughly with a mason's hoe. Slowly add water, and pull the dry ingredients from the sides into the water. Keep adding water and mixing until ridges cut in the concrete with a hoe hold their shape.

255 Formed versus Formless Piers

Concrete piers are used mainly to support decks, porches, and outbuildings. Whether you use form tubes or not depends on your soil. If the sides of the holes you dig do not crumble, you can use them as rough forms and save the cost of form tubes.

Piers are susceptible to shifting out of plumb in areas with freeze-thaw cycles, so you need to dig below the local frost depth to prevent heaving. Check with your local building department for the correct depth in your area. The holes for piers need to be deep and narrow. They are best dug with a power auger or a hand posthole digger. Don't use a shovel, because it will make a hole that's too wide near the top. Minimize settling by digging down to the required depth and pounding the dirt at the bottom of the hole with the end of a 2×4. The concrete pier must rest on a solid base. In most cases you'll also need to install a galvanized bracket to keep a post or girder securely in place.

If your pier is poured without a form tube, frame the top few inches with 2x4s staked in a level position.

Whether using form tubes or not, insert a threaded rod or an anchor bolt in the concrete. Hold in place with wires.

When the pier has cured, attach post- or girder-holding hardware to the rod or anchor bolt.

256 Reinforcing Concrete

It may come as a surprise to the uninitiated, but concrete, as strong as it is, needs to be reinforced to reduce cracking. A couple of different reinforcement methods exist, and it's important to choose the right one for your job. Moreover, critical steps must be followed along the way, or your efforts will go for naught.

Rebar Steel reinforcement bar (rebar, for short) is typically required by code in footings and foundations that carry heavy loads. The bars come in 20-foot lengths and in diameters ranging from ¼ to 1 inch. A typical 16-inch-wide footing for a house often requires two continuous ½-inch bars set about 8 inches apart down the center of the form. (Check local codes.) It's important to elevate the rebar (about 2 inches) so that it rests in the concrete instead of on the ground. You can support it with bricks or small fittings called chairs.

Mesh Reinforcing mesh, generally known as welded wire, is made of steel wires woven or welded into a grid. It's used in slabs to reduce cracking. Like rebar, welded wire should be elevated so that it rests in the slab instead of on the ground. You can rest the reinforcement on chairs or pieces of brick, block, or stone. If you need to reinforce an irregularly shaped slab, overlap sections of mesh at least 6 inches and bind them together with wire ties. Also keep welded wire back an inch or two from the outside edges of a slab.

1 Support rebar about 2 in. off the ground with pieces of brick, block, or small fittings, called chairs.

2 Secure rebar to masonry or special supports with wire ties to keep them from moving during the pour.

3 Lap and wire-tie adjoining rebar at least 12 in. around corners to provide unbroken support.

1 Welded wire mesh comes in rolls or sheets. You need to flatten the mesh inside forms.

2 Cut back mesh reinforcement so that it's separated from form boards by about 2 in. on all sides.

3 Use brick or block sections to support welded wire roughly 2 in. above the base of the excavation.

257 Tips for Pouring Concrete

You must work quickly when pouring concrete into forms. If the project requires a delivery of ready-mix concrete, have friends help with the pour. Before pouring, check the formwork. Add extra braces in key locations to resist the increased force of concrete pouring from a ready-mix truck chute. Spray the inside form surfaces and the soil or gravel base with water. This will prevent water from being drawn out of the concrete, which can produce a weak and crumbly surface.

For large projects, such as driveways, have at least two wheelbarrows for transporting the concrete to the forms. Lay 2×12s across lawn areas to protect them from the wheelbarrow tire, and build ramps over the forms so that you don't bump them out of place.

Begin piling concrete in the farthest corner of the forms, slightly higher than the formwork. Move the concrete with hoes and shovels. You may need to raise the wire mesh with a hammer claw to ensure that it stays in the middle of the pour. During the pour, repeatedly consolidate the concrete by moving a 2×4 up and down to release air bubbles. This is especially important near the edges and in corners. Don't overdo it though. If you overwork the concrete, the water will separate and rise to the top, weakening the mix. Further settle the concrete against the perimeter by tapping the outside of the form boards with a hammer.

1 Add extra form braces as needed. Use double-headed nails to make it easier to pull nails later.

2 Shovel the concrete into place without disrupting the overlapped rebar.

3 Fill the forms completely, tamping the concrete as you go to eliminate voids and air bubbles.

4 To form a smooth, sound edge, use a trowel to fill corners, sliding it along the sides of the forms.

5 Move a 2x4 screed back and forth across the forms to smooth and strike off excess concrete.

6 Embed anchor bolts in the concrete at 4-ft. centers and within 12 in. of each corner or opening.

258 Creed for Screeding

Once a form has been filled with concrete and tamped, begin screeding, or striking off, the surface level with the top of the forms. Use a length of 2×4 slightly wider than the forms. Try to use a straight piece of lumber, but if there is a bow to the wood, screed with the convex side up. Move the screed back and forth as you slide it along the tops of the forms. Keep both ends pressed down on top of the forms to force all of the aggregate into the concrete. Fill hollow areas with a shovelful of concrete, and level them. For a large pour, two people can begin screeding as concrete is placed ahead of them.

Work a straight 2x4 in a back-and-forth motion across the forms to smooth and level the mix.

259 Forming Pipe Sleeves

Before pouring concrete into foundation forms, install blockouts, also referred to as barriers, to accommodate electrical conduits and gas and water pipes. Create a blockout by drilling holes through each side of the form and sliding a piece of PVC drainpipe through the holes.

Pipe Measures Leave the pipes long, and trim them flush once the forms are stripped. Pipe diameters should be slightly oversize to allow easy access.

1 **Use a hole saw or saber saw to cut holes matching the pipe diameter.**

2 **Install plastic pipe through the holes to provide access for utilities.**

260 Secrets to a Good Finish

Floating is the first step in the finishing of concrete and is done immediately after screeding. Initial floating with a bull float or a darby depresses large aggregates and knocks down small ridges. To use a bull float, push it across the surface with the front edge raised a bit. When pulling it back, keep its blade flat to cut off bumps and fill holes. At the end of each stroke, lift the float and move it over, creating a parallel stroke. A darby is smaller and easier to control than a bull float. Use two hands to move it in sweeping arcs across the concrete surface. Do not allow the edges or end of the tool to dig into the concrete.

After the first floating, lightly sweep the surface with a broom, which will make the concrete less slippery. Then wait for the water sheen to leave the concrete surface. If you begin edging and further finishing while there is water on the surface, the concrete quality, especially at the surface, may be reduced. Of course, if you wait too long, the concrete will be unworkable.

Around the Edges When the water sheen is gone from the first floating, it's time to run an edger along the forms. Edging gives the pour rounded edges that resist cracking. Use the point of a small trowel to cut the top inch or so of concrete away from the face of the form. Then run an edging trowel along the perimeter to form an attractive finished edge. Run the edger back and forth to smooth the surface, without gouging the concrete. Raise the front edge slightly when moving the edger forward, and raise the back edge when moving the tool backward.

1 Rent a bull float with a long handle to create a smooth finish on the surface of the slab.

2 Lightly sweep the concrete with a broom to create a rougher, more slip-resistant surface.

3 Use a jointing trowel against a straightedge to cut control joints about every 10 ft.

4 Run an edging trowel around the perimeter to provide a clean, crack-resistant edge.

261 Controlling Cracks

Shrinkage cracks in concrete are controlled by control joints tooled into the surface. Control joints allow the concrete to crack in straight lines at planned locations. They can be hand-tooled into fresh concrete with a special jointing tool or cut into partially cured concrete with a circular saw fitted with a masonry blade. Tooled and saw-cut joints must be at least one-fourth of the thickness of the concrete. This weakens the section, causing cracks to occur at the bottom of the joints where they will be inconspicuous.

It is best to subdivide concrete into panels that are square, rather than elongated. Rectangular areas more than one and one half times as long as they are wide are prone to cracking in the middle across the width. On a sidewalk, concrete will be less likely to crack if the joints form square panels spaced 3 feet apart.

The jointing trowel leaves a smooth groove in the surface, but you may need to clear out the interior seam.

262 Finding the Right Cure

Concrete should cure for at least a week to allow the portland cement in the mix to harden properly. When moisture is pulled from the concrete too quickly, the surface can develop hairline cracks or have a chalky residue. Hot, dry, or windy weather increases evaporation, making it more difficult to keep the slab moist. Cold weather requires special precautions for curing.

Keeping It Moist There are several ways to cure concrete properly. You can cover and seal the surface completely with large sheets of plastic, or you can lay burlap over the surface and spray it with a garden hose twice daily to keep it wet. (Weigh down the edges of the sheets with bricks.) Another option is to set a sprinkler to continually but gradually pool water on the surface. But first be sure that the surface has hardened enough to resist being marred by the spray. Another way to lock in moisture is to apply a curing compound to the damp surface with a paint roller.

Concrete hardens best between 50 and 70° F. If concrete freezes before at least two days of curing, it will be weak and basically ruined. If you expect cold weather, apply a heavy layer of straw or blankets covered with plastic sheeting. In very hot weather, simply keep the concrete moist.

1 Spray the surface of finished concrete lightly but thoroughly with water from a garden hose.

2 Cover and seal the fresh concrete with overlapped plastic sheeting to lock in moisture.

3 A curing compound applied to concrete with a paint roller will also retard moisture loss during curing.

263 Easier Form Release

Forms can be removed after a wait of at least one day, but keep in mind that the pour is still easily damaged. During form removal, prying and hammering can cause large chips to break from edges and corners. You'll make the job a lot easier and lessen the risk of damaging the pour if you use double-headed nails or screws when building your forms. Both are much easier to remove than regular nails. Good finishing technique will help, too. Rounded-over edges will help keep forms from sticking to the concrete. After the forms are stripped, the concrete will continue to cure and reach nearly its full strength in about a month. But it is safe to walk on and use the surface after one week.

Edging walks, steps, and patios allows for a clean release of form boards and creates stronger edges that resist chipping.

264 Choosing Masonry Blocks for Your Project

Masonry blocks are easier to use than concrete when building foundations and walls. Although some strength is sacrificed, you work at your own pace, and if you make a mistake, it won't be a catastrophe.

Blocks range from open-faced decorative units used in screen walls to the basic concrete block used on house foundations. Standard blocks have a face size of 7⅝ inches by 15⅝ inches. When you add the thickness of a standard ⅜-inch mortar joint, the block measures 8 by 16 inches—its nominal size. The most commonly used block thickness is also nominally 8 inches (7⅝ inches actual dimension), but you can get nominal 4-, 6-, 10-, and 12-inch thicknesses, too.

The basic concrete block unit is called a stretcher. Stretchers are cored with two or three holes to reduce the weight as much as possible. If your project will incorporate vertical reinforcing steel (rebar) in the cores, the wall will be easier to build using special two-core units with open ends.

Consider your many options when designing a concrete block wall. Some concrete blocks are gray and have flat faces with a texture that may range from coarse to relatively fine. Other blocks are more decorative and come in a variety of colors and textures. Many manufacturers also produce blocks that look like natural stone, as well as blocks with ribs, raised geometric patterns, and smooth-ground faces.

There are also several specialty blocks, such as units molded with open faces that provide some privacy without blocking out a breeze. There are also many types of interlocking blocks that don't require mortar that you can use to build retaining walls.

Stretchers' end flanges butt in a mortar joint.

End blocks have at least one finished end.

Cap blocks finish off the tops of block walls.

Decorative blocks have webs on the vertical faces.

265 Laying Block like a Pro

Pros build up the corners, called leads, of block walls before filling in the blocks along each course. The first course of a lead should be three units long. The rest are set back one-half block in each course. This establishes a running bond pattern in which the units of one course are offset one-half block from the courses above and below. Build the wall by filling in between the leads. Then start over with new leads.

Filling In Stretch a mason's line to mark the top of each course as you build up the wall, checking for level with a line level. Use line blocks to hold the string an inch away from the wall face. Fill in the first course between leads, buttering the flanges as you lay blocks. Check for block alignment and for plumb with a 4-foot level. The last block to place is called the closure block. You should have just enough space left for this block plus a mortar joint on each end.

Use a mason's line, offset 1 in. from the wall surface, to keep blocks level and aligned.

266 Cutting Concrete Blocks with Common Tools

If you are building something that requires a lot of blocks, it's best to order specialty blocks, such as preformed half blocks and corner blocks, to eliminate a lot of cutting and speed up the job. But there will always be some cutting to do because there's not a specialty block made for every situation. Fortunately, this is an easy job if you have a few simple tools on hand. The first is a circular saw fitted with a masonry blade. The others are a 3-pound maul and a 3½-inch-wide cold chisel. Start by marking the cut line on the block. Then either cut along the line with the circular saw, or score the cut line with the cold chisel and break it in two with the maul.

A circular saw makes a clean cut, but it also makes a lot of noise and creates a lot of dust.

You can also cut blocks by scoring the cut line with a cold chisel and using a maul to make the break.

A chisel and maul are quieter and produce less dust than a circular saw, but they make a rougher cut.

267 Picking the Right Mortar

Mortar is made of various cements, sand, and lime, but there are different types. Pick the one that's right for your job to make sure you'll get the best results. For big jobs, contractors often buy the mortar ingredients in bulk and mix them on site. For most homeowners, it makes more sense to buy mortar in premixed bags. This ensures that the mix proportions will be right (and the same) for every batch. Some types of mortar include:

Type M: A high-strength mortar used for masonry walls below grade and walls subject to high lateral or compressive loads or severe frost heaving.

Type S: A medium-high-strength mortar used for walls requiring strength to resist high lateral loads.

Type N: A medium-strength mortar used for most masonry work that is above grade.

Type O: A low-strength mortar used for interior nonbearing partitions.

Type K: A low-strength lime-sand mortar used for repointing mortar joints.

268 Providing Drainage for Retaining Walls

Every block retaining wall that is more than 3 feet high should have weep tubes and drainage pipes. These pipes allow most of the water that collects in the soil behind the wall to drain away, reducing the hydrostatic pressure that might otherwise, over time, tip the wall over. Weep tubes are set in joints every third block. Drainage pipes are usually placed next to the bottom course of blocks, covered with gravel, and backfilled with soil when the wall is complete. Make sure to slope all drainpipes down so the water can run from behind the wall.

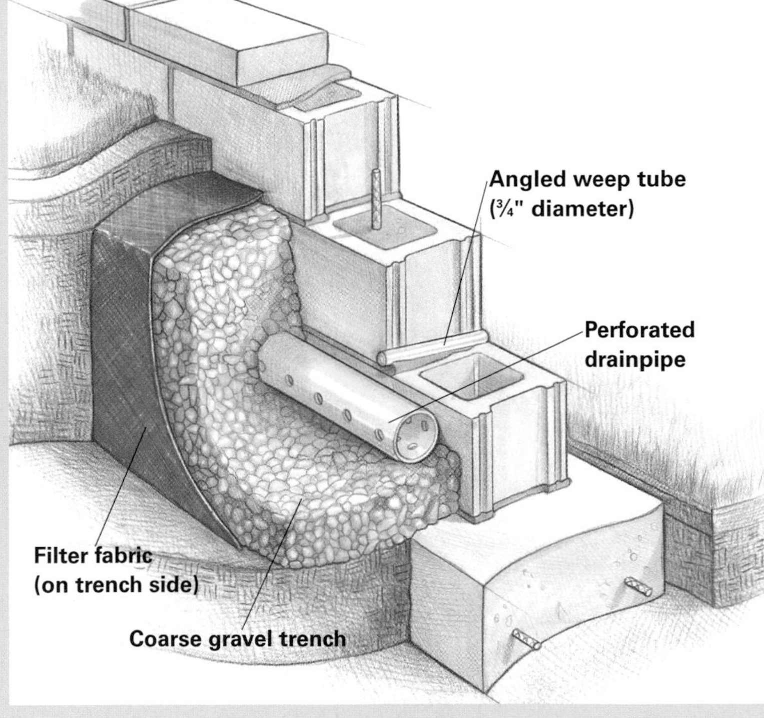

Install weep tubes every third block, and cover the "inlet" end with a wire basket.

Greener Ways

269 Masonry's Low Impact

Masonry is one of the greenest building products. When it's quarried or mined, there's nothing left over for the landfill—unlike the waste generated when mining for metal ores. Masonry construction is long lasting, reducing the demands on forests and related resources. Masonry surfaces do not require plastic or oil-based finishes.

270 Interlocking Block for Easier Garden Walls

If mortaring a masonry garden wall seems like too much work, or just too complicated, try one of the interlocking designs that are available at many home centers. Interlocking concrete blocks with attractive outside faces are a great material to use for building simple retaining walls. They are usually recommended for walls up to 3 feet high. If you need a higher wall, the blocks need to be reinforced, which complicates the job quite a bit. Available in many different sizes, shapes, and colors, all these blocks are designed to be stacked without mortar. Some have a lip on the bottom back of each block that hooks over the back of the blocks on the previous course. Others use rigid plastic locking pins that work like dowels to align blocks horizontally and vertically. (See below.) And some systems feature half blocks and corner blocks to make the job easier.

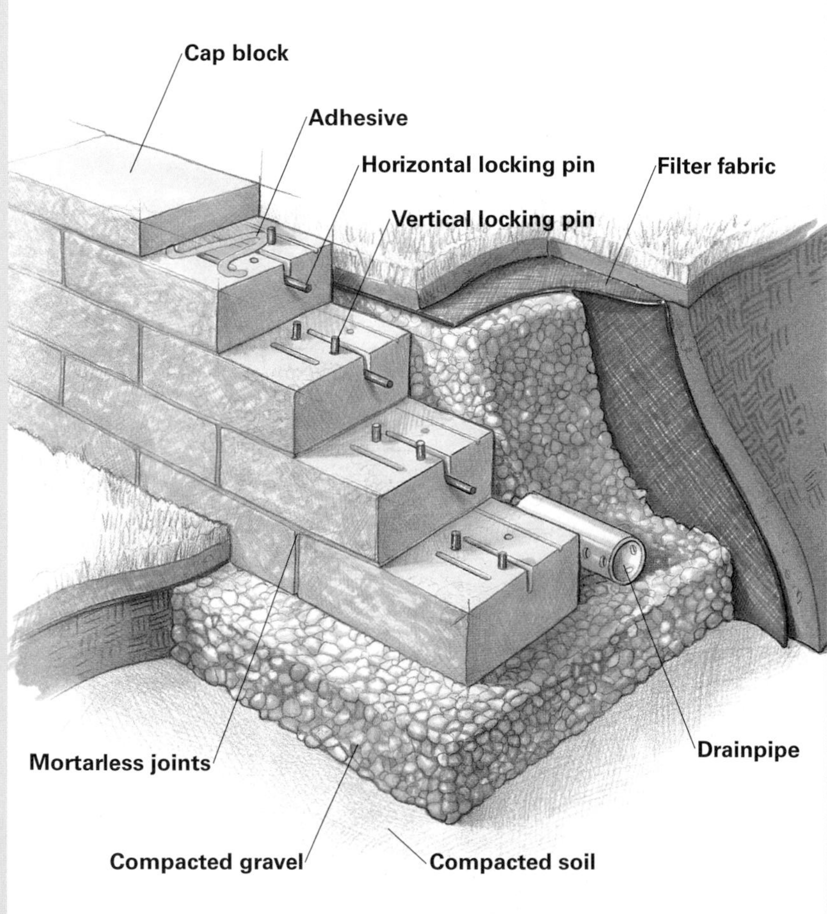

Vertical locking pins placed in preformed holes help align the courses.

Horizontal locking pins go in preformed slots between mating blocks.

271 Getting Beautiful Brick Joints

A lot of technique is involved in laying bricks, especially if you work quickly. But if you're doing a small job, it makes more sense to get good-looking joints, even if it does take longer. After all, the mortar joints catch your eye almost as much as the brick does. The steps shown here will minimize the mess and make cleaning up what mess is made much easier. Your results, however, will be only as good as your comfort level with a mason's trowel. In the beginning, this tool can feel awkward, but after a few hours it will feel more natural.

Less Is Best Start with a smaller amount of mortar for each step of the process because less is almost always more controllable. In this way, working with mortar and a trowel is much like spreading joint compound with a drywall knife. Start with the knife only half full and you'll spill a lot less compound.

1 Spread enough mortar to create a bed that's ⅜ in. thick

2 Compact and form the outer edge of the bed using a trowel.

3 Make a shallow furrow down the center of the bed.

4 Spread and shape mortar on the head end of the next brick.

5 Set the brick in place, and tap it using the heel of the trowel.

6 Scrape off excess mortar from the joints using the trowel.

272 Finishing Brick Joints

You can tell when joints are ready for tooling when you can press your thumb against the mortar and leave an impression without any sticking to your thumb. The concave joint (shown at right) is the most common shape. Check the mortar frequently, and tool the joints a few at a time when the surface is just the right consistency. As you tool the joints, small pieces of mortar called tailings will be squeezed out at the edges. Remove them with the edge of your trowel.

273 Moving Large Stones

The best way to handle large stones is by improving your leverage. In fact, sometimes mechanical advantage will seem like the only advantage you have. Large stones can weigh as much as three times the weight of water. This means that one cubic foot of stone can tip the scales at more than 185 pounds. Moving something like this around is a full day's work. That's why you should have a long pry bar and a hand truck on the job.

Bar or Truck? A good bar can move a heavy stone easily, especially when it only has to go a few inches. But for long distances, a hand truck is the best choice. Use the bar to move the stone onto the truck, and then wheel the truck where you need the stone.

When you're moving stones, a pry bar applies exceptional leverage—and helps to prevent back injuries.

If you have to move heavy stones a long distance, a hand truck comes in handy.

274 Mortar Bag: Faster, Neater

Mortar bags, sometimes called grout bags, are heavy-duty versions of the bags that chefs use to decorate cakes and other pastries. They are designed to make filling the gaps between stones in a wall much easier—and a lot neater. Masonry supply outlets sell them with different-size nozzles to fit different width joints.

Make Like a Pastry Chef To use a mortar bag, just fill it with a slightly soupy mix; close the end; and squeeze it to dispense the mortar.

1 Mix the mortar so it is slightly wet, and trowel it into the grout bag.

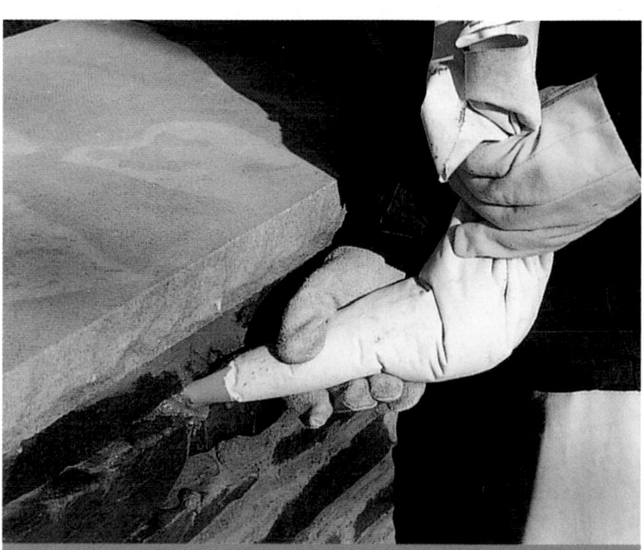

2 Use the bag like a caulking gun, pushing the nozzle into gaps and moving it as you squeeze.

11 Landscaping

- MULCHING AND EDGING • PATHS AND PATIOS
- BUILDING STONE WALLS • LAWN RESTORATION

275 Ringing Trees with Mulch

Mulching around trees is a smart move all the way around. It saves mowing time, minimizes time spent weeding, and protects your trees from being injured by the mower or string trimmer. In addition, it keeps the tree roots cool and moist.

Precautions Be careful to use proper mulching techniques. Don't pile mulch too high up the trunk. Referred to as volcano mulching, it can stress and eventually smother and kill an otherwise healthy tree. Also, leave a 3-inch space around the root flare of the tree so that the mulch does not touch the tree trunk. For best results with mulched beds, lay down sheets of water-permeable landscape fabric prior to planting. Shredded cedar, hardwood mulch, shells, gravel, and pine needles are good top mulches. But take note: pine can be a magnet for ants in some areas.

1 Use a sharp spade to cut an edge, but avoid cutting through the surface roots.

2 Put water-permeable landscape fabric—cut to the shape of the ring using scissors—around the tree trunk.

3 Cover with 3 in. of mulch. Shredded cedar is a good choice but will need to be replenished periodically.

276 Getting an Edge

A neat edge between lawn and garden looks good and helps to bring a sense of order to your landscape. Ragged, unmaintained borders are breeding grounds for weeds, which can eventually invade the lawn itself. You can create a neat edge by making a simple cut with a manual or power edger. Edges can also be made of stone, brick, masonry, wood, metal, or plastic. For a time-saving approach, use materials that allow you to create edgings with a flat surface that's wide enough for mower wheels to roll on. In this way, you can trim borders as you mow. For best results, the edging height should be an inch or two above grade level.

Flat-surface edging made of brick creates a low-maintenance edge that mower wheels can ride on. (Less weeding and trimming!)

277 A Good Foundation

Many landscape plans call for masonry, or "hard," walks. They make it easier to walk or wheel to entrances and to outlying structures, such as sheds, garages, and gazebos. Masonry walks may be built from poured concrete, brick, stone, concrete paver, or quarry tile. Whatever you choose, the hard walk must be laid on a firm, well-drained base or it may buckle, crack, or sink. A base consisting of 4 inches of compacted gravel topped by 2 inches of builder's sand (also called torpedo sand) should suffice. The gravel and sand not only provide a solid, well-drained base but also make it easier to level the paving units as they are installed. Poorly drained soils or those subject to frost heave, settling, and erosion may require a sub-base of 6 to 8 inches of gravel or crushed stone.

Lower Cost A less costly and low-labor solution is a "soft" walk. It consists of wood or any loose aggregate, such as gravel, decorative rock, crushed shells, wood chips, or bark. Unlike masonry walks, soft walks are not affected by unstable soil or frost heave, so you don't need to be as particular about the base. Tamped earth will do. Loose materials usually have to be replenished every year or two because material scatters or gets worked into the ground. Install edging to keep the loose paving material from spreading into surrounding areas.

Place landscape fabric under a soft walk to help prevent the paving material from mixing with the soil and to stop weed growth.

278 Edging Paths

Path edging is placed along the sides of a walk to define its borders and to contain the walk material. All soft walks require raised edging to keep the material in place. Brick and other masonry walks also need edging if they are to be dry-laid on a sand bed. In such cases, the edging not only holds the pavement in place but also serves to contain the bed on which the paving is set. If the walk materials will be mortared in place, edging is more decorative than structural, and its use is optional.

For edges that are mostly straight, landscape ties (usually 4×6s or 6×6s) are the least expensive approach. They work well with paths consisting of a loose aggregate because they can help prevent material from scattering. Just install the ties an inch or two higher than the path.

For curved edges, brick, concrete edging blocks, or stone works well for either soft or hard paths. They can be set to almost any contour. If the blocks or bricks do shift, they're easy to reset.

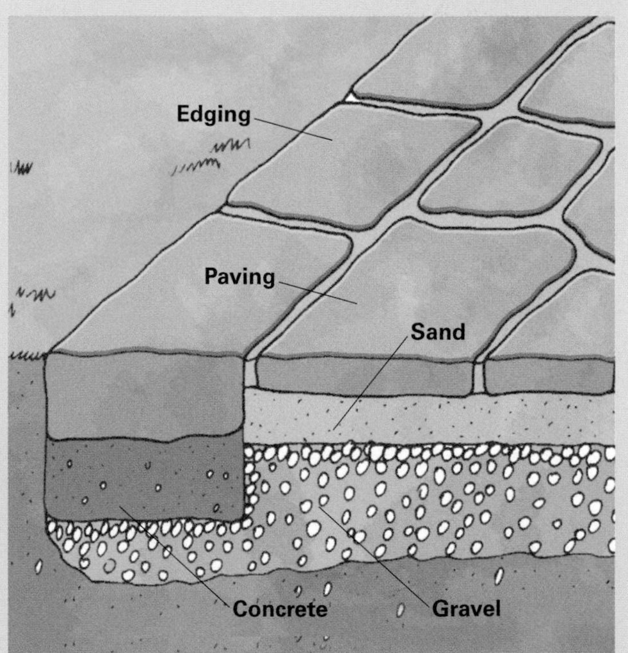

For added stability, set masonry edging on a 2- or 3-in. bed of concrete. With a well-drained base, however, such materials may be set without concrete.

Saving Money

279 Saving on Additives

Test lawn and garden soil to determine its pH level before applying fertilizer, lime, sulfur, or other amendments. By doing so, you may find that your soil needs less. In any case, you will get better growing results by eliminating guesswork. Although do-it-yourself soil-testing kits are available, it's best to have soil samples tested by a professional testing service. Contact your local Cooperative Extension Service or a commercial soil-testing lab.

280 Plotting Curves

Landscaping is largely a collection of pleasing curves, lawn, plantings, and focal points. Getting the right curves, however, is not always easy. For free-form curves, a long length of hose or rope will allow you to experiment until you have the contour you want. For more regular curves, such as an arc or circle, use rope. Stake one end in the center of the bed or tree ring. Then, keeping the rope taut, pace off the arc or circle. Mark the line with sand, and use it to guide your spadework.

281 Mulching Garden Beds

For many of the same reasons given for mulching around trees, garden beds should also be mulched. A mulched bed is going to be much easier to maintain than one that is not. The mulching technique, however, is slightly different. Prepare the bed soil first, adding amendments as required. Then rake level and spread landscape fabric over the entire bed. Use large landscape fabric "staples" to secure the fabric to the ground.

Next, cut openings for plantings. Two intersecting, perpendicular cuts will allow you to pull back the fabric and dig a hole for your plant. Once the plants are in the ground, replace any landscape fabric you've lifted for digging and cover the entire area with 3 inches of mulch. If new plantings are to be added later, simply rake back the mulch, cut a new hole, plant, and replace the fabric and mulch.

This well-maintained edge and the mulched woodland garden beyond it help prevent weeds from spreading.

282 Planning Steps

This will require a little math, but it's not difficult and doesn't need to be precise. First, determine the total rise (height) and run (length) of the proposed steps. (See the illustrations at right.) Then estimate the number of steps you'll need by finding a whole number between 5 and 7 that divides into your total rise as evenly as possible. (If your rise is 32, 6 would be the number.)

Test Your Numbers Next, test to see if this number of steps will work by dividing it into the total run. If the result is between 11 and 17, you're all set. (If your run is 72 inches, 12 would be your tread depth.) If it's less than 11, you will probably have to add to the overall run, which often requires adding fill to the base of the steps. If it's greater than 17, you may consider adding a landing. This will allow you to shorten the tread depths to an acceptable measure.

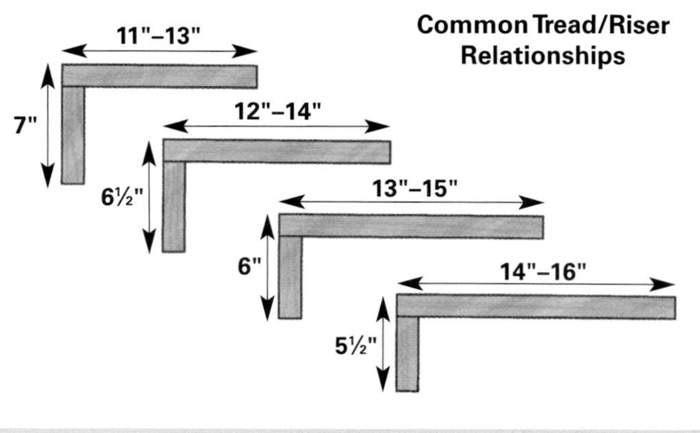

Working Safer

283 Stepping It Up

Building steps on grades that require them is a surprisingly simple job, unlike building stairs from wood. The existing terrain, with a little digging, can often supply all the support you'll need. Here are a few helpful rules to ensure comfort and safety:

- **Make the steps wide enough. Steps 3 feet wide are usually adequate for one person to stroll comfortably. But the tension may limit the width.**
- **Choose a comfortable step height (the rise). The maximum rise between any two steps should be the amount most people are comfortable stepping up—between 5 and 7 inches. Don't vary step heights! Irregular steps are a common cause of tripping.**
- **Maintain a safe tread/riser relationship, as shown in the stone stairs at right. The greater the total rise, the shallower the tread. For exterior steps, the rule of thumb is that twice the riser height plus the tread depth should equal 25 to 27 inches. That means the tread depth should be between 11 and 17 inches. A 7-inch riser and 12-inch tread is optimal for easy climbing, but you can vary the ratio.**

284 Tamping for Success

Tamping is a critical step when installing paths or patios. It can be done by hand, but for large projects, such as long paths and patios, do your arms and shoulders a favor by renting a vibrating tamper. You can use it to compact gravel, sand, and the like—and to make sure the paving material is set firmly.

Use a vibrating power tamper to smooth out and compact the gravel or sand base that should be used under most paths and patios.

Working Safer

285 Self-Draining Paths

Avoid creating a walkway from which water cannot drain easily; otherwise you'll end up with a hazardous path in freezing weather. The way to do this is by "crowning" the path—making it higher in the center. Make the crown high enough so that the slope to the path's edges is about ⅛ inch per foot. A 4-foot-wide path, for example, is crowned ¼ inch (⅛ inch per foot to each side of center). Walks that are next to the house or a garden wall should be sloped away from the structure.

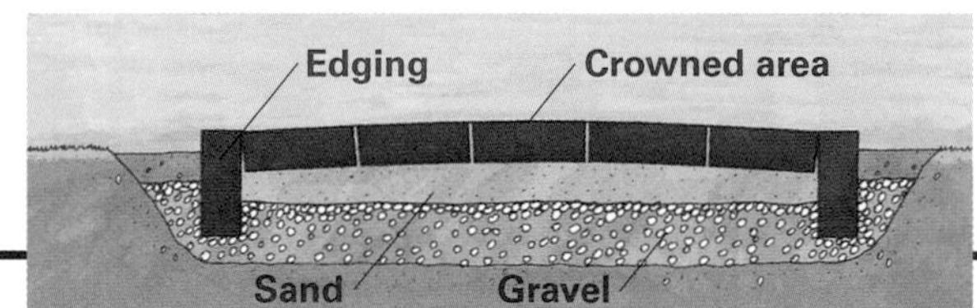

286 Better Patio Foundations

Patios are much like walks, in that you can lay them over one of two kinds of bases. The simplest is a sand-and-gravel base, which will support flagstone, brick, or interlocking pavers. Mortared brick and stone patios, on the other hand, sit in a mortar bed on top of a concrete pad that's laid slightly below grade.

The easiest patio you can build uses concrete pavers, brick, flagstone, or adobe block laid on a sand-and-gravel base. Pavers and flagstone of various shapes, colors, and textures come in a variety of sizes, but anything thinner than 1¼ inches may crack with use. The secret of success in dry-laid paving is a proper base, which minimizes settling. The base consists of a 4-inch layer of gravel, topped off with a sand layer. On poorly drained soils and in very cold climates, the drainage base should be 6 inches thick. With well-drained soils and in areas where the ground does not freeze and thaw, you may be able to do without the gravel entirely.

Patio edging holds pavers in place. If the patio is built at ground level, the earth can serve as an edging.

Use a 2x4 screed board to level the sand base. Embed 1½-in.-dia. pipes to use as a guide for your screed board.

Seat each paver using a rubber mallet, and check for level. Then brush dry sand into the joints.

287 Building Stone Walls

The "easiest" masonry wall to build is a dry-laid stone wall. Many do-it-yourselfers achieve success with little or no experience.

How It's Done The walls are typically stacked two stones thick; these parallel face courses are called wythes. To tie the wythes together, place bond stones at each end of the wall and at 4- to 6-foot intervals in each course. The more bond stones, the stronger the wall. As you build each successive course, stagger the joints between stones so that each stone rests on at least two supporting stones. Fill gaps with small rubble stones. Here are a few more tips to ensure success:

- Whether you buy or scrounge them, choose stones with at least three flat sides: the top, bottom, and the side to be used for the face of the wall.
- Although walls less than 3 feet high normally do not require footings, it's wise to dig a 3-inch-deep trench. Lay the first course in the trench, making it as level as possible.
- Dry-laid stone walls more than 2 feet high should slope inward slightly. Use a batter gauge to keep the "batter" (angle of inward slope) 1 inch for every 2 feet of rise. (See Step 5 below.)
- Use stakes and mason's twine to keep the courses level. Adjust the height of the twine as the courses get higher, using a line level to keep it level.

1 Use a flat, double-width stone at the head of both rows at the ends of the wall.

2 Orient stones so that a straight edge faces out. Fill gaps between larger stones with smaller stones and rubble.

3 Span the width of the wall using a double-wide stone. This helps tie the wall together.

4 In alternating courses at the ends of the wall, install square-edged cross stones.

5 Dry-laid stone walls should slope inward slightly. Check your work with a level and batter gauge made of 1x2s.

6 For added stability, you may trowel mortar over the top course and install cap stones.

288 pH for Healthier Lawns

When renovating a lawn, lime is the amendment to use for raising pH. It comes in various forms, from ground oyster shells to liquids. For lawns, agricultural ground limestone is the preferred type because it is readily available and can be safely, easily, and accurately applied with a drop or rotary spreader.

Agricultural ground limestone is either dolomitic or calcitic. Each contains calcium carbonate, a grass nutrient, and a neutralizer for acidic soil. Dolomitic limestone also contains magnesium, another important nutrient, as well as calcium carbonate. Use dolomitic limestone if your soil is deficient in magnesium. Calcitic limestone does not contain magnesium, making it more appropriate if your soil is already high in magnesium. However, adding dolomitic limestone to soil already high in magnesium has not been shown to cause lawn problems.

For Faster Results Finely ground limestone will begin to correct the soil pH faster than coarse grinds. Coarsely ground limestone acts slowly and is better suited for use once you have raised your pH to a desirable range. You can tell fine lime from coarse if you understand the information on the package. The higher the percentage of ground lime that passes through the finer sieves, the finer the grind. Sieves are graded by number: the higher the number, the smaller the sieve holes. Look for a product stating on the label that at a minimum, 50 percent of the ground limestone will pass through a Number 100 sieve.

For a beautiful lawn, apply lime to raise the pH of an overly acidic soil. A pH between 5.8 and 6.6 allows a lawn to better absorb nutrients already in the soil.

To lower the pH of a lawn, spread sulfur according to your soil test recommendations. Sulfur amendments are also available in the form of compounds, such as ammonium sulfate. These compounds can be used in place of elemental sulfur, but they can burn turf if used in excess. See amendment packaging for details on amounts that can be safely applied to turfgrass. To avoid applying too much, don't try to make your correction all at once. To meet recommended amounts, make several surface applications a few weeks apart, and water the grass after each application.

Greener Ways

289 Less Leaching

When buying fertilizer, choose water-insoluble types or other slow-release forms. Using slow-release fertilizers will allow you to reduce the amount of time you spend behind your spreader. They last much longer and don't have to be applied as frequently as quick-release fertilizers, saving you money as well as time. They are also less likely to leach into nearby sewers and waterways or to burn foliage. Determine the type of fertilizer you have by reading the guaranteed analysis on the bag. Note: many fertilizers have a combination of both fast-release and slow-release types of nitrogen. You should check carefully to find products that derive a majority of their nitrogen from slow-release sources.

290 When to Mow

Most cool-season grasses should be cut when they reach heights of 3 to 3½ inches. Warm-season grasses should be cut when they reach 2 to 2½ inches. Not ready to begin measuring the height of your lawn? Remember this simple rule: cut no more than one-third of the grass height at each mowing to avoid damaging the plants. If the lawn grows too high for you to cut off one-third of the height and have an acceptable length, cut off one-third now and cut off one-third again in two or three days. Cutting more than one-third the height results in clumps of clippings that tend to lie on top of the lawn, decompose more slowly, and give the grass a less attractive, open, bristly appearance. In addition, very short cutting will stunt or slow root growth and weaken the grass plants.

291 Sod Cutter You Make Yourself

You'll spend most of your time cutting, fitting, and leveling when laying sod, so it pays to fashion yourself this handy sod-layer's tool before you begin. Buy a mason's trowel and sharpen one edge using a file or grinder. It will serve as a knife for sod cutting and is handy for leveling the soil prior to laying the sod. Keep the file handy so you can resharpen the tool edge; cutting through sod will dull it quickly.

A sod-cutting tool (top), made from a trowel, makes cutting both curves (above) and crosscuts easier.

292 A Better Way to Overseed

If your lawn is looking scruffy, with small patches of weeds or bare soil, you can restore it by overseeding. Many homeowners choose to perform this task by spreading the seed by hand or by using a hand-held or walk-behind spreader. The better tool, especially if you were not able to remove all thatch prior to overseeding, is a slit seeder. These machines, available at many rental stores, cut shallow slits in the soil and sow seed at the same time.

Thatch is a layer of dead grass roots and stems that accumulate on the soil surface. When it exceeds ½ in., remove it using a dethatching rake or power dethatcher. This is especially important when you're overseeding.

If you will be spreading seed by hand or with a spreader, first use a thatching rake to roughen the exposed soil to a depth of ½ inch. Set the spreader to deliver the seed that's recommended by the seed producer for seeding a new lawn. If you were not able to remove all thatch, sow a little extra seed.

Begin around the Edges Apply seed to the edges of the area you are sowing first. Then divide your seed, and apply half while walking in one direction and the other half while walking in a perpendicular direction. Spread extra seed on bare or weedy areas, and lightly cover the seed with a mixture of compost and topsoil. Next, roll all seeded areas with a water-weighted roller that is one-third full. Apply water at least twice a day until germination and once a day after that until the seedlings are about 2 inches tall.

In the North, the best time to overseed is in late summer and early fall, although you may also try this technique in early spring. In the South, the recommended time to overseed is spring or early summer.

293 Protecting the Young

Whether you're planting a new lawn from seed or just patching a worn-out area, it's wise to spread a layer of straw mulch over seeded areas to protect young seedlings from drying out in warm weather. Here's how to get this task right:

- Choose a clean mulching straw that's free of seed, such as wheat straw.
- Avoid putting down a heavy layer that would inhibit grass growth. Evenly spread about 50 to 80 pounds (one or two bales) per 1,000 square feet.
- In windy areas, stretch string over the mulch every few feet to keep it from blowing away.
- Burlap and agricultural fleece (a textile mulch that admits water and sunlight) are other mulches that will protect the seed from drying sun and wind. They are particularly helpful in preventing erosion and seed runoff when staked over seeded slopes.
- Remove mulches about three weeks after germination.

Spread straw mulch over a new lawn to slow evaporation, provide shade, and disperse raindrops that might otherwise dislodge seedlings.

Greener Ways

294 Choosing the Right Grass

Choosing the right grass for your yard can make the difference between having an environmentally friendly lawn that uses fewer resources, such as fertilizer and water, and one that is susceptible to diseases, pests, and weed invasion and that requires a lot of upkeep. The type of seed you choose for either a new or restored lawn should depend on several factors.

First, how do you want your lawn to look? Grasses vary in their color, leaf width, growth habit, and density. Second, how much time and money are you willing to spend tending your lawn? Higher-maintenance grasses mean greater commitments. Third, your seed choice will be affected by your site's growing conditions: the amount of sun and shade your site gets, the soil type and its level of fertility and dryness or wetness, and your climate. Lastly, consider how your lawn will be used—for decorative landscaping, for erosion control, or as a play area.

Grass seed can be purchased in one of two ways. You can visit the garden section of a retail store and pick out a package labeled with intended use, such as "Shade Mix," or you can buy the latest cultivars and make your own mix. For the latter, you will need to do some research. Begin by contacting your Cooperative Extension Service and speaking with a turfgrass specialist. Other excellent resources are the National Turfgrass Evaluation Program (ntep.org) and the Guelph Turfgrass Institute (guelphturfgrass.ca).

295 Cutting Short Your Short Cuts

Many homeowners set their mower's blade height to the lowest setting in order to mow less frequently. This and using a dull mower blade are not the best ways to maintain a healthy lawn. Here's why you shouldn't cut your grass too short:

- Grass grows from the crown, not the blade tips. This trait makes grass ideal for lawns because it keeps on growing despite the regular mowing off of its upper stem, leaf sheath, and blades. No crown, no grass!
- Keeping grass on the longer side allows the leaf blades to have greater surface area to carry out photosynthesis. This in turn results in healthier plants.
- Taller grass grows slower than shorter grass. You can use this simple fact to eliminate up to 20 percent of the mowing you do annually. That's a saving of about eight hours a year for the average homeowner, not to mention gasoline savings and less pollution.
- By keeping your grass at the upper end of its recommended mowing height, you can prevent most weeds from germinating, reducing the need for herbicides.

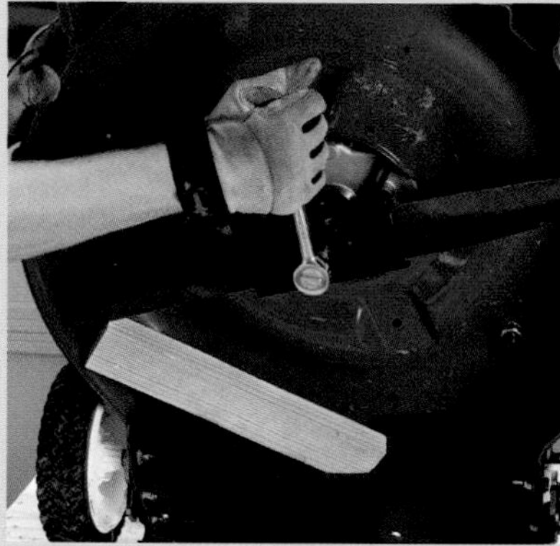

1 Resharpen your mower blade at least every season. Remove the blade using a wrench and block as shown.

2 Use a mill bastard file to remove equal amounts of metal from each side, and then check the blade's balance.

3 Reinstall new or resharpened blades using a torque wrench set to the torque specified in your manual.

296 Sensor Advances

Rain sensors have long been a recommended (and often mandated) accessory to lawn sprinkler systems. When it begins to rain, the sensor sends a signal to the controller to stop all watering. Some rain sensors are a bit smarter. They won't turn off until a significant amount of rain has fallen. With some of these, you can set the amount of rainfall needed to shut down the valves. The latest offerings include wireless rain sensors that reduce labor. Some wireless units are trickle-charged with a photovoltaic solar module. Others run on 9-volt batteries.

Manufacturers have added other types of sensors. Wind sensors signal the controller to cease watering when wind speeds would cause unacceptable water loss. Similarly, freeze sensors cause systems to stop operating when air temperatures get close to freezing.

Rain sensors will shut down an irrigation system after it begins to rain, conserving water.

Working Safer

297 Minimizing Hazards from Pesticides

When using pesticides or herbicides, take all basic precautions, including the use of goggles, disposable dust masks (for pesticide dusts), and tight-fitting respirators when using liquid sprays. Buy the least toxic, most target-specific chemical in the amount needed to do the job. Read product labels thoroughly, and apply products with care. Wear protective clothing, gloves, and gear as directed.

298 Smarter Watering

The smart approach to watering a lawn is to give it the water it needs—and no more. This moderate approach conserves an important resource, saves money, and helps prevent grass diseases caused by too much water. How often you should water your lawn depends on the health of your lawn and soil, the amount of rainfall your lawn gets, and the climate. It may be as little as twice a year or as much as twice a week.

The best approach to watering grass and many other plants is to follow nature's pattern of rainy periods followed by brief dry spells. Apply enough water all at once to penetrate the roots; let the soil almost dry out; and apply water again. Grass signals that it needs water by losing its spring: when your lawn shows footprints, it probably needs to be watered.

299 Benefits of Clippings

Leave clippings where they fall. This not only saves you the labor of collecting and composting them but also reduces the need for adding fertilizer because the clippings add nitrogen to the soil as they decompose. Clippings also act as a light mulch that helps to conserve soil moisture. However, if you have neglected your mowing or must mow in wet conditions, the long clippings are likely to form heavy clumps that cover the grass. In such cases, remove the clippings so that they do not smother the grass plants beneath them.

The idea of leaving clippings on the lawn is not new, but today's mulching mowers, also called recycling mowers, make it even easier to leave clippings where they fall. The deck and blade designs allow these mowers to cut each grass blade several times, producing a finely chopped clipping.

300 Time to Fertilize

Nitrogen is important to sustaining a thick, vigorous lawn. In addition to bringing on a deep green color, nitrogen is responsible for the sturdy growth and shoot density needed to fight off weeds and stand up to diseases, bugs, and traffic. All these positive effects can easily turn into negatives if you apply nitrogen at the wrong time. The common practice of fertilizing in early spring is actually not the best time in northern climates. It not only encourages excess blade growth, which means more mowing, but also gives your weeds a boost and increases thatch! Weeds need nitrogen, too. Excessive spring growth also produces thin-walled grass-blade cells that are more prone to injury and disease. Late summer to early fall is the preferred time for feeding northern lawns; midspring is the recommendation for the South.

Resource Guide

This list of manufacturers and associations is meant to be a general guide to additional industry and product-related sources. It is not intended as a listing of products and manufacturers represented by the photographs in this book.

Andersen Corporation

100 Fourth Ave. North
Bayport, MN 55003
Phone: 800-426-4261
www.andersenwindows.com
A company that offers a full line of entry doors, patio doors, storm doors, and many types of windows.

Cooperative State Research, Education, and Extension Service (CSREES)

U.S. Department of Agriculture
Waterfront Centre
800 Ninth St. SW
Washington, DC 20024
Phone: 202-720-7441
www.csrees.usda.gov
An agency that helps fund—at the state and local levels—research, education, and extension programs in order to advance knowledge of agriculture, the environment, and human health and well-being.

Environmental Protection Agency

Ariel Rios Building
1200 Pennsylvania Ave. NW
Washington, DC 20460
Phone: 202-272-0167
www.epa.gov
A federal agency committed to protecting human health and the environment. The EPA's Web site includes a wealth of information on environmental toxins, indoor air quality, and household hazardous waste.

Forest Stewardship Council – U.S.

1155 30th St. NW, Ste. 300
Washington, DC 20007
Phone: 202-342-0413
www.fscus.org
The U.S. chapter of a nonprofit, international organization created to promote responsible management of forests worldwide. The Web site includes information on policies, standards, and certification regarding forestry policies.

Guelph Turfgrass Institute

328 Victoria Rd. South, R.R. #2
Guelph, ON, Canada N1H 6H8
Phone: 519-767-5009
www.uoguelph.ca/GTI/
The center for research, extension, and professional development in areas such as pesticide use, evaluation of grass species, and seeding methods.

Gypsum Association

6525 Belcrest Rd., Ste. 480
Hyattsville, MD 20782
Phone: 301-277-8686
www.gypsum.org
A not-for-profit trade organization founded in 1930 that promotes the gypsum industry in the United States and Canada. The Web site provides technical information and industry statistics.

National Fire Protection Association

1 Batterymarch Park
Quincy, MA 02169
Phone: 617-770-3000
www.nfpa.org
A nonprofit, international association established in 1896 whose mission is to reduce the worldwide burden of fire and other hazards on the quality of life by providing and advocating consensus codes and standards, research, training, and education.

National Institute for Occupational Safety and Health

395 East St. SW, Ste. 9200
Patriots Plaza Building
Washington, DC 20201
Phone: 800-232-4636
www.cdc.gov/niosh
The federal agency responsible for conducting research and making recommendations for the prevention of

work-related injury and illness. Its Web site is a good source for researching the health risks of a particular chemical.

National Lead Information Center

422 South Clinton Ave.
Rochester, NY 14620
Phone: 800-424-5323
www.epa.gov/lead/pubs/nlic.htm
A resource that provides information about lead hazards and their prevention. The NLIC operates under a contract with the Environmental Protection Agency.

National Turfgrass Evaluation Program

Beltsville Agricultural Research Center West
10300 Baltimore Ave.
Bldg. 003, Rm. 218
Beltsville, MD 20705
Phone: 301-504-5125
www.ntep.org
A research program that tests, evaluates, and identifies turfgrass species in the United States and Canada. NTEP data is used to find environmentally sound turfgrasses.

Occupational Safety & Health Administration

U.S. Department of Labor
200 Constitution Ave.
Washington, DC 20210
Phone: 800-321-6742
www.osha.gov
An agency of the U.S. Department of Labor whose mission is to prevent injuries and protect the health of America's workers by ensuring safe and healthful workplaces. Created in 1970.

Overhead Door Corporation

2501 South State Hwy. 121, Ste. 200
Lewisville, TX 75067
Phone: 800-929-3667
www.overheaddoor.com
A company that manufactures integrated door and operator systems for commercial, industrial, and residential applications. The company's product lines include insulated garage doors.

Progress Lighting

P.O. Box 6701
Greenville, SC 29606
Phone: 864-678-1000
www.progresslighting.com
Makes more than 5,000 lighting fixtures for residential and commercial lighting, including entryway lights fitted with LEDs.

Serious Materials

1250 Elko Dr.
Sunnyvale, CA 94089
Phone: 800-797-8159
www.seriousmaterials.com
A green company that develops and manufactures sustainable building products.

Sustainable Forestry Initiative

1600 Wilson Blvd., Ste. 810
Arlington, VA 22209
Phone: 703-875-9500
www.aboutsfi.org
A comprehensive, independent forest certification program developed by the American Forest & Paper Association. SFI conducts site visits and chain-of-custody audits to ensure wood is grown and harvested in an earth-friendly manner.

USG Corporation

550 West Adams St.
Chicago, IL 60661
Phone: 800-874-4968
www.usg.com
A company that manufactures and supplies building materials, including gypsum wallboard and joint compound. The company's Web site features its history, product information, and a resource guide.

VELUX America Inc.

450 Old Brickyard Rd.
P.O. Box 5001
Greenwood, SC 29648
Phone: 800-888-3589
www.velux.com
A company that manufactures a wide range of roof windows and skylights. VELUX Group also offers sun screens, roller shutters, thermal solar panels, and solar tubes.

Glossary

Anchor bolt A bolt set in concrete that is used to fasten lumber, columns, girders, brackets, or hangers to concrete or masonry walls.

Blocking The installation of short pieces of lumber between joists or studs.

Bottom plate The horizontal lumber at the base of a wall.

Butt joint Two pieces of wood joined at their square cut ends.

Butter To place mortar on a masonry unit with a trowel before setting the unit in place.

Casing The exposed trim boards around the surfaces of windows and doors.

Clapboards Overlapping horizontal boards used as siding.

Cleat A piece of wood or metal that is fastened to a structural member to support or provide a point of attachment for another member or fixture.

Clinching To drive an overlong nail through two boards and bend the protruding end over.

Conduit Metal or plastic protective tubing that encloses electrical wires.

Control joint A surface joint that allows concrete stress cracks to form at planned locations.

Coped joint A curving profile cut on a piece of trim that makes the reverse image of the piece against which it must butt; made with a coping saw.

Corner board A vertical trim member that caps the corner of a building.

Coupling A fitting that joins pipes end to end.

Crosscuts Cuts to a board that are perpendicular to the direction of the wood grain.

Curing The process by which concrete, paint, adhesive, or other material dries completely and reaches its final degree of hardness.

Daylighting The use of natural light from windows, skylights, and other openings to supplement or replace electric light in a home or building.

Deadman A wooden device consisting of a short cross brace at the end of a support that is used to pin and hold a drywall ceiling panel in place until it is fastened. Also called a T-support or T-brace.

Dentil molding A molding detail that includes alternating blocks and spaces—suggestive of teeth.

Drip cap Molding at the top of a window or door.

Drip edge A metal piece bent to fit over the edge of roof sheathing, designed to shun rain.

Eave The lower edge of a roof that overhangs a wall.

End grain The end of a crosscut piece of wood.

Engineered wood Flooring made up of thin plies of wood and topped with a hardwood veneer.

Fascia Horizontal board that covers the ends of roof rafters.

Feathering In drywall, to create a smooth transition between joint compound and the drywall panel.

Fish tape A flexible metal or nonmetal strip used to pull cables through walls and conduit.

Fixture Any number of water-using devices hooked up to the main water supply network: sinks, showers, bathtubs, and toilets.

Flashing Pieces of metal or other materials inserted, especially on a roof, to keep water out.

Floating The process of smoothing the surface of a concrete pour with a tool called a float.

Footing A concrete pad, usually at or below the frost line, that supports posts, piers, or stairs.

Form A mold in which concrete is placed to set.

Frieze A horizontal band of decoration that runs along the wall of a room just under the ceiling.

Furring Wood strips fastened to a wall or other surface to form an even base for the application of other finish materials, such as wallboard or siding.

Gauge A measurement of wire thickness. The higher the gauge, the thinner the wire.

Glazing Transparent material, such as glass, used for windows. Double glazing is two layers of glass set in a window, to reduce heat flow.

Grade The finished level of the ground surrounding a landscaping or construction project.

Ground-fault circuit interrupter (GFCI) A device that monitors the loss of current in an electrical circuit. If an interruption occurs, the GFCI quickly shuts off current to that circuit.

Gypsum A mineral (calcium sulfate) that, after processing, forms the core of drywall panels.

Header The thick horizontal structural member that runs above rough openings, such as doors and windows, in a building frame.

Jamb Boards that fit into window and door openings, covering the rough framing.

Jig A device used to maintain the correct positional relationship between a piece of work and the tool.

Joist A horizontal member in house framing that supports a floor or ceiling.

Joist hanger A metal framing connector used to join joists to a ledger board and header joists.

Kilowatt-hour (kWh) Amount of electrical energy expended in an hour by one kilowatt (1,000 watts).

Mastic A thick, pasty adhesive.

Miter A joint in which two boards are joined at angles, typically 45 degrees, to form a corner.

Molding A decorative strip installed along edges of walls, floors, ceilings, doors, and windows.

Mortar A compound of cement, sand, water, and sometimes lime that provides a stable base for stone or ceramic tile.

Mud An informal term for joint compound.

Muntin A strip separating panes of glass in a sash.

Nap A hairy surface (as on a paint roller cover).

On center The distance between the centers of regularly spaced structural members, such as studs.

PEX Acronym for cross-linked polyethylene plastic tubing. PEX is a strong, flexible water tube.

Pigtail Flexible conductor that connects an electrical device or component to an electrical circuit.

Pilot hole A hole drilled before a screw is inserted to defeat splitting.

Pitch In roofing, the ratio of a roof's rise to its span. A 24-foot-wide roof that rises 8 feet has a 1/3 pitch.

Plumb Exactly vertical (in two planes).

Plumb bob A pointed metal weight with a string used to determine vertical alignment.

Portland cement A material made of lime and clay combined with sand; hardens and becomes water resistant when mixed with water.

Primer An undercoat layer of paint that covers stains, retards moisture absorption, and provides a good surface for a top coat of paint to adhere.

Rake board A trim board that follows the slope of the roof at its outer edge—generally on a gable.

Rebar Metal bars laid in a grid used to reinforce concrete. Short for "reinforcement bar."

Rip A cut made parallel with the length of a board.

R-value A measurement of a material's resistance to heat loss. The higher the R-value, the better its insulating qualities.

Sash The framework into which window glass is set.

Scarf joint A 45-degree joint that is used to join two boards or moldings end to end.

Screeding Moving a straight board back and forth across the tops of forms to smooth and level sand or concrete.

Scribe To mark and shape a trim member to fit against another irregular surface.

Sheathing Panels or boards applied to a building's framing and upon which siding is installed.

Shim A narrow wedge of wood driven between a fixed surface and a movable member to alter the position of the movable member.

Sill A horizontal board at the bottom of a window frame.

Sill plate Horizontal lumber attached to the foundation on which stand the building's walls.

Slope In roofing, a description of the slant of a roof described in the ratio: inches of rise per 12 inches of horizontal run. For example, a 4-in-12 roof slope is one that rises 4 inches for each foot of horizontal run.

Soffit The underside of a structural member; the board that runs the length of the wall on the underside of the rafters, covering the space between the wall and the fascia.

Solar heat gain coefficient (SHGC) A measurement of how well a window blocks heat from sunlight—expressed as a number between 0 and 1. The lower a window's SHGC, the less solar heat it transmits.

Solder A metal or metallic alloy used, when melted, to join metallic surfaces. Also, to unite by solder.

Stud A vertical member in a frame wall, usually placed every 16 inches to facilitate covering with standard 48-inch-wide panels.

Subfloor Plywood or other board that is installed on joists to form the base of the finish flooring.

Terminal A position in a circuit or device at which a connection is normally established or broken.

Terminal screw A screw on a device where a wire connection is made.

Top plate The framing member(s) on top of a stud wall, upon which joists rest.

Underlayment Highly stable, often water-resistant panel, installed on top of a subfloor but beneath resilient flooring or other finish floor material.

Wainscoting Wooden paneling or decorative boards applied to the lower portion of a wall.

Wythe The vertical section of a wall that is equal to the width of the masonry unit.

Index

Metric Equivalents

Length

1 inch	25.4mm
1 foot	0.3048m
1 yard	0.9144m
1 mile	1.61km

Area

1 square inch	645mm^2
1 square foot	0.0929m^2
1 square yard	0.8361m^2
1 acre	4046.86m^2
1 square mile	2.59km^2

Volume

1 cubic inch	16.3870cm^3
1 cubic foot	0.03m^3
1 cubic yard	0.77m^3

Common Lumber Equivalents

Sizes: Metric cross sections are so close to their U.S. sizes, as noted below, that for most purposes they may be considered equivalents.

Dimensional lumber	1 x 2	19 x 38mm
	1 x 4	19 x 89mm
	2 x 2	38 x 38mm
	2 x 4	38 x 89mm
	2 x 6	38 x 140mm
	2 x 8	38 x 184mm
	2 x 10	38 x 235mm
	2 x 12	38 x 286mm
Sheet sizes	4 x 8 ft.	1200 x 2400mm
	4 x 10 ft.	1200 x 3000mm
Sheet thicknesses	¼ in.	6mm
	⅜ in.	9mm
	½ in.	12mm
	¾ in.	19mm
Stud/joist spacing	16 in. o.c.	400mm o.c.
	24 in. o.c.	600mm o.c.

Capacity

1 fluid ounce	29.57mL
1 pint	473.18mL
1 quart	0.95L
1 gallon	3.79L

Weight

1 ounce	28.35g
1 pound	0.45kg

Temperature

Fahrenheit = Celsius x 1.8 + 32
Celsius = Fahrenheit - 32 x 5/9

Nail Size and Length

Penny Size	Nail Length
2d	1"
3d	1¼"
4d	1½"
5d	1¾"
6d	2"
7d	2¼"
8d	2½"
9d	2¾"
10d	3"
12d	3¼"
16d	3½"

Credits

page 1: Gary David Gold **page 2:** John Parsekian **page 5:** John Parsekian **page 8:** *left* **Merle Henkenius;** *right* Brian C. Nieves **page 9:** courtesy of Werner Ladder **page 10:** *top left* Kim Jin Hong Photo Studio; *top right* courtesy of iLevel; *bottom left* courtesy of Puleio; *bottom right* **courtesy of Dupont page 12: John Parsekian page 14: John Parsekian page 16:** *top* courtesy of iLevel; *bottom* Brian C. Nieves **page 20:** *left* John Parsekian; *center* courtesy of Certainteed; *right* courtesy of Certainteed **page 22:** *top left* courtesy of Fypon; *top right* Neal Barrett; *bottom left* John Parsekian; *bottom right* Gary David Gold **page 23:** Neal Barrett **page 24:** *top & bottom left* John Parsekian; *bottom right* Neal Barrett **page 25:** *top & bottom right* Neal Barrett; *bottom left & bottom center* Gary David Gold **page 26:** *top sequence* Gary David Gold; *bottom* John Parsekian **page 27:** *top, bottom left & bottom right* John Parsekian; *middle left & middle right* Neal Barrett **page 28:** *top* Neal Barrett; *bottom* **Brian C. Nieves page 29:** *top left, top right, bottom left & bottom center* Neal Barrett; *bottom right* courtesy of Fypon **page 30:** *top left & top right* John Parsekian; *bottom sequence* Neal Barrett **page 31:** Neal Barrett **page 32:** *top left & bottom right* Nancy Hill; *top right & bottom left* Merle Henkenius **page 33: Merle Henkenius page 34:** *top left* Freeze Frame Studio; *top right, bottom left & bottom right* Merle Henkenius **page 35:** *top sequence* **Merle Henkenius;** *bottom* David Geer **page 36:** *top* John Parsekian; *bottom sequence* Merle Henkenius **pages 37–41:** Merle Henkenius **page 42:** courtesy of State Industries **page 43:** Merle Henkenius **pages 44–57: Brian C. Nieves page 58:** *top left* courtesy of U.S. Gypsum; *top right* courtesy of Stanley Tools; *bottom left* David Baer of Smith-Baer Studios; *bottom right* courtesy of USG Drywall **page 59:** John Parsekian **page 60:** *top* David Baer of Smith-Baer Studios; *bottom* John Parsekian **page 61:** *top* courtesy of U.S. Gypsum; *bottom* courtesy of USG Drywall **page 62:** courtesy of USG Drywall **page 63:** John Parsekian **page 64:** courtesy of Celotex **page 65:** *bottom left* David Baer of Smith-Baer Studios; *bottom right* John Parsekian **page 67:** John Parsekian **page 70:** David Baer of Smith-Baer Studios **page 73:** Home & Garden Editorial Services **page 74:** *top left* Mark Samu; *top right* Neal Barrett; *bottom left* John Parsekian; *bottom right* courtesy of VELUX **page 75:** courtesy of Andersen Corp. **page 76: John Parsekian page 77:** *top* courtesy of Sunpipe; *bottom sequence* courtesy of VELUX **page 78:** *top* John Parsekian; *bottom sequence* Freeze Frame Studio **page 79:** John Parsekian **page 80:** *top* iStockphoto.com/Terry Healy; *bottom four* Neal Barrett **page 81:** *top left, top right & bottom right* Neal Barrett; *bottom left* Mark Samu **page 82:** *top* courtesy of Andersen Corp.; *bottom sequence* Neal Barrett **page 83:** *bottom left* courtesy of CraftMaster Door Design; *right three* John Parsekian **page 84:** *top left & top center* Neal Barrett; *top right* Rob Melnychuk; *bottom* courtesy of Pella **page 85:** *top* courtesy of Western Red Cedar Lumber Association; *bottom* courtesy of Progress Lighting **page 86:** *top left* Jesse Walker; *top right* John Parsekian; *bottom left* Freeze Frame Studio; *bottom right* courtesy of Armstrong **page 87:** *top* courtesy of Gobbetto; *bottom* Freeze Frame Studio **page 88:** *top* Mark Samu; *bottom* courtesy of Hartco/Armstrong **page 89:** *top* Home & Garden Editorial Services; *bottom sequence* John Parsekian **page 90:** *top left & bottom sequence* John Parsekian; *top right* Freeze Frame Studio **page 91:** *top sequence* Freeze Frame Studio; *bottom left & bottom right* John Parsekian **page 92:** John Parsekian **page 93:** *top left & top right* Freeze Frame Studio; *bottom three* **John Parsekian page 94:** *top* courtesy of Bondex International, Inc.; *bottom sequence* John Parsekian **page 95:** John Parsekian **page 96:** *top left* iStockphoto.com/Jan Pietruszka; *top right & bottom left* John Parsekian; *bottom right* iStockphoto.com/Jason Cheng **page 97:** *top* John Parsekian; *bottom* John Puleio **pages 98–101:** John Puleio **page 102:** *top & middle* **John Puleio;** *bottom* Brian C. Nieves **page 103:** John Puleio **page 104:** *top three* John Puleio; *bottom three* John Parsekian **page 105:** *top* Home & Garden Editorial Services; *bottom* John Puleio **pages 106–108: John Puleio page 109:** *top* courtesy of Werner Ladder; *bottom left & bottom right* John Puleio **page 110:** iStockphoto.com/Jason Cheng **page 111:** *top right & bottom right* John Puleio; *middle left & middle right* John Parsekian **page 112:** courtesy of Werner Ladder **page 113:** *top left & bottom left* **courtesy of Werner Ladder;** *right* iStockphoto.com/Mike Clarke **page 114:** *top left* courtesy of Calgary Cupola; *top right* Brian Vanden Brink; *bottom left* Jessie Walker; *bottom right* John Parsekian **page 116:** Brian C. Nieves **page 117:** *top* Donna Chiarelli; *bottom left & bottom right* courtesy of Calgary Cupola **page 121:** Donna Chiarelli **page 122:** *top* John Parsekian; *bottom* courtesy of Tomko **page 123:** courtesy of Celotex **page 124:** *left & center* Donna Chiarelli; *right* John Parsekian **page 125:** John Parsekian **page 126:** *top left* Alan & Linda Detrick, designer: Cording Landscape Design, Inc.; *top right, bottom left & bottom right* John Parsekian **page 127:** *top* Brian C. Nieves; *bottom sequence* John Parsekian **pages 128–132:** John Parsekian **page 133:** *top* Merle Henkenius; *bottom sequence* John Parsekian **pages 134–139: John Parsekian page 140:** *top left* Jessie Walker; *top right* Brian C. Nieves; *bottom left* John Parsekian; *bottom right* Home & Garden Editorial Services **page 141:** *top sequence* **Home & Garden Editorial Services;** *bottom* Crandall & Crandall **page 142:** Jerry Howard/Positive Images **page 143:** Home & Garden Editorial Services **page 144:** Charles Mann **page 145: Brian C. Nieves page 146: John Parsekian page 147:** Home & Garden Editorial Services **page 148:** *top & bottom* Home & Garden Editorial Services; *middle* Larry Lefever from Grant Heilman Photography **page 149:** Home & Garden Editorial Services **page 150:** *top sequence* Home & Garden Editorial Services; *bottom* courtesy of The Toro Company **page 151:** *top* courtesy of Gardens Alive!; *bottom* courtesy of The Toro Company **page 157:** courtesy of Hartco/Armstrong **page 158:** Charles Mann

Photo credits in bold also appear on front or back cover.

Illustrations:

Vincent Alessi, Vincent Babak, Clarke Barre, Glee Barre, Ron Carboni, Tony Davis, Cathy Dean, Mario Ferro, Craig Franklin, Ron Hildebrand, Steve Karp, Bob LaPointe, Ed Lipinski, Greg Maxson, Thomas Moore, Jim Randolph, Frank Rohrbach, Paul M. Schumm, Ray Sibinski, Robert Strauch, Charles Van Vooren, Ian Warpole